GEORGIC MODERNITY AND BRITISH ROMANTICISM

Poetry and the Mediation of History

This book traces connections between georgic verse and developments in other spheres that were placing unprecedented emphasis on mediation from the late seventeenth to the early nineteenth centuries: the mediation of perception by scientific instruments, of events by newspapers, of knowledge by the feelings, of the past by narrative. Kevis Goodman argues that because of the georgic's concern for the transmission of knowledge and the extension of the senses over time and space, the verse of this period, far from burying history in nature (a position more often associated with Romanticism), instead presents new ways of perceiving history in terms of sensation. In this way Goodman opens up the subject of georgic to larger areas of literary and cultural study including the history of the feelings and the prehistory of modern media concerns in relation to print culture and early scientific technology.

KEVIS GOODMAN is Associate Professor of English Literature at the University of California, Berkeley. She has published articles in *Studies in Romanticism, ELH* and *South Atlantic Quarterly.*

CAMBRIDGE STUDIES IN ROMANTICISM

General editors

Professor Marilyn Butler
University of Oxford

Professor James Chandler
University of Chicago

Editorial board
John Barrell, *University of York*
Paul Hamilton, *University of London*
Mary Jacobus, *University of Cambridge*
Kenneth Johnston, *Indiana University*
Alan Liu, *University of California, Santa Barbara*
Jerome McGann, *University of Virginia*
David Simpson, *University of California, Davis*

This series aims to foster the best new work in one of the most challenging fields within English literary studies. From the early 1780s to the early 1830s a formidable array of talented men and women took to literary composition, not just in poetry, which some of them famously transformed, but in many modes of writing. The expansion of publishing created new opportunities for writers, and the political stakes of what they wrote were raised again by what Wordsworth called those "great national events" that were "almost daily taking place": the French Revolution, the Napoleonic and American wars, urbanization, industrialization, religious revival, an expanded empire abroad and the reform movement at home. This was an enormous ambition, even when it pretended otherwise. The relations between science, philosophy, religion and literature were reworked in texts such as *Frankenstein* and *Biographia Literaria*; gender relations in *A Vindication of the Rights of Woman* and *Don Juan*; journalism by Cobbett and Hazlitt; poetic form, content and style by the Lake School and the Cockney School. Outside Shakespeare studies, probably no body of writing has produced such a wealth of comment or done so much to shape the responses of modern criticism. This indeed is the period that saw the emergence of those notions of 'literature' and of literary history, especially national literary history, on which modern scholarship in English has been founded.

The categories produced by Romanticism have also been challenged by recent historicist arguments. The task of the series is to engage both with a challenging corpus of Romantic writings and with the changing field of criticism they have helped to shape. As with other literary series published by Cambridge, this one will represent the work of both younger and more established scholars, on either side of the Atlantic and elsewhere.

For a complete list of titles published see end of book.

GEORGIC MODERNITY
AND BRITISH
ROMANTICISM

Poetry and the Mediation of History

KEVIS GOODMAN

University of California, Berkeley

CAMBRIDGE
UNIVERSITY PRESS

PUBLISHED BY THE PRESS SYNDICATE OF THE UNIVERSITY OF CAMBRIDGE
The Pitt Building, Trumpington Street, Cambridge, United Kingdom

CAMBRIDGE UNIVERSITY PRESS
The Edinburgh Building, Cambridge, CB2 2RU, UK
40 West 20th Street, New York, NY 10011–4211, USA
477 Williamstown Road, Port Melbourne, VIC 3207, Australia
Ruiz de Alarcón 13, 28014 Madrid, Spain
Dock House, The Waterfront, Cape Town 8001, South Africa

http://www.cambridge.org

First published 2004
Reprinted 2006

Printed in the United Kingdom at the University Press, Cambridge

Typeface Adobe Garamond 11/12.5 pt   *System* LATEX 2ε   [TB]

A catalogue record for this book is available from the British Library

ISBN 0 521 83168 7 hardback

For my parents,
Marjorie and David Z. Goodman,
one of a kind – each.

Contents

ix

Illustrations

Acknowledgments

If it is remarkable that one book should have acquired so many debts of gratitude, it will always be a source of wonder and joy to me how much support this one has received. I am well aware how lucky I have been.

Lucky in my first mentors: Leslie Brisman and Geoffrey Hartman taught me how to read; later, as loyal friends, they never gave up when the dissertation they directed did not become a book. Great teachers are measured in their students' ability to diverge, as much as not. The influence of Geoffrey Hartman's body of published work, playful, diverse, and never labelable, will be apparent – maybe in those traits, too. At Yale, where I trained and first taught, I learned much from others on the faculty: Jill Campbell, who made eighteenth-century studies come alive, deserves special mention. So, too, do a number of colleagues now elsewhere: Heather James, Cathy Caruth, Priscilla Gilman, and Blakey Vermeule, whose auspicious dare, as it turned out, changed my career and my life.

Lucky, too, to move three thousand miles and find myself among such remarkable and inimitable colleagues at Berkeley, who welcomed me warmly and tolerated the unpredictable, sustaining it where it looked productive. It has been exciting to be a Romanticist here, thanks to Celeste Langan and Steve Goldsmith, who came first and set the brilliant standard, and to Ian Duncan and Anne-Lise François, who joined shortly afterwards – great sources of happiness and trust. These four scholars have read draft after draft, providing inspired commentary and equal patience. So did Catherine Gallagher, whose luminous insight and uncanny economy of expression one can only dream of attaining. I am also indebted to Richard Feingold and Paul Alpers for early tenacious support and to James Turner and George Starr for probing criticisms, productive misunderstandings, valuable bibliographic suggestions, and tolerating my border-crossings. For walks, talks, meals, and other forms of friendship, I thank Elizabeth Abel and Janet Adelman (who will know what I mean when I say that this is like touching the bush); Alex Zwerdling; Katie Snyder; and, from the beginning, Colleen Lye, Stephen Best, and Chris Nealon, all three ever "mod."

The larger world of the academy has proved hospitable in ways I never expected, distinguished by the number who have performed completely unobligated acts of kindness. Long ago, Alan Liu took a first-year graduate student's course paper very seriously when he did not have to and, in so doing, did much to make her feel real in this world; since then both he and his work have been presiding genii, if not of place. James Chandler intervened to rescue this book and its author from an uncertain future, displaying such genuine interest, enthusiasm, and efficiency as would be remarkable in a scholar one-eighth as busy and productive as he. David Simpson and Marshall Brown were no usual press readers: they read promptly at inconvenient times, contributed their wide learning and deep wit, and saw much that I didn't. (All remaining shortcomings, including any scarcity of short, declarative topic sentences, are my own.) Along the way, portions or the entirety of this manuscript benefited greatly from the encouragement and scrupulous readings of Mary Favret, Susan Stewart and Peter Manning; an important earlier portion of this manuscript was written while subletting Peter's Los Angeles home, living amidst his books and his good will. All of these scholars have modeled the kind of professional and friendly assistance one can only repay by extending some version of it to one's own students and colleagues.

I owe thanks to a number of institutions, as well, for material support of this book. Research and writing were facilitated by generous grants from the University of California, including a Career Development Grant, a junior faculty fellowship from the Townsend Center for the Humanities, and a Humanities Research Fellowship. The last, combined with financial assistance from the Hellman Family Foundation, helped to supplement and make possible a year of research at the Huntington Library, where I held a Barbara Thom fellowship during 1999–2000. The air-conditioned halls of that library were warmed by the assistance, companionship, and laughter of many, particularly Jesse Matz, fellow traveler in many things, and the Huntington's witty Director of Research, Roy Ritchie.

Helen Tartar has supported my work since I was in graduate school. I salute her formidable talents as an editor, noting the role of the many books she has brought into print in my own work. When this book moved to Cambridge University Press, I was extremely fortunate to come into the expert hands of Linda Bree, who acted promptly at a decisive moment, and has since then been at once professional and humane. I thank also Lesley Atkin for her hard work combating the perils of long endnotes and long distance copy-editing, and I am grateful to Duke University Press for permission to reprint an earlier version of part of Chapter 3, which appeared in *SAQ* 102 (2003).

The quotidian life of writing and manuscript preparation can be dreary, especially under the felt pressures of a tenure review, but mine has been cheered and sustained by a number of very special, gifted, graduate-student colleagues at Berkeley, who have taught with me, laughed with me, and in many cases, worked on the more laborious aspects of manuscript preparation. For inspired wit, intellectual exchange, research assistance, reading with excitement, proof-reading with care, and coping patiently with my notoriously bad typing skills, I am particularly grateful to Mike Farry, Michael Ferguson, Kathryn Evans, Paul Stasi and Nicholas Nace. Kimberly Johnson is as greatly gifted a friend as a poet, and Alison Hurley and Fiona Murphy have been a fund of information and conversation, eighteenth-century and otherwise.

At every stage, going back to 1988, Cliff Spargo has helped to sharpen my thought and bring many a precarious idea into existence; he has discussed every page of this manscript and its several discarded precursors, during which time he has written at least three of his own. I am honored by his friendship and collaboration.

My originary and greatest debt is expressed by the dedication. From Gramercy Park to Berkeley: *hic est quod unum est pro laboribus tantis.*

Introduction
Georgic modernity: sensory media and the affect of history

scilicet et tempus veniet, cum finibus illis agricola incurvo terram moli-
tus aratro exesa inveniet scabra robigine pila, aut gravibus rastris galeas
pulsabit inanis, grandiaque effossis mirabitur ossa sepulcris.

Georgics, 1.493–97

Here, at the end of the first *Georgic*, Virgil famously imagined his own violent present as the future's past: "A time shall come when in those lands, as the farmer toils at the soil with crooked plough, he shall find javelins eaten up with rusty mould, or with his heavy hoes shall strike on empty helms, and marvel at the giant bones in the upturned graves."[1] If one had to choose a representative anecdote for the pervasive georgic influence in eighteenth-century poetry, this scene would make a good candidate.[2] Again and again, with notable flexibility, it makes its appearance in poems of varying political sympathies, whether these are explicit formal imitations of Virgil's poem, such as John Philips's celebratory 1708 *Cyder* (where "Coins, and mould'ring Urns, / And huge unwieldy Bones . . . the Plowman haply finds, / Appall'd"), or topographical verse where the influence is more diffuse but still strong, as in Charlotte Smith's less complacent *Beachy Head* (published in 1807), where "wondering hinds" gaze on the enormous bones of a captive elephant from a Roman campaign and "in giants dwelling on the hills / Believed and marvell'd."[3]

The tableau could also be said to organize much scholarship on georgic-descriptive poetry from the seventeenth century through Romanticism, whether the focus has been on georgic as a strictly defined genre or, more loosely, on georgic as a mode exerting a rhizomatic underpresence across a variety of affiliated descriptive and didactic verse genres. But with a crucial difference: under critical scrutiny the *versus*, which in Virgil's generative pun designate both the furrows of the field and the lines of verse on the page, are seen to turn the debris of history the other way, not up but under. So Alan Liu's extraordinary study of 1989, *Wordsworth: the Sense of*

I

History, offered this formulation, which remains influential in the study of topographical verse:

Georgic is the supreme mediational form by which to bury history in nature, epic in pastoral. Like the tour mode, it is the form in which history turns into the background, the manure, for landscape. Through georgic, Wordsworth is able, at least at first glance, to make the entire under-narrative of the Revolution sink into unbroken invisibility. . . . The purpose of the mirror of georgic nature is to hide history in order, finally, to reflect the self.[4]

The trope of overturning has a long, distinguished genealogy in British rural ideology critique. Before Liu, and treating a different period, James Turner put the case as follows: "Rural poetry of the civil war period [1630–60] does not simply embellish or ignore the things of the world; it inverts them." Raymond Williams described the table-turning as a "magical extraction of the curse of labour" by the "simple extraction of the existence of labourers" in his classic analysis of Jonson's and Carew's country house poems. What the work of art buries or extracts the critic can recover. "[W]e must peer under the classical draperies of this personified Industry," wrote John Barrell of a passage in James Thomson's *The Seasons*, "and ask who she is imagined to be."[5] Even Kurt Heinzelman's recent and ongoing work on Romantic genre, which has maintained that *Virgilian* georgic did possess "a requisite sense of history," argues nonetheless that "eighteenth-century uses of georgic already tended to undermine, to the point of silencing, the genre's capacity for historicist thinking" – and that after the 1760s, "the genre quite suddenly disappeared, at least by name, from literary practice" into the fissure of a Foucauldian epistemic break.[6] (Heinzelman's qualification, "at least by name," like Liu's "at least at first glance," is important, and so we will return more than once to the work of both scholars.) Before the scholars, there were the poets: George Crabbe's exclamation – "Then shall I dare these real ills to hide / In tinsel trappings of poetic pride?" – anticipates the twentieth-century discussion.[7] Much of the strongest work we have to date has shown us the ways in which the georgic influence on historical representation in eighteenth-century and Romantic poetry has worked like Marx's and Engels's famous *camera obscura* of ideology: "If in all ideology men and their circumstances appear upside-down as in a *camera obscura*, this phenomenon arises just as much from their historical life-process as the inversion of objects on the retina does from the physical life process."[8]

These analyses have been immensely productive: both directly and indirectly, they have done much both to invigorate the study of the georgic in particular, which for some time had lagged considerably behind our versions of pastoral, and to reanimate topographical poetry from the seventeenth century through the first phase of Romanticism more generally. One would not want to forfeit the acuity of the negative hermeneutic or the awareness it has given us of the constraints placed on representing the rural poor, those documentable hard facts that lie on what Barrell aptly calls "the dark side of the landscape."[9] Still, it seems time to ask whether there are ways in which the poetry can and does offer a substantial register of "history." Do those georgic *versus* in some instances "work" as agents of disclosure in ways we have not been able to recognize, even as they attempt ideological closure in ways that we have? What happens if we – not naively but heuristically – take Virgil's tableau at its word and explore the possibility that the problem is sometimes not that the plough or the pen buries what should be disclosed, but that the critic's predicament, like that of the farmer and the poet, is the difficulty of recognizing the historical meanings of what does get turned up, not under, by their lines?

This book proposes that those material georgic *versus* can be complexly communicative sites for certain kinds of history, particularly that aspect of the flux of historical process that Raymond Williams called social experience "in solution," not yet or never quite precipitated out in the form of the "known relationships, institutions, formations, positions" or other familiar terms. When Williams spoke and wrote gropingly of "the experience of the present" or history as "presence," he did not necessarily mean the temporal present, which is equally susceptible to the "precipitating" and fixative effects of analysis as the historical past, but that immanent, collective perception of any moment as a seething mix of unsettled elements.[10] The issue he points us to is not "presence" or immediacy, as is often concluded, but, as his late interviews with the *New Left Review* make much clearer, *presentness*.[11] And presentness can be analyzed as a mediated problem or a problem within mediation. However uncertain Williams's talk of "experience" and "feeling" was – and in the pages and chapters that follow I will treat it as a problem, with *its* own history – nevertheless, the analytic and conceptual dilemma he tried to diagnose remains a real one. It is a version of the Heisenberg uncertainty principle: the difficulty of recording and recognizing history-on-the-move, or, to invoke grammar rather than physics, the difficulty of treating or recreating the historical process as a present participle ("the present tense, so to speak grammatically," he insisted) rather than as a past perfect.

My overarching argument will be that historical presentness is often "turned up" by georgic as *unpleasurable* feeling: as sensory discomfort, as

disturbance in affect and related phenomena that we variously term perceptive, sensorial, or affective – I refer to the noise of living (the aural trope will
be examined), rather than to shapely, staged, or well-defined emotions (the
sentiment of a Yorick, the feeling of a Harley).[12] It is no doubt true, as we
have come to say almost ritually, that affects have a history, are conditioned
by specific material circumstances, etc. Certain affective positions may indeed belong to the set of coping practices that Pierre Bourdieu designates
"habitus": "durable, transposable *dispositions*, structured structures predis-
posed to function as structuring structures." However, I hope to show that
other affects, especially affective dissonance, can conversely be a neglected
postern of certain kinds of history. (That is not to say that they are the only
postern, merely an important one that needs more analysis.) As discomfort,
they are not well described by the term that Bourdieu, sounding remarkably like a modern reader of the *Georgics*, uses: "habitus, history turned into
nature, i.e., denied as such."[13] Nor are they particularly well encompassed
by most definitions of ideology, even Louis Althusser's sophisticated and
capacious sense of ideology as a "representation of the imaginary relationship of individuals to their real conditions of existence," since Althusser's
corollary question ("why do men '*need*' this imaginary transposition of
their real conditions of existence in order to 'represent to themselves' their
real conditions of existence?") indicates that he, too, considers ideology a
coping practice, a way of preserving as much as possible the pleasure principle, or at least the pleasure principle modified and restricted by the reality
principle.

In a rhetorical flourish at the end of the important first chapter of *The
Political Unconscious*, Fredric Jameson wrote that "History is what hurts."
The aphorism has been so often cited that I suspect Jameson himself might
now want to retract or rephrase it, but, if so, then it is all the more interesting to ask, and to understand, how something like "hurt" became a
powerful index of what Jameson calls, by turns, the Real (after Lacan) and
(after Althusser, following Spinoza) the "absent cause."[14] As unlikely as this
proposition may at first sound, I will examine this uncomfortable affect
of history as a production and a legacy of the georgic mode as it inflects
British poetry of the "long" eighteenth century.

While my argument thus clearly resists the demystifying charge of the
Romantic new historicism and its forerunners in British ideology critique,
it does take its cue from them in one important respect. The significance of some kind of "feeling" ("sense," "hurt") as a mode of historical manifestation is an underexplored or undeveloped insight of the most
articulate exponents of both methods. Again, I think of Liu, who asks

toward the beginning of his study:

> How precisely does literature "sense" the sense of history? The solution to this inquiry, I suggest, requires that we unthink the "idea," which from Locke through modern history of ideas has as much blocked as facilitated the passage between historical context and historical knowledge . . . [I]deas and their influence are always after the fact. Historical context first makes itself known to an author in concrete, highly charged phenomena that are accepted as material because they are prior or unacceptable to idea . . . It is the excess of negativity in such markers of difference [constitutive of historical context] that manifests itself in the author's *pre-ideational consciousness* as an elementary *feel* for representation.[15]

Liu does not often return to this (collective, even if here connected to the author) "pre-ideational consciousness." His project is to write *The Sense of History*, not the history of the "sense of history," and it may also be that History steals the show from Sense in his study. Nonetheless, this passage and ones like it are wonderfully suggestive, and they prompt me to wonder about such a *history of* the *sense of history*, not only in Wordsworth but as it preceded him and is later inherited by twentieth-century thought. As we will see in the chapters that follow, the Lockean "idea" is problematic from its inception, and its "unthinking" is a process scrutinized in the writing of the period bounded, roughly, by Locke's *Essay Concerning Human Understanding* (1690) and Wordsworth's *The Excursion* (1815).

Although Liu is not directly indebted to Raymond Williams, and apparently different in his Althusserian commitment to History as "the absence that is the very possibility of the 'here and now,'"[16] Liu's collective pre-ideational consciousness resembles the "feeling" of history-in-motion that Williams tried to give some theoretical standing and dignity, perhaps better in such later works as *Marxism and Literature* (1977) and *Politics and Letters* (1981) than in *The Long Revolution* (1961), the first time he discussed his elusive signature phrase, "structures of feeling," at any length. For Williams as much as for Liu, "ideas" are after the fact. Protesting what he considered the settled habit of treating the "social" or historical present as "past, in the sense that it is always formed" (or, in his favored chemical analogy, already "precipitated"), Williams argued that we turn by default "to find other terms [than the social] for our undeniable experience of the present." If the terms of analysis, "the known relationships, institutions, formations, positions," are fixed and explicit, then "all that escapes from the fixed and the explicit and the known, is grasped and defined as the personal[,] this, here, now, alive, active 'subjective.'" Yet this is a misrecognition: what the historian or sociologist has often "taken to be private, idiosyncratic, and even isolating" misconstrues "social experiences in solution."[17]

However, as I suggested above, Williams's appeal to "experience," the "lived," and "feeling" sets off all sorts of alarm bells among many of his readers, who have heard the sound of a Leavis or a naive empiricism. The interviewers from the *New Left Review* wondered if his commitment to the possibility of "an emergent experience beyond ideology seem[ed] to presuppose a kind of pristine contact between the subject and the reality in which this subject is immersed," and Joan Scott has since accused him of making experience a foundational authority whose discursive construction goes naively unexamined.[18] The phrase "lived experience" seemed particularly disabling because it seemed to coincide too perfectly with Williams's reticence on the significance of Britain's empire to the "country and city" model. After all, his critics have pointed out, in the periods Williams most frequently wrote about, an entire account of the conditions that made possible any experience in England, Scotland, or Wales would have to account for far-flung coordinates not verifiable at the level of sense, by first-hand sight, touch, hearing, etc.[19] As Fredric Jameson writes (with a later stage of imperialism in mind, but the problem holds for earlier stages as well): increasingly, "the truth of [any individual] experience no longer coincides with the place in which it takes place. The truth of that limited daily experience of London lies, rather, in India or Jamaica or Hong Kong; it is bound up with the whole colonial system of the British Empire. . . . Yet those structural coordinates are no longer accessible to immediate lived experience and are often not even conceptualizable for most people." History is thus, for Jameson that "absent cause," a system of relations inaccessible at the level of individual cognition.[20]

During his life Williams resisted these and similar charges. His "feeling" was not attached to isolated subjects, he explained; rather, the category of the "merely subjective" precipitates out during the process of analysis when our categories cannot accommodate the flux or the excess of events. Nor was he supposing a "pristine contact between the subject and the reality in which this subject is immersed." In response to that question from his interviewers, he answered firmly: "No. That should be very clear. For after all the basic argument of the first chapter of *The Long Revolution* is precisely that there is no natural seeing and therefore there cannot be a direct and unmediated contact with reality." However, he continued more enigmatically:

[I]n the whole process of consciousness – here I would put a lot of stress on phenomena for which there is no easy knowing because there is too easy a name, the too easy name is "the unconscious" – all sorts of occurrences cut across the established or offered relations between a signification and a reference. The formalist position that there is no signified without a signifier amounts to saying that it is only in articulation that we live at all. . . . I have found that areas which I would call structures of feeling as often as not initially form as a certain kind of disturbance or unease, a particular type of tension, for which when you stand back or recall them you can sometimes find a referent. To put it another way, the peculiar location of a structure of feeling is the endless comparison that must occur in the process of consciousness between the articulated and the lived. The lived is only another word, if you like, for experience: but we have to find a word for that level. For all that is not fully articulated, all that comes through as disturbance, tension, blockage, emotional trouble seems to me precisely a source of major changes in the relation between the signifier and the signified. . . . [O]ne has to seek a term for that which is not fully articulated or not fully comfortable in various silences.[21]

Let us not forget that Williams was an expert on modern communications media. He knew, as he put it in a 1978 essay, that "means of communication" are always "means of production" because they frame and filter their content in determinate and recognizable ways.[22] To my mind he cannot be accused of a naive empiricism or a cult of the "lived"; at the same time, however, he was not willing to settle for the equally naive position that all experience is reducible to its discursive or technological mediation.[23] What interests him, this passage suggests, is the fact that all received articulations have their interference, their static, or their uneasy silence ("all sorts of occurrences cut across the established or offered relations between a signification and a reference"). However inadequate or misleading it proved to be, "feeling" – not as unmediated experience but as that elusive "present participle" for the historical process – was the name he gave to such cognitive noise. He groped, in a wayward, occasional, even baffled way (perhaps all too well matched to his object of study), to give such dissonances some meaning, to find for those interferences and shifts in signification a referent which is not merely personal; for example it can be glimpsed, he suggested, in the wide recurrence of a suddenly charged "semantic figure."[24] Although he probably would have resented the comparison since, notwithstanding his appreciation of Lucien Goldmann, his Anglophilic preferences remained largely resistant to currents in French thought, the later Williams seems to me at certain points quite close to Jean-François Lyotard's conception of the "differend": "the unstable state and instant of language wherein something which must be able to be put into phrases cannot yet be." "This state is signaled by what one ordinarily calls a feeling," Lyotard writes, then adds, significantly: "What is at stake in a literature, in a philosophy, in a politics perhaps, is to bear witness to differends by finding idioms for them."[25]

The conditions of the "here and now" may not, then, be any less absent for the later Williams than for Althusser, Jameson, or Liu; or rather they are absent as *idea* and present as that uncomfortable suprasensory *feeling*. Nonetheless, it is true that Williams never did give a full account of the relationship between those elusive excesses and the media or discourses that collaborate to shape them. He may have been too busy avoiding another "too easy" thesis, at the time being advocated by Marshall McLuhan and other technological determinists.[26] Nor was he eager to examine his own relation to Locke and British empiricism, whose central aporias, particularly a difficulty theorizing a pre-ideational or extra-ideational feeling, he inherited – they are evident in his wary shying away from Freud in the extended passage quoted above. Perhaps for that reason the "structure of feeling," as David Simpson has observed, "has not proved an exportable concept."[27]

I do not plan to import it. But I would like to dilate and give a literary prehistory to the insight, lurking in the formulations of Williams, Liu, Jameson, as well as Simpson,[28] that some sort of affect or cognitive dissonance registers those unfixed elements of history that elude or exceed the Lockean idea. Rather than start from the premise that this is the case, however, I will study those affects, *not* as they emerge from some kind of immediate contact with the real (that infamous "lived experience" that Williams was suspected of harboring a nostalgia for), but rather as they are produced in selected long poems of the later eighteenth century and Romantic periods when their verses compete and clash with rival media, or pathways of perception and communication. Each of the poems I study at greatest length, James Thomson's *The Seasons*, William Cowper's *The Task*, and William Wordsworth's *The Excursion*, is in its own way written under the sign of the georgic mode, and the focus of my readings falls on those moments in which each confronts the *failure* of mediation to produce what Joseph Addison, reading Virgil's *Georgics* most carefully at the turn of the eighteenth century, called, by turns, "Pleasure," an "Idea," and, later, as he elaborated his early "Essay on the Georgics" in *The Spectator* papers, "the Principle of Pleasure." Of course, Addison's influential reading of georgic, whether in his "Essay" on Virgil or as disseminated in *The Spectator* papers, has no monopoly on the discussion of pleasure or displeasure, but it will be key to my argument that the georgic mode allows an intense and historically situated focus on early developments in and conceptualizations of media or "mediums"[29] (the more frequently employed contemporary plural). Poetry invested in the georgic mode obsessively tests its mediating power, and even when it attempts to narrate or otherwise contain history, something else – an affective residue – will out. I am interested in these moments of excess and dissonance as records of an otherwise unknowable history. (I should caution however, that my interest in history-on-the-move and its affect does not produce an analysis of the sort that explains a poem by showing the relevance of some particular event or cultural force; part of the challenge is to find a way to give rigor to processes whose resistance to clear apperception is part of my very subject.) This book's focus on the legacy of georgic, in other words, is not motivated by a *quid pro quo* impulse to overturn ideology critique on the georgic ground that founds many of its influential analyses, although it will be clear that I am critical of simpler versions of the *camera-obscura*-of-ideology interpretations of the genre. Rather, I am prompted by what I take to be a difficult and un-developed connection between "mediation" and "media" in Williams and those he has widely influenced. And I believe these are concepts which the later eighteenth-century and Romantic fate of the georgic can illuminate in return.

Over the course of this book, then, I offer the following proximate the-ses, which may sound counterintuitive at first and are nothing unless they acquire more detailed textual substance. (1) A curious, quirky blend of pro-saic subject matter and self-consciously opulent diction and figuration, the georgic in its Virgilian and post-Virgilian incarnations is a mode distinc-tively concerned with the transmission of precept and intelligence over time and space. Moreover, as it moves from its classical sources into English, the history of the georgic mode was intimately intertwined with the history of efforts to extend, by means of an array of artificial "organs," what Francis Bacon called "the reports of the sences" in *The Advancement of Learning* – the project that he also called (not coincidentally) "these Georgickes of the mind."[30] (2) Within and in part under the influence of georgic, the poetry of the long eighteenth century underwent a process whereby it became conscious of itself as one "sensible path" among others (I take the phrase from the microscopist Robert Hooke).[31] Such verse inhabits a cultural sit-uation in which it has to define itself not only against an array of prose genres, whose material it often usurps, but also in relation to non-written means of perception and communication, whose several mystiques it often courts. This second category includes both optical technology (explored in chapters 1 and 2 , best read together if possible) and oral interchange – the latter ranging from *à la mode* urbane conversation (chapter 3) to residual, rural storytelling (chapter 4). (3) Where almost every scholar to date has concentrated on the "smoothness" of georgic's apparent pleasures – its eas-ing of contradiction – I am most interested instead in the communicative or perceptual interferences that emerge within the poetry in its rivalry with other "sensible paths," during a period that both promoted fast changes in the notions of space, place, and time and suffered the anxieties of its own expansions. These clashes are the ground, as it were, out of which georgic can plow a sensation of history as affective discomfort, cognitive "noise."

By calling the georgic mode a site for exploration or heuristic, I have tried to indicate that *Georgic Modernity and British Romanticism* is not a genre survey (e.g., *The Modern Georgic*), especially in the sense that its motives are obviously not anthological, nor are they merely restitutive. While I very much hope that the poems studied will seem newly interesting in what follows, and while I believe that literary history and criticism have not been able to account fully for their high profile in their own time, I come not (simply) to praise georgic, nor to bury it. Having read both the original *Georgics* and British georgics carefully for some time, I would like to open up relatively specialist matters (as work on those subjects has tended to be) to a wider purview: to the history of the feelings, to a revised historicist method that reserves a place at the table for sensation and affect, and, perhaps above all, to the early history of contemporary media in relation to print culture – and thus to the pre-history of concerns that dominate modern and postmodern "media theory." For a comprehensive picture of the literary history of the georgic as a genre with a set of formal conventions, we already have a variety of fine studies; I have learned much from them and will engage them in the main discussion, where relevant, and more extensively in the notes (I hope some of these can offer bibliographical essays of sorts).[32] Moreover, particularly after chapter 2 which treats Virgil's *Georgics* and their Restoration and early eighteenth-century critical reception, my emphasis is not on what James Turner and others have called real or "true Georgics" – the flurry of full-scale formal imitations that succeeded Dryden's translation of 1697 (works by Philips, Gay, Somervile, Smart, Dyer, Grainger, and even as late as Jago) – but rather on texts that appeared, at least in full, from mid-century on, when purer instances of the genre were waning or fully in decline.[33] My conviction is that georgic is most influential, if less well understood, not as a relatively short-lived Augustan genre but when and where it persists afterwards as a subtle underpresence and discipline. As such georgic became, I argue, a subtle foundation for poetic practices during the later eighteenth century, offering itself to that period as an occasion for negotiating temporal flux, spatial extension, and concerns about the transmission not only of traditional precept (Virgil's *praecepta*) but also of new scientific information and "intelligence" (a term from the period's news culture). In this respect I concur with Kurt Heinzelman, whose comment that after 1760 the georgic "quite simply disappeared, at least by name, from literary practice" is strongly qualified by his intuition that it does so "*only* in name, not as a cultural practice" – although the "entailments" that we consider as the main legacies of the genre differ considerably, as I will explain at the end of chapter 1.[34]

Nonetheless, more should be said at the outset – and by way of a preview of the chapters to come – about why I think that georgic provides a surprisingly apt site for exploring matters of considerable and ongoing theoretical as well as historical significance in the longer course of modernity and – as is certainly the case for "media" – postmodernity. Why georgic, that unlovely "ugly duckling" of a mode which, as Heinzelman wryly notes, has "not usually prompted critical fireworks"?[35] The answer has several parts, which occupy three sequential phases in the history of the mode. The first, I have already suggested, concerns Virgil's *Georgics* themselves. As their double sense of *versus* suggests, these books are as much about the tending of words as they are about agriculture and other forms of terraculture: they are concerned not only with words (*verba*) as bearers of things (*res*) but also with words *as* things, exerting friction within representation and requiring labor and care. With their deliberately "soaring words" amplifying the rural *res* of their subject matter, the *Georgics* displayed, and were understood by their seventeenth-century readers to display, a gorgeous verbal *tekhnē*. Here I part from the critical consensus, which has located the attraction of Virgil's "middle term" to contemporary readers in the *Georgics'* promise of matters more "realistic" or workaday than other genres (and has faulted them for defaulting on a promise they do not entirely make) – I suspect that this may be a misprision induced by later readers' greater distance from the Latin and from routine Latin training. My first chapter begins by suggesting that the poem's first readers liked what one Restoration reader (Robert Wolseley) called Virgil's "poetical daemonianism": the ability to "beautifie the vilest dirt" and "enliven the deadest Lump."

This Restoration and then early eighteenth-century reception constitutes the second phase, also considered in chapter 1, but informing each of the chapters that follow. I argue that the paradoxical logic suggested in such comments as Wolseley's, whereby the power and the interest of the real depends on a deliberate heightening and transformation of the real, is also the logic at work in the period's experimental philosophy and its corollary linguistic projects. The microscopist Robert Hooke praised the use of "artificial Organs"; the *Georgics* were understood by his contemporaries to *be* a kind of artificial organ. Certainly this is the premise of the young Joseph Addison, publishing his "Essay on the Georgics" in John Dryden's

1697 translation. The heir of the preceding generation's enthusiasm for scientific (especially optical) instruments before he became famous as "Mr. Spectator," Addison used Virgil's poem to explore the specificity of poetry as one epistemological instrument among others. That distinctiveness, he claimed, inhered in the *Georgics*' "By-ways," the poem's capacity to place its reader in a teasingly and, above all, pleasingly indirect relation to objects that might repel. Addison's reading of the *Georgics* was influential in its own right, but even more so, I argue, because it became the foundation for the aesthetics advanced in his famous "Pleasures of the Imagination" series of 1712, which sought to shape the taste by which descriptive writing – and indeed much of polite culture – was to be enjoyed. Hence, although by the 1760s the taste for formal georgic imitation had receded, the legacy of the mode persisted as a concern for positioning and "proper" sense reception.

However, while Bacon, Hooke, Addison, and others mentioned in chapter 1 sound a celebratory note, those "sensible paths" become increasingly difficult to maintain as pleasurable byways, with the result that the Addisonian "principle of pleasure" was not so easy to uphold in verse inflected by the georgic mode during the middle and late decades of the eighteenth century. These constitute a third phase, and they are my emphasis in this book. The technologies and prostheses both of the new science and of the proliferating eighteenth-century print culture occasion a concern about sensory over-extension, perceived initially perhaps as an influx of opportunity, but increasingly, and more negatively, sustained as a wounding of perception. Such epistemological crises present a challenge to the place- and time-commanding ambitions of this largely locodescriptive or topographical mode, which responded by attempting to establish what Barrell has called "the idea of the landscape." At the same time, I argue, georgic points beyond the forms of ideational and pleasurable mastery it has been understood to promote. It does so frequently, as I try to show in chapters 2 and 3, where concerns about sensory influx became attached to that other, concurrent, area of expansion surcharging experience and feeling well in excess of "the idea of the landscape" – territorial expansion, or the dark side of empire. In such instances, the georgic mode can act as a shield against the possibility of sensory over-extension that shadows both the technologies of the new science and the territorial growth of nation and empire, but it is also an *aperture*, disclosing the pressures it might seek to cover.

New media and new worlds bring home information not verifiable by the ordinary powers of vision, hearing, or touch; they simulate sense-experience from positions or vantages where the body cannot literally be situated, dislocating both body and place. The "semantic figure" (Williams's term) of the "microscopic eye," whose history I explore in chapter 2, can, for instance, be seen as the dialectical extension and nightmare version of the often-studied *camera obscura*, abolishing the camera's dualism between subject and object world, exteriority and interiority, and disclosing the vulnerability that attends scientific ambitions, like Robert Hooke's, for the "inlargement of the dominion of the senses." Its history leads from the matrix of seventeenth-century optics and linguistics to Locke's *Essay Concerning Human Understanding*, where it signals a feared impasse in the formation of ideas and the power to name things; from Locke it moves into didactic-philosophical poetry of the earlier eighteenth century. Chapter 2 explores the optical poetics of James Thomson's phenomenally popular version of English georgic, *The Seasons*, where the "microscopic eye" takes a decisive turn, and sensory extension becomes a figure for the dependence, within an enlarged imperial dominion, on the labors and suffering of "nameless nations." Their pressure, not pleasurably distanced in Addisonian "By-ways," now bursts on the senses as "noise" – this is a powerful figure that marked Locke's *Essay* as well, where it signaled the separation of sound from "Idea" and the failure of consensual understanding, and I explore noise's relation to Thomson's often-maligned, periphrastic poetic diction. If the threat of noise that lurks beyond the "microscopic eye" offers an ancestral trace of Williams's historical "discomfort, tension, blockage, emotional disturbance," as I think it does, then it also shows us that "feeling," sensory and affective discomfort, seemingly personal, was never quite separable from the problem of spatial expansion and conquest, a point that Williams recognized but refrained from studying at any length.[36]

Near becomes far and far near in chapter 3, too, where I turn to the "sensible paths" provided by the eighteenth-century daily newspaper, which aspired to make its readers virtual witnesses of an increasingly far-flung reality, to link the bodily and phenomenological life of the individual with an expanding imperial system. While I try in this chapter to offer an overall glimpse of the larger eighteenth-century culture of "news," my focus falls on the rivalry that took shape during the early 1780s between the newspaper and the didactic, georgic-inflected poetry of William Cowper as distinct vehicles of "intelligence." This competition was occasioned by Cowper's habit in *The Task* (a poem that would rival Thomson's earlier *Seasons* in its popularity) of turning the contents of the daily news into poetry. In this remarkable practice of conversion, or "remediation,"[37] Cowper exploits Virgil's pun on *vertere* to the fullest: his intentional strategy, or his hope, is to "turn" the random or dissociated particles of news from the daily newsprint into con*vers*ation – that is, to render the "noise" of history as the measured sound of polite parlor interchange. Like Addison, who praised the *Georgics* for its conversion of overly direct "sensible paths" into pleasurable "Byways," Cowper hoped to establish poetry as a distinctive medium for sifting the present, one able to turn the chaos of presentness into what David Hume had dubbed "the conversable world," where conversability marked both an epistemological and stylistic ideal. Yet the world in part represented and in part suggested by the daily newsprint cannot be made readily "conversable" – that is, communicable or comprehensible. I turn, therefore, to explore the ways in which *The Task*, a poem burdened by silence as well as noise – each equally resistant to the simulation of polite conversation – renders elements of Cowper's "unconversable" present. Such elements emerge in a mode of affective perception that the poet called "indolent vacuity of thought" (in order to describe the interstices and absences between ideas), and they are palpable in the poem at the level of figure rather than articulated as direct statement. This paradoxically full but non-ideational vacuity, I want to suggest, is itself an unlikely mode of historical knowledge. Others besides Cowper associated this condition with the distinctive experience of the present as a flux of news, and I conclude by examining the semantic shift, in which Cowper played a significant part, that attempts to stabilize these vacuities, and the vertiginous experience of space that they entail, in the form and experience of aesthetic perception.

With chapter 4, I come to Wordsworth, careful reader and translator of the *Georgics*, acute reader of Thomson and Cowper, and heir to the affect of history that troubles the "sensible paths" of perception and communication. This chapter discusses *The Excursion* as an experiment in the historiography of the past, and it returns us to the signature Virgilian scene of the first *Georgic* – that farmer at his furrow, disclosing the matter of history – which provides the organizational principle of Wordsworth's long refractory poem. Here, therefore, I consider extension backwards in time rather than outward in space, but the history under consideration is equally "in solution," not because it is still unresolved (as in chapters 2 and 3), but because it never was resolved, never "precipitated" into record. The "microscopic eye" returns here as the stethoscopic ear, concerned that the earth will speak, "capable / Of yielding its contents," and the microscopist's "sensible paths" take the form of *The Excursion*'s "passages of life." This remarkably polysemous phrase – which includes the passing of oral anecdotes between characters, of sound through what Wordsworth calls the "strict passage" of the ear, of text between poem and reader, and of animation between the living and the dead – becomes my focus in all of its several meanings. In its sober scrutiny of each of these "passages," Wordsworth's *Excursion* offers a complex meditation on the plausibility and improbities of asking the past to yield the Addisonian "principle of pleasure" to the present, whether by way of therapeutic intervention ("cure"), aesthetic compensation (narrative), or epistemological gratification (the "Idea"). Yet, at the same time that it is aware of the falsifications entailed in such consolations, the poem is also wary of defining history only as that which lies beyond the pleasure principle. It is mindful that there are states of discomfort which preclude the will or desire to historicize – let alone, as in Jameson's transhistorical injunction: "*always* [to] *historicize!*"³⁸ What work of words confronts that which is elusive about history but also refuses to disclaim historical knowledge altogether with the excuse that it is unknowable? What kinds of communication keep hearts and minds responsive to historical suffering without becoming so invasive that both shut down, as Wordsworth puts it, "dead" to "public care"? In *The Excursion*, the answer resides, as in the earlier poems I consider, in a complex husbandry of distance and sense, in this case carried out at the site of the production of the past.

Many of the anxieties concerning the expansion and inundation of the senses that I examine in *Georgic Modernity and British Romanticism* have been taken up in recent media theory, where the assumption has often been that they are unique to the postmodern condition or at least to modern communications technology. Friedrich Kittler's postulate that before the late nineteenth-century invention of sound broadcast and storage technologies (phonograph and cinematograph in particular) "writing functioned as a universal medium – in times when there was no concept of medium" is too restrictive.³⁹ Both the term and the concept *did*, of course, exist before 1900, or 1800, or 1700. As we will see in the next chapter, which addresses the question of definition and early history, it enters English in translations of Aristotle at the turn of the seventeenth century and gains currency within seventeenth-century science and linguistics, precisely the movements for which the *Georgics* (as Bacon's famous phrase, "these Georgickes of the mind," suggests) provided a literary signature. Seeking to uncover a portion of this earlier story, my analysis tries to follow a double imperative. I do not assume – I do not believe – that the problems of our so-called media culture are unique, even if our technologies are different. At the same time, one must resist the backward imposition of late modern and postmodern assumptions onto a rich concept with a long history, assumptions that include the conscious or unconscious reduction of media to technology, as well as the homogenization of the work of the several senses under the too easily abstracted, too easily singular category, "The Media," which is often accorded determining powers. In practice, this double imperative will translate into a definition of the term "medium" that is more inductive than *a priori*, while, at the same time, confronting the poets of the past with theorists of the present – and modern theorists with their literary pre-history. If I am lucky, *Georgic Modernity and British Romanticism* can suggest the persistence of the past in the changed and changing present, and that on two planes: a study of the long eighteenth century and a portion of Romanticism as fields of contest in their own right, and then a leverage of that past for our critical present, so that the reapprehension of Addison, Thomson, Cowper, Wordsworth and others can become evidence for re-thinking Raymond Williams and Walter Benjamin (my main exponents of a georgic modernity), as well as Jameson, Liu, Lyotard, and others still to be mentioned. One of them (it will have escaped no one) made famous in the modern era the existence of areas "beyond the pleasure principle." But as Freud said – and I maintain by considering him only in my final chapter *as* the author of a version of georgic – the poets were there before him.

CHAPTER I

The Georgics *and the cultivation of "mediums," 1660–1712: "sensible paths" and pleasurable "By-ways"*

[T]he Science of Nature has been already too long made only a work of the *Brain* and the *Fancy:* It is now high time that it should return to the plainness and soundness of *Observations* on *material* and *obvious* things . . . [Philosophy] can never be recovered, or continued, but by returning into the same *sensible paths*, in which it did at first proceed.

Hooke, *Micrographia* (1665)

This is wonderfully diverting to the Understanding, thus to receive a Precept, that enters as it were through a By-way.

Addison, "An Essay on the Georgics" (1697)

INTRODUCTION

If, as I noted at the end of my introduction, Friedrich Kittler's claim – that, before the invention of sound storage and broadcasting technologies, "writing functioned as a universal medium" and for that reason "there was no concept of medium" – is too restrictive, perhaps too blithe in its relative presentism and reduction of media to technology, just where would one look for a "media theory" around 1600, when the term first entered the English language?

Some of its earliest English uses and conceptualizations occur in translations of Aristotle. George Chapman's marginal gloss to *Ovid's Banquet of Sence* (1595) notes that "sight is one of the three sences that hath his medium extrinsically," while Robert Burton, writing "Of the Sensible Soul" in *The Anatomy of Melancholy* (1621), observes that "to the Sight three things are required, the Object, the Organ, and the Medium."[1] In these instances, both Chapman and Burton are rendering a sequence from *De Anima*, which defines as indispensable to all perception an "in-between thing or area," τo μεταξύ (*to metaxu*) – literally "the in-between," a noun formed by prefixing the adverb μεταξύ with an article. This "in-between" is both an activity and a substance; affected by the sensible object, it in turn affects and moves

17

the organ of sense. Without it, Aristotle insists, there would be no sight, hearing, smell, taste or touch:

Democritus is mistaken in thinking that if the intervening space [*to metaxu*] were empty, even an ant in the sky would be clearly visible; for this is impossible. For vision occurs when the faculty of sense is affected; as it cannot be acted upon by the seen color [i.e., of the object] itself, there only remains the medium [*to metaxu*] to act on it, so that some medium [*metaxu*] must exist; in fact, if it [*metaxu* implied from previous clause] were empty, sight would not only be not accurate but we would see nothing altogether.[2]

Hearing and smell, the other senses that depend on what Chapman calls an "extrinsic" medium, also have their *metaxu:* air, water, wool, bronze, or other conducting bodies for hearing; air or water for smell. Touch and taste, where taste is a version of touch, initially give Aristotle more trouble, but they too function only because of a conducting in-between: flesh, the intrinsic medium. The difference here is just that in the case of touch we perceive "at the same time as the medium" (εῶ μεταξύ) rather than after it.[3] In each case, however, the *metaxu* is essential: for Aristotle there is a palpable world of objects beyond the media of each sense, but without those media, we would not know it, for they are requisite for perception.

  De Anima offers a remarkable preview of many features that will recur in discussions of media to the present day, and it usefully suggests what might define *medium-consciousness* as distinct from an awareness of form, with which it might easily be merged. Media are a necessary condition of sense perception, although not a sufficient one (for Aristotle, they are part of a complex relationship that includes the accessibility of the object and the development of the faculty of sense). For this reason, as in the example of the ether, they can easily escape notice, lurking somewhere beneath conscious perception. They may, however, force attention to themselves with a sudden shift in the distribution, a display of heterogeneity, among the several senses, for although Aristotle does not reduce the difference between media to the difference between the faculties of sense, nevertheless, the two differences are closely related, and each medium will act on certain organs more than others. Next, Aristotelian media are functions of distance, no matter how large (an expanse of air) or small (a membrane of skin). Scholastic commentary on Aristotle translated the Greek into the Latin *medium*, which had a two-fold spatial reference – midpoint and intermediary agent – although increasingly, as Leo Spitzer has shown, the spatial relationship acquired a functional interpretation. Isaac Newton, whose optics were so influential for eighteenth-century poetry, used the word frequently in Latin and English (the "aetherial medium," or the "transparent," "refracting," "reflecting," or "ambient medium") in such a way that a medium is invariably an element placed so as to become a factor.[4] Niklas Luhmann's enigmatic but useful formulation of the distinction between form and medium from the perspective of twentieth-century systems theory undoubtedly draws on this semantic history. As Luhmann puts it: "Differences between places qualify the medium, whereas differences between objects define its forms"; hence these are two sides "that cannot be thought of in isolation."[5] It also informs Samuel Weber's observation that modern media "call attention to the irreducible significance of the space in-between." For Weber, this interstitial space, within which movement can occur, distinguishes the discussion of media from "aesthetically oriented notions of art and reality, form and work."[6] We will see that a poem's consciousness of itself as a medium is frequently represented by a vertiginous shift in space, whereby near becomes far, or far near.

If, from its inception, the concept of a medium responded to a question of relative places in space, then it also lent itself easily to the problem of rhetoric and therefore to the negotiation of different positions in time as well. Aside from Chapman's and Burton's, another of the earliest uses of the word occurs in *The Advancement of Learning*, when Bacon turns to the problem of "Tradition or Delivery," the "expressing or transferring our knowledge to others":

For the ORGANE OF TRADITION, it is either SPEECH OR WRITING: for *Aristotle* sayth well: ["]*Wordes are the Images of Cogitations, and Letters are the Images of Wordes*["]; but yet it is not of necessitie, that *Cogitations* bee expressed by the *Medium of Wordes*. For *whatsoeuer is capable of sufficient differences, and those perceptible by the sense; is in Nature competent to expresse Cogitations.*[7]

What Aristotle actually says, in *On Interpretation*, is that things spoken are the σύμβολα, or symbols, of παθημάτων (*pathematon*, or affections), just as written words are the σύμβολα of the spoken.[8] By modulating from Aristotle's σύμβολα to his own "*Medium*" in the first of the sentences just quoted from *Advancement*, Bacon subtly but consequentially convenes, under the term "medium," the organic, physical intermediaries of *De Anima* with the man-made, instrumental "organs" of linguistics and science. The human faculty (eye, ear, etc.) stimulated *by* the "in-between" in Aristotle becomes, in Bacon's text, a new "Organe" that *is* the in-between: Bacon here cites language, writing, hieroglyphics, and non-iconic sign-systems. George Snell, a later acolyte of the Baconian new science, intertwines the organic and the technological applications of the word together in his 1649 attempt to naturalize and ratify the vernacular as the national language, *The Right Teaching of Useful Knowledge*: "It is more facil for an English man, by the eie of reason, to see through the medium, and light of the English tongue; then by the more obscure light of anie forrein language."[9] (One might apprehend the seeds of a much later abstraction and reification whereby the "medium" becomes independent of its human sense activity, *à la* McLuhan and others, but neither Bacon nor Snell goes that far.)

These several examples – more could be cited – point to the fact that we can find many of the elements of a seventeenth-century media theory at the intersection of the new science (especially optics, the flagship science) and its corollary linguistics. This junction is also the place where one also finds new attention to Virgil's *Georgics* and, more generally, an intensified interest in "Englishing" the mode. One task of this chapter will be to explain why this convergence is not merely fortuitous, and then to begin to elaborate the peculiar role of the *Georgics*, and English interpretations of that poem, in the maneuvers that make up one early chapter in the history of attempts to "understand media."

Anthony Low has influentially made the case for a seventeenth-century "Georgic Revolution," and Ralph Cohen and Alastair Fowler, while preferring more evolutionary terms, have argued similarly that the georgic presence in English cannot be limited to sedulous imitations or strict full-scale instances of the georgic as a genre, which flourished only during the seventy years following Dryden's translation of Virgil in 1697, the Act of Union in 1701, and the Peace of Utrecht of 1713.[10] The earlier modal presence intensified within and because of the new science, where the *Georgics* themselves served as a kind of poster-poem – a signature and source of quotations or mottos – for the program of scientific and agricultural reform, and where the concept of a "georgics" as a discipline or meta-theory also begins to emerge. This honorific status is apparent as early as Bacon's often-cited description of *The Advancement of Learning* as "these Georgickes of the Mind, concerning the husbandry & tillage therof" (I return to this passage shortly in more detail), and it later appears in the new plans for agriculture, beekeeping, gardening, and education sponsored by the members of the Hartlib circle at mid-century, including Snell, whose *Right Teaching of Useful Knowledge* was appropriately dedicated to Samuel Hartlib. It is particularly evident in the constitution of the Royal Society after the Restoration, which included a "Georgical Committee" (John Evelyn, Abraham Cowley, John Beale, and others) and generated a number of georgic essays, the most famous of which is Cowley's *Of Agriculture* (1688). Dryden's hyperbolic promotion of the *Georgics* as the "best poem by the best poet" in the dedication of his 1697 translation of *The Works of Virgil in English* is well remembered, but we should see this praise in the context of his earlier membership in the Royal Society (1662–66), followed by his defense of the method of the *Essay of Dramatic Poesy* by comparing it to the "modest inquisitions" of the Society.[11]

Low, Michael Leslie, Timothy Raylor, and others following Low have noted that the *Georgics* became a textual touchstone for the new science and its forays into linguistics, and they have accounted for this role by focusing on the poem's thematic appeal to these movements: its authorization of the general culture of active estate management and terracultural experiment, as well as its promotion of a cult of retirement, figuring the gentleman-farmer as the Happy Man, ostensibly free of the care of politics and strife. Certainly, the figure of Virgil's vigilant *agricola*, "ever at his post to discipline the ground [*exercetque frequens tellurem*] and give his orders to the field" (*Georgics*, 1.99), is well-suited to a political and social program for disciplining both ground and sense. Yet the thematic account is not in itself sufficient. As Rachel Crawford has noted, for example, all of the factors which in Low's account earned the georgic prestige – "the linking of scientific method with agriculture, the growth of societies that supported this endeavor, growing numbers of agricultural treatises, and new attitudes toward the relationship between gentlemen and labor" – similarly describe movements at the end of the eighteenth-century.[12] My own resistance is more basic still; it responds to the premise, which founds Low's and almost all critical narratives about English georgic, that Virgil's middle term chiefly promised more workaday, practical, and realistic representations than a more courtly taste had permitted. The premise makes good sense on thematic grounds, but it neglects the degree to which the *Georgics* also offered, and were understood by the linguistically self-conscious seventeenth century to offer, a glittering verbal *tekhnē*, producing a medium (*to metaxu*, that "in-between") capable of stimulating a work of reading that was not assumed to be the same as the work it described or – since the *Georgics* are *not* after all very realistic – the work it simulated. If the role of georgic as the literary sign of the new science has gone under the radar of intellectual or scientific histories, then both the highly-"worked" quality of Virgil's *Georgics* and the appeal of its heightening powers to an initial audience – well-trained in the classics – have not received enough attention or play from recent seventeenth- and eighteenth-century literary historians, and with considerable consequences for understanding its later residual legacy.

This chapter therefore locates the *Georgics* within a movement fascinated by optical and linguistic media or "mediums"[13] as well as intent on scrutinizing its own discursive and literary mediums. I argue first that the paradoxical logic at work within the new science, whereby the demand for sense-immediacy was met by a multiplication of the techniques of mediation, was also a considerable part of the original lure of the *Georgics*, even as its glossy artifice is much later responsible for the subsequent muting of the genre. Here I am less interested in revising our accounts of literary change than I am in laying the ground for how it came to be that, after the taste for formal imitation subsided, the georgic mode could persist in concerns for positioning and sense reception, for the instruments and feelings – the channels of sensation and perception – by which later readers sought to know the world. Joseph Addison, the focus of the third section of this chapter, occupies a pivotal place in this history not only because of his early commentary on the *Georgics* but also, and more so, because of his use of that essay as the basis for the aesthetics advanced in *The Spectator*'s "Pleasures of the Imagination" sequence. Having used the *Georgics* to define the advantages of poetry as an epistemological instrument, one capable of positioning the subject so that percept and precept "ente[r] as it were through a By-way," Addison, as Mr. Spectator, implicitly asks the other arts to pass through its rationale. Whether they do or not is another matter altogether, which future chapters will explore.

THE *GEORGICS* AS "ARTIFICIAL ORGAN": MAGNIFYING SMALL THINGS AFTER THE RESTORATION

Robert Hooke, Curator of Experiments for the Royal Society, articulates in revealing terms the ambitions of the new experimental philosophy practiced by that Society in the "Preface" to his *Micrographia* (1665). In the text that would do so much to make the microscope something of a sensation within England for the next hundred years, Hooke announces:

The first thing to be undertaken in this weighty work, is a *watchfulness over the failings* and an *inlargement of the dominion*, of the Senses. . . . The next care to be taken, in respect of the Senses, is a supplying of their infirmities with *Instruments*, and, as it were, the adding of *artificial Organs* to the *natural*; this in one of them has been of late years accomplisht with prodigous benefit of all sorts of useful knowledge, by the invention of Optical Glasses. . . . The truth is, the Science of Nature has been already too long made only a work of the *Brain* and the *Fancy*: It is now high time that it should return to the plainness and soundness of *Observations* on *material* and *obvious* things. It is said of great Empires, That *the best way to preserve them from decay, is to bring them back to the first Principles, and Arts, on which they did begin*. The same is undoubtedly true in Philosophy, that by wandring far away into *invisible Notions*, has almost quite destroy'd it self, and it can never be recovered, or continued, but by returning into the same *sensible paths*, in which it did at first proceed.[14]

Although his expertise remained in "optical glasses," Hooke's ambitions did not stop at enhancing the organ of sight, as this next remarkable comment suggests:

It has not been yet thoroughly examined, how far *Otocousticons* may be improv'd, nor what other ways there may be of *quickning* our hearing, or *conveying* sound through *other bodies* then the *Air*: for that that is not the only *medium*, I can assure the Reader, that I have, by the help of a *distended wire*, propagated the sound to a very considerable distance in an *instant*.[15]

Hooke's return to the "*sensible paths*" (pathways of sensation) is in each instance a return with a difference. The optical "*artificial Organs*" and acoustic "*medium*" offer a remedial extension and transformation of the Aristotelian *to metaxu*, or what Jay David Bolter and Richard Grusin have called a "remediation" (with the implicit conjunction of remedy and mediation).[16] Aristotle's science was founded on the "postulate of the visible,"[17] but Hooke's new prostheses or "helps," as he claims, will "discipline" and newly empower the senses – "both in the surveying the already visible World, and for the discovery of many others hitherto unknown, and to make us, with the great Conqueror, to be affected that we have not yet overcome one World when there are so many others to be discovered, every considerable improvement of *Telescopes* or *Microscopes* producing new Worlds and *Terra-Incognita's* to our view."[18] Hooke's metaphors for sensory extension are portentous, as we will see.

New worlds require lots of documentation and "histories"; they call up the need for what Hooke calls a "sincere hand." Many accordingly hastened to legislate, innovate, and otherwise attend with new zeal to Bacon's "organs of tradition" or delivery. The proliferation of aspiring language legislators and improvers during the Civil War and Restoration periods is a well-known story;[19] I will outline the points that seem most salient for understanding the paradoxes that reside in the popularity of Virgil's *Georgics*. Too often Thomas Sprat's notorious resolution on behalf of the Royal Society "to turn back to the primitive purity, and shortness, when men deliver'd so many *things*, almost in an equal number of *words*" or Abraham Cowley's "Ode to the Royal Society" (prefixed to Sprat's *History* and sporting the motto, "From Words which are but Pictures of the Thought / . . . to things, the Mind's right Object be it brought") are taken at face value as authoritative accounts of the Restoration's faith in the "neutrality and transparency" of discourse; the actual picture is more complicated.[20] Regretting what they considered the lost "language of Adam," in which "all things live stand operate and speak out," such men as John Webster, George Dalgarno, Walter Charleton, Seth Ward, the aptly named Cave Beck, and others sought to repair the ruins of lost paradise and "restore Babel" with a universal language and character, but the descriptions Webster offered for such a putative language are not particularly reassuring, at least on the score of undoing Babel: "*Hieroglyphical, Emblematical, Symbolical, and Cryptographical*"; "*Polygraphy* or *Steganography*."[21]

The most famous of these schemers was, of course, John Wilkins, whose *Essay Towards a Real Character and a Philosophical Language* (1668) had no modest goals: it set out to provide tables and charts for "the distinct expression of all things and notions that fall under discourse," to facilitate "easy Conversation" and "mutual Commerce, amongst the Several Nations of the World," and to install a gentlemanly civility into domestic (national) intercourse: "This design will likewise contribute much to the clearing of some of our Modern differences in Religion, by unmasking many wild errors, that shelter themselves under the disguise of affected phrases."[22] The political stakes and motivations for this linguistic economy are clear enough, for in such urgent fantasies that one might turn from wheeling words and sectarian enthusiasms to discrete "facts" – to say nothing of the premise, underlying a universal philosophy, that all minds operate in just the same way – one hears the bad memories of mid-seventeenth-century civil war and factionalism. Wilkins included in his *Essay* an appendix containing the Lord's Prayer and Nicene Creed in his universal language, as well as transcriptions of that language in the "real character," and the choice of these illustrative texts is hardly accidental. The hope is that we will perhaps be less likely to argue about the theology behind the words, if the words are not words at all, but universally accepted graphic markers for exchange and consent.

But the *effect* of consulting Wilkins's Lord's Prayer is, of course, altogether different (see figure 1). We find there the parallel lines of numbers, surrounded both by hieroglyphs to represent ideas, plus a completely different set of phonetic symbols to denote sounds, and only then succeeded by the familiar English words: "Our Father who art in Heaven. . . ." So, too, the effect of the period's proliferating handbooks of grammar, the various plans for sign languages, the debates about printers' cues, or the multiplication of punctuation marks – Wilkins and others suggested the installation of a special mark to denote irony, an inverted exclamation point [¡] – is to bare the device with a vengeance, rather like activating the "reveal codes"

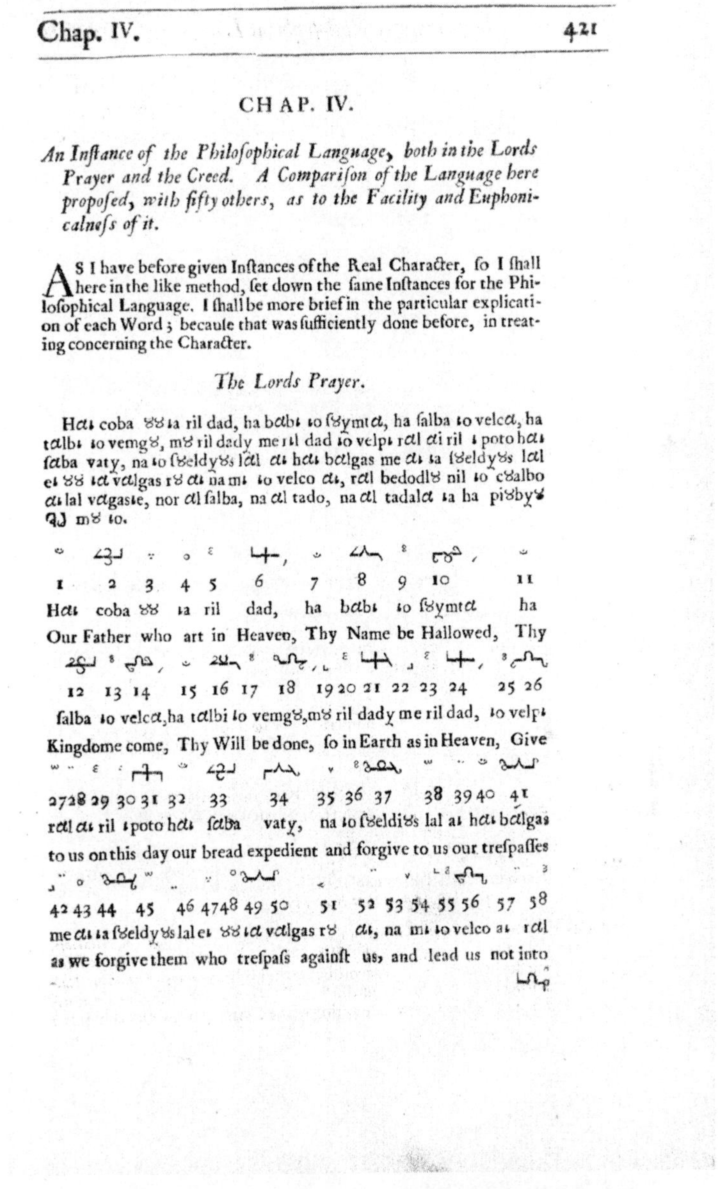

Chap. IV.   421

CHAP. IV.

*An Inſtance of the Philoſophical Language, both in the Lords
Prayer and the Creed.   A Compariſon of the Language here
propoſed, with fifty others, as to the Facility and Euphoni-
calneſs of it.*

AS I have before given Inſtances of the Real Character, ſo I ſhall
here in the like method, ſet down the ſame Inſtances for the Philoſophical Language. I ſhall be more brief in the particular explicati-
on of each Word ; becauſe that was ſufficiently done before, in treating concerning the Character.

The Lords Prayer.

Haı coba ᴚᴚ ıa ril dad, ha baıbı ıo ſᴚymtaı, ha ſalba ıo velcaı, ha
taılbı ıo vemgᴚ, mᴚ ril dady me ril dad ıo velpı raıl aıi ril ı poto haı
ſaıba vaty, na ıo ſᴚeldyᴚs laıl aıı haı baılgas me aıı ıa ſᴚeldyᴚs laıl
eı ᴚᴚ ıaıvaılgas rᴚ aıı na mı ıo velco aıı, raıl bedodlᴚ nil ıo caᴚalbo
aıı lal vaıgasıe, nor aıl ſalba, na aıl tado, na aıl tadalaı ıa ha pıᴚbyᴚ
ꝗⱻ mᴚ ıo.

1	2	3	4 5	6	7	8	9	10		11

Haı   coba ᴚᴚ ıa ril   dad,   ha   baıbı ıo ſᴚymtaı   ha
Our Father who art in Heaven, Thy Name be Hallowed,   Thy

12	13 14	15 16 17	18	19 20 21 22 23 24	25 26

ſalba ıo velcaı,ha taılbi ıo vemgᴚ,mᴚ ril dady me ril dad, ıo velpı
Kingdome come, Thy Will be done, ſo in Earth as in Heaven, Give

27 28 29 30 31 32	33	34	35 36 37	38 39 40 41

raıl aıı ril ıpoto haı ſaıba   vaty, na ıo ſᴚeldiᴚs lal aı haı baılgas
to us on this day our bread expedient and forgive to us our treſpaſſes

42 43 44	45	46 47 48 49 50	51	52 53 54 55 56	57 58

me aıı ıa ſᴚeldyᴚs lal eı ᴚᴚ ıaı vaılgas rᴚ   aıı, na mı ıo velco aı raıl
as we forgive them who treſpaſs againſt us, and lead us not into

Figure 1 The Lord's Prayer in John Wilkins' "Philosophical Language" (*An Essay Towards
a Real Character, and A Philosophical Language,* 1668).

function in a word-processing program today.[23] All these strategies elicited Swift's hilarity in *Gulliver's Travels*, but they call into question the narrative often told about this period by more than one important modern historian: "word and thing are brought to coincide in the sense that the former is a completely adequate and transparent representation of the latter."[24] Universal language schemes did not restore Adamic language. They generated more universal language schemes.

In other words, the desire for what Wilkins and others called a "noise"-free, pure system of words or signs (Sprat: a "primitive purity," a "naked natural way of speaking") was just that: a desire. It was the statement of a problem, a signal that especially in the wake of "our Modern differences in Religions" a crisis was detectable in the "sensible paths" of communication and perception. It was not enough just to ban political controversy from the meetings of the Society (as in fact its members did); the fault might be in language itself, in the fact that language is inevitably political and historical. Additionally, we need to recognize that the desire for sense-immediacy in optics, acoustics, and linguistics was just that, too: a desire, insatiable perhaps, but one whose remedy for the infirmities of the senses was in practice sought for by the multiplication and intensification of the technologies of mediation. Bolter and Grusin, cited earlier, would call this paradox the "double logic of remediation," whereby the fiction of improved immediacy depends on an exertion of what they call "hypermediacy," the self-conscious display of diverse pictorial, phonic, and numerical techniques.[25]

This paradox, I suggest, gives us a view of the appeal of Virgil's *Georgics* in the later seventeenth century that differs considerably from the one established by Low and others. Beyond the poem's *thematic* appeal to the new husbandry, its availability as a source of mottos, and its tacit acknowledgment of imperial ambition, it was also compelling as a distinctive text precisely because in it a version of the same paradoxical logic is at work. In Virgil's *Georgics*, in other words, the power and interest of the real depends on a self-conscious heightening and restatement of the real. The contradiction seems already, if covertly, acknowledged in Bacon's use of quotation in the famous "Georgickes of the mind" sequence:

Neyther needed men of so excellent parts to haue despaired of a Fortune, (which the Poet *Virgill* promised himselfe, and indeed obtained) who got as much glory of eloquence, wit, and learning in the expressing of the obseruacions of husbandry, as of the heroicall acts of *Æneas*:–
    Nec sum animi dubius, verbis ea vincere magnum,
    Quam sit & angustis his addere rebus honorem.

And surely if the purpose be in good earnest not to write at leasure that which me*n* may read at leasure, but really to instruct and suborne Action and actiue life, these Georgickes of the mind concerning the husba*n*dry & tillage therof, are no less worth the*n* the heroical descriptio*n*s of *vertue, duty, & felicity. . . .*[26]

Bacon is, at this moment, advocating the study of "ordinary and common matters," arguing that if these have been shunned, it is because men "haue compounded Sciences chiefly of a certaine resplendent and lustrous masse of matter chosen to give glory either to the subtillity of disputacions, or to the eloquence of discourses." If we are to acquire knowledge of practical things, near to hand, then we must withdraw our language from the "treasury of eloquence" and set matters forth with economy.[27] The phrase "Georgickes of the mind" thus refers not only to a particular program of study ("ordinary and common matters") but also to a concern for what the *Advancement* had just called "the medium of Wordes," which Bacon ostensibly wants to *oppose* to the "resplendent or lustrouse masse of matter" of classical eloquence. Rhetorical and epistemological economy are nominally conjoined under the designation of a "georgics."

But if one is really shunning the resplendent and lustrous matter of words for the naked, unadorned thing, the *Georgics* themselves make a notably strange literary correlative. Bacon seems well aware of the irony, since the citation from the third *Georgic*, "For well I know how hard it is to elevate these things with words (*verbis*), and to bring to slight things (*angustis rebus*) this honour due" (3.289–90), does not suit his ostensible argument at all.[28] Although Virgil is writing about quotidian wisdom at this point (the care of cattle and goats), he is explicitly underlining the *dissonance* between the two kinds of "matter" yoked together by that common word in Bacon's *Advancement* – between, that is, his own "soaring words" (*magno . . . ore* [3.296]) and the *angustis rebus* (literally, the narrow or confined things) of his subject.[29] *Res* and *verba*, things and words, the materials of the husbandman's and the poet's labors respectively, exist at once in a collaborative and a competitive relation to each other here as throughout the *Georgics*. Although its series of opening relative clauses presents the text as an instructional manual on the various arts of husbandry by beginning with a series of "how-to's" – *Quid faciat laetas segetes . . . quo sidere . . . quae cura . . . qui cultus . . . quanta experientia* ("What makes the crops joyous . . . beneath what star . . . what tending . . . what care . . . what skill . . ." [*Georgics*, 1.1–4]) – nonetheless no actual farmer in Virgil's time, and few afterward, could have followed the *Georgics* for advice on the rules of cultivation or meteorology. The text did promote an ethos of improvement, and in particular Frans De Bruyn has argued that the eighteenth-century discourse on agricultural improvement was happy to "piggy-back" on the culturally prestigious form of georgic, but anyone who followed it literally would not have had what the first line promises: *laetas segetes* ("joyous" [i.e., fertile] crops).[30] Messengers of the details of husbandry, carrying them to Rome and the circle of Augustus, the poet's *verba* inlay and amplify those rural *res* with their own glossy thingliness, creating a marked density within representation. The poem does not lose contact with the cycle of the seasons and the improbities of labor (the famous *labor improbus*); as the classicist Richard F. Thomas has shown, Virgil worked very carefully with the Greek and Roman prose agricultural treatises by Varro (*Res Rusticae*), Theophrastus (*Historia Plantarum*), and Cato (*De Agricultura*).[31] Yet by expanding some details and subduing others, Virgil reshaped the prose material and offered his erudite and urban audiences a splendid virtual reality.[32]

Moreover, although Virgil "courts the burden of referentiality," as Kurt Heinzelman has pointed out, the poet's references are just as often literary and intertextual as terracultural or extra-textual: "*The Georgics* is one of the most allusive texts we have," Heinzelman acknowledges elsewhere.[33] Its "art of allusion," studied by Thomas and more minutely by Joseph Farrell, is extremely sophisticated, offering a compendium of the work of Lucretius, Homer, Hesiod, and so many others.[34] Even more so than in Milton, who learned this technique from Virgil, and more than in the *Eclogues* or the *Aeneid*, every line teems with the buried and multiple voices of other poets. Those *versus* are a crowded palimpsest of classical culture, and they have been diligently probed for their multiple sources, generating marginal notes and glosses deeper than any underworld. The glorious laboriousness of reading the *Georgics* results from a complex, non-mimetic practice of reference; *verba* in the poem point in two directions at once – ostensibly, but not transparently, toward the details and cycles of agricultural work, and diachronically toward layers of previous poetic works. Writing the preface to *Sylvae* (1685), the second volume of his *Poetical Miscellanies*, twelve years before his translation with its famous declaration of the *Georgics* as the "best poem by the best poet," Dryden understands Virgil's various nesting, intensifying, and heightening techniques quite well. Since Dryden also sounds as if he is describing the crowding of rays upon the specimen within the microscope, one might want to call this an insight into Virgil's syn-optics:

I look'd on Virgil, as . . . one who weigh'd not only every thought, but every Word and Syllable. Who was still aiming to crowd his sence into as narrow a compass as possibly he cou'd; for which reason he is so very Figurative, that he requires, (I may almost say) a Grammar apart to construe him.[35]

A poem reputedly written at the average rate of one line per day, the *Georgics* are as much about the labor of language as an in-between as they are about what Virgil calls the "*variae . . . artes*" (*Georgics*, 1.145), the "diverse arts" or techniques of cultivation. The *cultus* and *cura* celebrated from the first to the last lines of the poem at every point also imbue the tending and the upkeep of words.

Richard Thomas thus rightly cautions against treating the *Georgics* as a "bipartite poem, alternating between the 'technical' (i.e., 'dull' or 'unimportant') and the 'lyrical' (i.e., 'interesting' or 'meaningful')," for the *Georgics* are about poetry as *tekhnē*.[36] They, too, are an "artifical Organ," and proud of it. Writing in the same year as the publication of Dryden's *Sylvae*, Robert Wolseley praised Virgil for the "Operations of his vivifying Power," which – at least to Wolseley's sensibility – consists in the ability to "enliven the deadest Lump, beautifie the vilest Dirt, and sweeten the most offensive Filth . . . and by a poetical Daemonianism, possesse it with the spirit of good sence and gracefulnesse."[37] These magnifying powers, I have been suggesting, were a large part of the lure of this text to the intellectual culture of experimental philosophy, which delighted, as Henry Power does here with the help of the microscope, in "The Common Fly": "[H]er body," writes Power, "is as it were from head to tayl studded with silver and black Armour, stuck all over with great black Bristles, like Porcupine quills . . . her wings look like a Sea-fan with black thick ribs or fibers, dispers'd and branch'd through them, which are webb'd between with a thin membrane or film, like a slice of Muscovy-glasse."[38]

JOSEPH ADDISON'S "BY-WAYS": THE POLITE PLEASURES OF INFORMATION

Georgic's transformation of "slight," quotidian matters by "lofty words" became the focus of the series of prefaces, essays, and lectures that accompanied or swiftly followed Dryden's complete 1697 edition and his particular promotion of Virgil's middle work. The first wave of these writings begins with Joseph Addison's "An Essay on the Georgics," prefixed at Dryden's request to the 1697 volume but probably written before it, as early as 1693.[39] Addison discusses Virgil only, but his essay was soon followed by Joseph Trapp's "Of Didactic or Preceptive Poetry," published in 1711 and reissued throughout the first three decades of the eighteenth century, and

Thomas Tickell's *De Poesi Didactica*, a lecture delivered in 1711. Like Joseph Wharton and John Aikin later in the eighteenth century, Trapp and Tickell follow Addison closely, citing and quoting him as their original. Since both are, unlike Addison, in the position to respond to the first English georgic imitations, such as *Cyder*, they also seek to expand the range of Virgilian farming and husbandry to include local and national historiography, moral philosophy, and natural science, sometimes by amalgamating the poem to Lucretius's *De Rerum Natura* – the "culture" in agriculture is undergoing a rapid expansion. All of them, however, are equally engaged by the question of the relationship between what Trapp calls the "technical words, or *Terms of Art*" (e.g., skill or craft) and the "poetry."[40]

This tension between the technical and the poetical is not just the Horatian commonplace about negotiating a harmonious balance between instruction and pleasure (*utile* and *dulci*), soon to become a familiar refrain in essays on the new "novel or romance." The precepts and details that provide the ostensible subject matter and occasion for Virgil's "poetical Daemonianism" – sheep-dipping, soil-testing, animal-mating, manuring, irrigation – present in acute form a challenge to decorum and, as a result, an occasion to define the flexibility as well as the limits of "poetry"; the same is true to some degree for the subjects now enfranchised by the new science.[41] Addison complains that Hesiod has "much more of the Husbandman than the Poet in his Temper. . . . He is every where bent on Instruction, avoids all manner of Digressions, and does not stir out of the Field once in the whole *Georgic*. His Method in describing Month after Month with its proper Seasons and Employments . . . makes the whole look but like a modern Almanack in Verse." Virgil, by contrast, "delivers the meanest of his Precepts with a kind of Grandeur, he breaks the Clods and tosses the Dung about with an air of gracefulness."[42] This last, often-cited verdict may strike us now just as amusing evidence, if any were needed, of Addison's remove from the life of agricultural husbandry, but the question of the compatibility of practical "dung" and poetic "grace" was a serious one. What is the difference between an "almanack in verse" – or what Tickell just as unflatteringly characterizes as the mere "Packets of Precepts" in surviving fragments of Greek didactic poetry – and a poem, to say nothing of the "best poem"?[43] Can subjects usually reserved for "almanacks," whether in verse or in prose, become the stuff of a "poem"?

Later critics were increasingly dubious: "The subject, Sir, cannot be made poetical," sniffed Dr. Johnson in response to *The Fleece*, Dyer's 1757 georgic on sheepshearing and the cotton market: "How can a man write poetically of serges and druggets?"[44] Similarly, John Aikin would write in a

1795 preface to John Armstrong's 1744 medical georgic, *The Art of Preserving Health*, that even as fine an example as Virgil's *Georgics* will

> serve to shew the unfavorable Effect of attempting to express Matter purely technical in a Poetical Manner . . . [I]n many of the preceptive Passages, . . . he is overpowered by his Subject, and chained, as it were, to the Earth he is labouring, while on the other hand, as a Teacher of the Art [i.e., farming] he is frequently so obscure as to have embarrassed the whole Race of agricultural and literary Critics since his Time.[45]

Yet Addison, Trapp, and Tickell are not willing to give up the dung of technical matter as an occasion for poetic grace. Where Sir Philip Sidney had demoted the *Georgics* specifically and philosophical verse more generally for remaining too "wrapped within the fold of the proposed subject" over a century earlier, Trapp elevates both by insisting that "Precepts and Poetry are no ways inconsistent" as long as the "*technical words*, or *Terms of Art* . . . might be so dressed up, as to invite, not deter the Pains of the Listener."[46] For Trapp, that is, precept and poetry *should* be mutually wrapped in the fold. The fact is sometimes the sweetest dream that genteel poets know, to adapt Robert Frost's adage. These essays point to the new, distinctive, and pleasurable charge carried by information itself, by the parcel of practical or scientific knowledge contemplated as a kind of useful diversion. The Augustan "amateurs," as Barbara M. Stafford comments, "valued information couched in the refined displays consonant with the labor-free ideals of civic humanism" and "looked to the universe as a source on nontaxing learning achieved through contemplation."[47] More importantly for my purpose here, the georgic's heterogeneous yoking of "information" and poetic process brings the latter under scrutiny as an instrument that now exists as a complement or potential rival to other, new technologies of knowledge. The rivalry is implicit, if stated with some irony, in Trapp's comparison between modern poems and new scientific instruments of perception (including "the Microscope" and "the Telescope"): "As Natural Philosophy has, by the Help of Experiments, been lately brought to much greater Perfection than ever; this kind of Poetry [e.g., didactic or preceptive], no doubt, would have made proportionable Advances, if the same age that had shew'd a Boyle, a Halley, and a Newton, had produced a Virgil."[48] Tickell may have disparaged "Packets of Precept," but the packaging of precept is precisely his concern.

This intensified self-consciousness about poetry as one "organ" among others often occurs, as we will continue to see in chapter 2, because of the rhetorical and conceptual fluidity between accounts of optical instruments and textual helps for apprehension, but it does not depend on that analogy. In many cases, including Addison's, it occurs because of the apparent proximity of georgic poetry to instructional prose. "For there are several ways of conveying the same Truth to the Mind of Man," Addison writes in the 1697 discussion of the *Georgics*, "and to chuse the pleasantest of these ways, is that which chiefly distinguishes Poetry from Prose, and makes *Virgil*'s Rules of Husbandry pleasanter to read than *Varro*'s."[49] What is "pleasantness" for Addison? It is a function of a particular kind of imagined relationship between the text and an idealized Reader ("philosophically considered," as Wordsworth would put it), in which the "pleasure" is a measure of the text's productivity as a promoter of responsiveness. This relationship, a number of critics have nicely observed, makes the consumer not just a collaborator but a genteel co-laborer with the author in the joint production of meaning.[50] In Addison's words:

> [Virgil] loves to suggest a Truth indirectly, and without giving us a full and open view of it: To let us see just so much as will naturally lead the Imagination into all the parts that lie conceal'd. This is wonderfully diverting to the Understanding, thus to receive a Precept, that enters as it were through a By-way, and to apprehend an Idea that draws a whole train after it: For here the Mind, which is always delighted with its own Discoveries, only takes the hint from the Poetry, and seems to work out the rest by the strength of her own Faculties.[51]

Indirectness, or the tarrying of the "By-way," is what makes "*Virgil*'s Rules of Husbandry pleasanter to read than *Varro*'s," whose prose text, *Res Rusticae*, Virgil had combed for the *Georgics*. Prose plows straight ahead, as Addison would have it (punning on the etymology of "prose" from *prorsus*, straightforward, from *provertere*, to turn forward), while the *versus* coils back upon itself; it is "diverting," leaving more to readerly surmise. Its pleasure, and the young Addison assiduously courts what he will later call "the principle of pleasure," results from its operation as a "cool medium" – "hot media," wrote McLuhan in high Addisonian mode, "are low in participation, and cool media are high in participation or completion by an audience."[52] Texts merely sow the seeds, so that readers are pleased to reap the ideas.

Of the several striking things to note in Addison's essay, then, one is that where the poetry cannot be differentiated from prose on the basis of its subject matter, as in the case of the *Georgics*, Addison does not resort primarily to more traditional distinctions of form, meter, or even diction (although he does gesture toward the last when he praises Virgil's "Metaphors, *Grecisms*, and Circumlocutions").[53] Instead he defines the specificity of "Poetry" as a function of the manner in which it works upon another body – that is, by its properties as an "in between," *to metaxu,* which places the reader in a distinctive way, positioning him (or her) as if with a teasingly "indirect" rather than a "full and open view," leaving "parts concealed," and thereby drawing the mind into the supplementary production of "Idea." In short, Hooke's solicitude for improving "sensible paths," equally dependent on the management of space, has become Addison's concern for sustaining diverting "By-ways."[54] And, of course, although Addison does not say so, this imagined positioning contains a tacit social relationship: the reader is not an actual farmer in full view of the dung but a cultivator whose main activity is to apprehend and shape ideas.

Addison's account of those georgic by-ways may sound familiar: "The Mind . . . takes the hint from the Poetry, and seems to work out the rest by the strength of her own faculties." That formulation becomes the basis of what the older critic would come to call the "secondary pleasures of the Imagination" in the famous cluster of 1712 (*Spectator* Nos. 411–21).[55] To review the more widely known formulations in the *Spectator* papers: where the primary pleasures arise from "Objects as are before our Eyes," the secondary pleasures arise from our "Ideas of visible objects, when the objects are not actually before the Eye," but are called up by representations of those objects or by our memories of them.[56] Five days later, in *Spectator* 416, Addison elaborates the second category by arguing that the "pleasure" of the secondary pleasures derives not simply from the representation (or the memory) but more specifically from a comparison between the "Ideas" provided by each: "from that Action of the Mind, which compares the *Ideas* arising from the Original Objects with the Ideas we receive from the Statue, Picture, Description, or Sound that represents them."[57] Upon beholding even the smallest circumstance of such representations, and comparing or supplementing them from memory, Addison writes in *Spectator* No. 417 (now following the earlier formulation from the "Essay on the Georgics" quite closely), "*our Imagination takes the Hint, and leads us unexpectedly into Cities or Theatres, Plains or Meadows.*"[58] In spite of the hierarchy suggested by their names, it is the secondary, more mediated pleasures that possess the superior pleasure; following McLuhan, one might say they are cooler but better. The source of their superiority Addison locates again in consumerly collaboration: in the opportunity afforded for active mental comparison, which gives at least the illusion of mastery (the mind "seems to work out the rest by the strength of her own Faculties"). As in the *Georgics* essay, but now more insistently, such mastery is marked by the ability to form a mental "idea" out of bodily sense. As in that essay, too, ideational mastery in *The*

Spectator depends on a measure of distance from the original object, which is to remain at least partly concealed: if "the Object presses too close upon our Senses . . . it does not give us time or leisure to reflect on our selves."[59] Gently stirred sensation permits the imaginative cultivation even of the "Disagreeable" – especially of the disagreeable because, as Shaun Irlam has observed, "despite their frequent affirmations of propriety, Addison's essays will perversely pursue the pleasures of impropriety."[60] Virgil's farmer was praised for "fling[ing] the Dung with Grace" in the *Georgics* essay, and *Spectator* 418 accordingly considers what it calls the "new Principle of Pleasure" raised by the result. "The Description of a Dung-hill is pleasing to the Imagination, if the Image be represented to our Minds by suitable Expressions," Addison cheerfully writes, for "we are not so much delighted with the Image that is contained in the Description, as with the Aptness of the Description to excite the Image."[61]

Although accounts of eighteenth-century aesthetics have typically considered Locke, and in particular Locke's principle of association, as the primary source of the *Spectator*'s emphasis on affective response, the actual wording of the 1712 *Spectator* essay ("our Imagination takes the Hint") suggests that Addison is drawing on his own earlier "An Essay on the Georgics" at least as much as he is evoking Locke's account of the "madness" of association – especially since Addison wrote his essay on Virgil before he could have read Locke's chapter on association, which was added to the *Essay Concerning Human Understanding* only in 1700.[62] It is thus not only possible but necessary, I think, to read the papers on "The Pleasures of the Imagination" and their principle of productive response, of the working or exercising *reader*, as a development of the nascent aesthetic program first prompted for Addison by reading and writing about the *Georgics*. This is interesting as a matter of genealogy but not only as such. It also makes sense of an otherwise contradictory feature of *The Spectator*'s "Pleasures" sequence: although the cluster starts by praising "Our Sight [as] the most perfect and most delightful of our senses" and the "rough careless *Strokes*" of a painterly "Nature," by *Spectator* 416 Addison has completely substituted *verbal* description for the other arts (statues, painting, music) as the source of the secondary pleasures.[63] From this moment on, language, which does not appeal to the sense of sight (as "it is impossible to draw the little Connexions of Speech, or to give the Picture of a Conjunction or an Adverb"), provides the model according to which the other arts are conceived: "most of the Observations that agree with [verbal] Descriptions, are equally Applicable to Painting and Statuary."[64] This slippage, which results in the substitution of "Words" for the diversity of the several arts, is easy for

Addison – inadvertent perhaps – precisely because the secondary "Pleasures of the Imagination" started their conceptual life as a meditation on the pleasures of information in Virgil's *Georgics*.

Thus at several key moments in which Mr. Spectator surreptitiously displaces the particularity of the other arts with the principles of verbal description, and particularly "the Time of Reading" them (3:568), he is importing with only minor alterations some formulation from his author's "Essay on the Georgics." So, for example, *Spectator* 416's claim that *verbal* "Description often gives us more lively Ideas than the Sight of the Things themselves" echoes Addison's earlier reading of Virgil's poem, "where we receive more strong and lively *Ideas* of things from his words . . . and find our Imaginations more affected by his Descriptions, than they wou'd have been by the very sight of what he describes."[65] Ideas produced by words are more "lively," *Spectator* 416 makes clear, because words "run yet further from the things [they] represent than painting." They are, in other words, georgic "By-ways." They should not, however, run too far away from things. If the failure to form ideas issues from overdue proximity ("the Object press[ing] too closely upon our senses"), then it can equally result from too great a distance. That failure, for Mr. Spectator's paradoxically *writerly* aesthetic, is invited by *sound*: "It would be yet more strange, to represent visible objects by Sounds that have no Ideas annexed to them, and to make something like Description in *Musick*."[66]

Addison's *Spectator* papers on imaginative pleasure do in this way tend to elevate writing as a "universal medium" in the sense described by Kittler: "whatever else was going on dropped through the filter of letters or ideograms."[67] It does not therefore follow that "there was no concept of [a] medium." The poetry- and print-based homogeneity of Addison's pleasures, so conducive (he hoped) to the production of ideas and the individuality of the subject, is precariously shored up against the heterogeneity of the several senses which underlie it. We will see that such heterogeneity, as well as the artifice that sustains those verbal detours or "By-ways," can emerge, like a rough bearing from within a smooth wheel.

CODA: BEYOND THE "PRINCIPLE OF PLEASURE"

In a provocative article on British georgic in a "Georgian" age, Heinzelman has suggested that in the Romantic period, the "practice of representing aesthetics according to an economic model in which consumption is an alternative or supplemental kind of production . . . is sanctioned by the implicit belletristic model underlying the structure of Romantic age economics, and the name for that belletristic model, though no one used it at the time, is Georgic."[68] Heinzelman's eye is primarily on Wordsworth, but we can now see the bases of his intuition extend back considerably in time. As disseminated in the form of the extraordinarily influential *Spectator* papers on imaginative pleasure, Addison's descriptions (or prescriptions) *for* reading georgic could outlast the "true Georgics" or formal imitations of the early eighteenth century to become a set of foundational principles, a basic discipline, for the polite enjoyment of later topographical verse, even where the signature of genre is more muted. Any "Man of Polite Imagination," Mr. Spectator advises, can meet "with a secret Refreshment in a Description, and often feels a greater Satisfaction in the Prospect of Fields and Meadows, than another does in the Possession." As long as he possesses his own "Ideas" of the landscape, he acquires real estate with no maintenance: "[Description] gives him, indeed, a kind of Property in every thing he sees, and makes the most rude uncultivated Parts of Nature administer to his Pleasures."[69]

For Heinzelman, the "entailments" or legacies of the georgic include a utilitarian model of communication celebrating "perspicuity," the disciplinary development of economic writing, and, in Wordsworth's case, an obsession with the morphology of genres and forms.[70] Yet we might ask whether the georgic survives as an ideal of perspicuity, a model for reader empowerment, as ideology, only insofar as we do indeed let Addison set the terms for evaluating its cultural work. Certainly Addison gives us the *desideratum* of many later writers of georgic, in its explicit and implicit manifestations. Reading with a less polite imagination, however, I am not sure that the "principle of pleasure" always gets the upper hand.

What does this insistence on the "principle of pleasure" signal if not also an awareness that there lies something beyond it, too? Later versions of georgic do court the polite principle of pleasure, sometimes emphatically. However, as the rest of this book will argue, for that reason they also move ambivalently beyond it, toward aspects of reality that, as Addison's essay alerts us, are *not* manifest as "Idea." Addison's essay illuminates why these elements of the real will remain so elusive to positivist or history-of-ideas analysis, while at the same time they cannot exactly be defined as a simple absence (elision, denial, or other term of negation used powerfully by the "new historicist" method). They will lurk in the excesses that elude that unit of Lockean currency, the "Ideas," in the failure of mastery that registers in a poem as displeasure, discomfort, sensory and affective dissonance. Moreover, Addison's formulations are particularly useful for the unerring if inadvertent accuracy of their (wary) anticipation of where we might find such significant excesses and affects: in the vertiginous dissolution of that middle distance that facilitates "indirection" and idea-formation, in the disturbance of sense-perception, or the disclosure of a heterogeneity within writing that belies its status as a universal medium. In short, we need to heed the parasitical static, including that threat of "Sounds that have no Ideas annexed to them," which shadows perspicuous perception and communication.

Lastly, Robert Hooke's rhetoric has given us a premonition of one reason why the "sensible paths" may not always yield the "principle of pleasure." The *Micrographia*'s artificial organs are "helps" for "the surveying [of] the already visible World" – and from sensory extension it is only a short step to an implied design of territorial expansion: "the discovery of many others hitherto unknown." Hooke finds himself wondrously "affected that we have not yet overcome one World when there are so many others to be discovered . . . new Worlds and *Terra-Incognita's* [to be brought] to our view." But will all *terrae incognitae* yield "pleasure" and the affect of wonder? At what point does the "*inlargement of the dominion,* of the *senses*" create a short-circuit in the "By-ways" of "Idea"? I turn now to that question.

CHAPTER II

The microscopic eye and the noise of history in Thomson's The Seasons

If we had a keen vision and feeling of all ordinary human life, it would be like hearing the grass grow and the squirrel's heart beat, and we should die of the roar that lies on the other side of silence. As it is, the quickest of us walk about well wadded with stupidity.

George Eliot, *Middlemarch: a Study of Provincial Life*

INTRODUCTION

Recent readers of *The Seasons* in search of the realistic details of rural labor, or what John Barrell has called "the dark side of the landscape," have been largely disappointed.[1] Rather than particular laborers, the poem favors the personified "Industry, rough Power, whom Labour still attends, and Sweat, and Pain." When the laborers do emerge, they are neither sweating nor pained, but godlike ("the rustic youth" and "ruddy Maid"), or else represented by animated synecdoche ("stooping Age is here; and Infant-Hands / Trail the long Rake").[2] There are, of course, the exhortations to the affluent to "Be mindful of the rough laborious Hand, / That sinks you soft in Elegance and Ease" (*Au.*, 351–52). However, as Tim Fulford has observed, such invitations to compassion and charity increase the authority of the gentle or sentimental reader, removing the vulnerability that a more complete identification with the rustic would bring.[3] John Murdoch's incisive parody of eighteenth-century personification is largely representative of a consensus which sees the critical force of *The Seasons* diffused by its pastoralization of georgic or its movement toward the picturesque: for Murdoch, "the landscape of Labor is being transformed into the landscape of Nature: Labor, provided it is Mindless, is equated with Nature. And Nature has the capacity to assimilate all Labor, even Mindful Labor . . . into itself and redeem it."[4]

At least since Wordsworth's comment in 1815 that Thomson teaches "the art of seeing," readers have recognized that the instrument whose activity most engages Thomson is not the rake, hoe, or plough, but the eye, which in *The Seasons* has a whole battery of epithets attached to it: the "philosophic eye," "reason's eye," the "purer eye," the "sage instructed eye," and others (*Su.*, 102, *Wi.*, 1049, *Sp.*, 859, 210).[5] Among late twentieth-century readers, John Barrell's work has led the way, with several studies that have emphasized the importance of the prospect view and related conventions for organizing the landscape in Thomson. Barrell's work has had the advantage of bringing together Thomson's characteristic "equal, wide survey" (*Su.*, 1617, and the title of one of Barrell's books) – the contemplative, distanced, and selectively comprehensive perspective – with the discourse of political economy, which during the eighteenth century tried to recuperate occupational differences and competing interests as social coherence. For Barrell, the Thomsonian panoramic survey represents that poet's attempt to imagine a principle of social and economic coherence uniting Britain and her overseas possessions in one "great Design," a "Chain Indissoluble bound" (*Su.*, 1619, 98). Adam Smith's subsequent interest in the "invisible hand" guiding the separate labors and interests of the nation toward a "common" good – a concept as vexed as that of a common tongue and developing together with it – participates in a similar project, as does Smith's life-long penchant, from his early "History of Astronomy," for imagining all "invisible chains which bind together . . . disjointed objects" (gravity, rhetoric, sympathy, money).[6] And if such a "philosophic eye" in *The Seasons*, like Smith's "impartial spectator," remained distinctly more of a hypothesis than an actual body, it is nonetheless a possibility that Thomson, like George Dyer, who follows the progress of wool across professions from sheep to frock in *The Fleece*, tried to imagine and render. These efforts are chapters in the story of the attempt to conceive what Smith, in georgic fashion, calls "head-work," or intellectual labor: "Those who are called philosophers or men of speculation, whose trade it is, not to do anything, but to observe everything . . . are often capable of combining together the powers of the most distant and dissimilar objects," Smith would write in *The Wealth of Nations*. And even if speculation itself was increasingly "subdivided into a great number of different branches," as Smith put it, Thomson's *Seasons*, as well as his *Castle of Indolence*, often gropes – with mixed success – for a similar definition of intellectual labor as the capacity to stand above the "tangling Mass of low Desires / That bind the fluttering Crowd" (*Su.*, 1739–40).[7]

In contrast with recent readings, Thomson's own century was impressed less by the poet's panoramas than by his skill for delivering, in Joseph Warton's admiring terms, "a minute and particular enumeration of

circumstances judiciously selected." Patricia M. Spacks quotes a late
eighteenth-century essay that praises the poet because in *The Seasons* "it
is as if . . . every object [were] magnified by the microscope."[8] Two truths
are told: to read *The Seasons* is to be made aware of an ongoing dialectic
of distance and proximity, the vertiginous movement from the vision of a
bird's eye to the sight of gathering moisture on a bird's wing ("the plumy
People streak their Wings with Oil / To throw the lucid Moisture trickling
off" [*Sp.*, 166–67]) – and out again. If the narrator of *The Seasons* aspires
to a philosophic gaze, the early commentator is right to note that he also
courts a "microscopic eye" (*Su.*, 288, and part of a passage I will examine
at some length).

As a term and a charged semantic figure, the "microscopic eye" derives
from seventeenth-century natural science, which provided eighteenth-
century political economy and literature with its language and models for
conceiving intellectual labor. The new type of professional observer in the
early eighteenth century, whose trade it is to "observe everything" extends
the spectatorial model of intellectual labor from the laboratory scrutiny of
the natural world to public-sphere institutions and scrutiny of the social
world.[9] Mindful of this genealogy, I want to trace the movement of the "microscopic eye" from the late seventeenth century into Thomson's poem. The
topos leaves its mark in the prose of physico-theological conservatives like
Richard Bentley and that of early eighteenth-century rationalist philosophers like Berkeley and Locke; it informs the works of Swift and Pope;
and it moves into georgic-descriptive verse by John Philips, Christopher
Smart, Henry Baker, and Richard Jago, as well as in the memorable instance in *The Seasons* I discuss below. We will see that it is not only (or
even primarily) an eye for detail but also the fantasy-nightmare of what
it would be like if we were to live in such a state of enhanced sensation
that our eyes could not help but function as acute, and non-detachable,
microscopes, with our ears and sense of touch simultaneously amplified.
As my epigraph from George Eliot's *Middlemarch* suggests – and a recent
discussion of globalization by Bruce Robbins confirms[10] – versions of the
microscopic eye have outlived their original context by a good bit and have
become associated with a discordant affective awareness of one's place not
above "the tangling mass" and "fluttering crowd" but bound up within it.
It signals the instant at which "those who trade it is not to do anything but
observe everything" recognize their dependence on the anonymous labor
of other bodies, often on other continents. I will suggest that the decisive
turn, from optics to an uncomfortably charged international socio-optics,
occurs in *The Seasons*.

While the genealogy of the "microscopic eye" will not yield a comprehensive reading of Thomson's entire poem (which has by now been well surveyed), it can spark connections between that work and a range of texts and fields not usually associated with it. Most importantly, the microscopic eye permits us to confront a question which seems to me insisted on by *The Seasons*, although perhaps underemphasized by its recent critics: the operation of physical media of vision as they occur in nature and are wielded by humans – that "indispensable something in between" which makes all perception possible in classical natural science, as we have seen in chapter 1. Thomson, we know, was fascinated by Newtonian science: he taught at Watts, an academy for the dissemination of Newtonian philosophy, during the year in which he published the first of *The Seasons* ("Winter," 1726); he wrote "A Poem Sacred to the Memory of Sir Isaac Newton"; and he celebrated "the various Twine of Light . . . disclos'd / From the white mingling Maze" by the prism (*Sp.*, 211–12).[11] This and all the "dusky wreaths," "doubling vapours," and other mists that drift through the poem might alert us to Thomson's self-consciousness about sensory mediation and to the possibility that his grasp of other kinds of mediation and extension may be more complicated than it has seemed. The "microscopic eye," as I hope to establish by the end of my discussion, signals an acute, if limited, recognition of the problem of presentness, or what Lukács more precisely identified as "the problem of the present as a *historical* problem" rather than as an empirical and unmediated given.[12]

The end, in other words, will not just be to supplement Barrell's philosophic eye with my microscopic one, but to raise the question of literary mediation of the historical field in a rather different fashion. Not only Barrell's but most accounts of *The Seasons* have addressed the socio-historical contradictions that the poem's aesthetic strategies attempt to resolve. I am more interested in what they unleash. I am not, then, offering another account of the history that the poem undoubtedly falsifies at times but the inchoate, amorphous, and incompletely realized awareness of history it can record. In certain ways I take my cue from Fredric Jameson's comment that "if the ideological function of mass culture is understood as a process whereby otherwise dangerous and protopolitical impulses are 'managed' and defused, rechanneled and offered spurious objects, then some preliminary step must also be theorized in which these same impulses – the raw material upon which the process works – are initially awakened within the very text that seeks to still them."[13] And if "mass culture" seems an unlikely designation for a poem that has largely disappeared from our current curriculum and books-in-print lists (to say nothing about our taste), it is worth recalling that it had an unprecedented and genuinely wide appeal: we forget its phenomenal popularity both during the decades the several *Seasons* were first published and for almost a century afterwards, its remarkable publication history as a collected text, and its additional dissemination in various forms, including as excerpts in standard teaching anthologies of rhetoric and belles-lettres.[14] In 1818 Hazlitt reports that Thomson is still "perhaps the most popular of all our poets" – and reports a sighting of *The Seasons* "on the window-seat of an obscure country alehouse." An anonymous article from the *Penny Magazine* of 1842 observes that "his works are everywhere, and in all hands." Richard Altick's discussion of the nineteenth-century mass reading public concludes that *The Seasons* "seems to have penetrated where few other books did."[15] We know what it "knots together" (David Lloyd's phrase, invoked by Barrell and Harriet Guest).[16] What "various twine" does the poem disclose from the "white mingling maze," and how does it do so?

THE "MICROSCOPIC EYE" IN LOCKE AND OTHERS: TROUBLE IN THE "PRESENCE ROOM" OF THE MIND

Since Thomson's interest in optics looks back not merely to Newton but more generally to the matrix of experimental philosophy and linguistics that shaped Newtonian science during the decades just before Thomson's birth in 1700,[17] it will be helpful to recall some of the overt ambitions and the signature paradoxes of the virtuosi, outlined in chapter 1. Foremost among the ambitions was, in Robert Hooke's phrase, a "watchfulness over the failings *and* an inlargement of the dominion, *of the senses.*" Hooke's and others' desire to "command things" in the known world and master "*Terra-Incognita's*" was pursued by remedying those failings with "artificial Organs" able to apprehend the subvisible world; within accompanying schemes for universal communication, like John Wilkins's *Essay Toward a Real Character and a Philosophical Language*, similar ambitions sought to "rectify" the naming power, or linguistic control, over things newly visible to mortal sight.[18] We saw that the *Georgics*, Virgil's "poem of the earth," is a work peculiarly suited to these ambitions not only for evident thematic reasons (its celebration of the difficult disciplining of a nature conceived as an unruly battlefield; its linkage of local cultivation with imperial expansion) but also for less thematic and less obvious ones, notably its selective amplication of the real and simulated immediacy of the things of this world. It is a fallacy of many readers past and present to assume that Virgil's most detailed poem is necessarily a "realistic" one. The relationship between words and things in the *Georgics* lies far from the ideal of perspicuity that the poem is often supposed to endorse; it consists rather of the delivery of quotidian things in soaring words.[19] The *Georgics* are truly a "gorgeous" poem in the original sense of that word, and they insist on the work of verbal mediation. The phrase that Bacon singled out to announce his "Georgickes of the mind" – *verbis ea vincere magnum quam sit et angustis hunc addere rebus honorem* (in a 1628 translation, "how great / A paine [i.e., effort] twill be in words . . . to give such lustre to a subject slight") – nicely describes as well the eloquent curiosity of the experimental scientist. Henry Power's wonder bears quoting again here, since we are about to return to the common fly: "The Common Fly," wrote Power in 1664, "her body is as it were from head to tayl studded with silver and black Armour, stuck all over with great black Bristles, like Porcupine quills . . . her wings look like a Sea-fan with black thick ribs or fibers, dispers'd and branched through them, which are webb'd between with a thin membrane or film, like a slice of Muscovy-glasse."[20]

Yet the fortunes of the microscope itself, which Cowley had made the emblem of the new science in his ode "To the Royal Society," were in decline by the 1690s. Hooke himself became disgusted at what he considered the degradation of the instrument from laboratory tool to leisured hobby: aside from "Mr. *Leewenhoek*," he wrote in 1692, "I hear of none that make any other Use of that Instrument, but for Diversion and Pasttime, and that by reason it is become a portable Instrument, and easy to be carried in one's Pocket."[21] Pepys and his wife entertained themselves with one after dinner; Swift contemplated buying another for Stella as something of a joke – she was near-sighted. (If their children needed assistance, Henry Baker, Defoe's son-in-law, would publish in 1742 *The Microscope Made Easy* for the help of the amateur – an enduring genre.[22]) Probably more irksome to Hooke and fellow ex-enthusiasts were those who took the instrument seriously but emphasized its distortions rather than its accomplishments. Among its earlier and most trenchant critics, Margaret Cavendish, the first woman permitted to visit the Royal Society, offered her rebuttal within a year of Hooke's *Micrographia* and two years after the publication of Power's *Experimental Philosophy*. Cavendish's 1666 *Observations upon Experimental Philosophy* has two distinct complaints against vision-enhancing instruments. First, such "Art doth more easily alter than inform," representing "the figure of an object in no part exactly and truly, but very deformed and misshaped," for "there are so many alterations made by several lights, their shadows, refractions, reflexions, as also several lines, points, mediums, interposed and intermixing parts, forms, and positions, as the truth of an object will hardly be known."[23] Second, even if "they can present the natural figure of the object," there are consequences to the disruption to proportion when

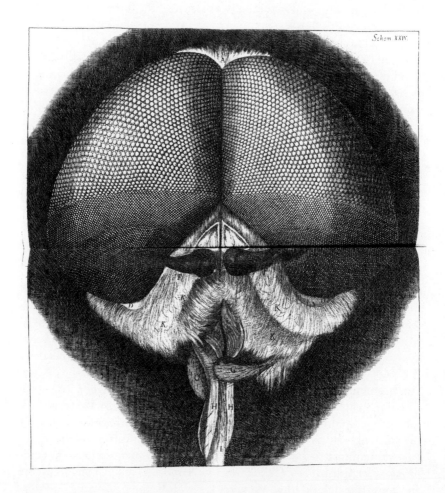

Figure 2 Robert Hooke's illustration of the eye of a grey drone fly, viewed by microscope (*Micrographia*, 1665).

"a louse by the help of a magnifying glass appears like a lobster," as she dryly puts it, with Hooke's enormous, beautiful-grotesque foldouts of various insects probably in mind (see figures 2 and 3). After all, she writes, anticipating the mode of *Gulliver's Travels*, whose protagonist will confront a monstrous female Brodingnagian breast:

[I]f the picture of a young beautiful lady should be drawn according to the representation of the microscope, or according to the various refraction and reflexion of

Figure 3 Robert Hooke's illustration of the blue fly, viewed by microscope
(*Micrographia*, 1665).

light through such like glasses, it would be so far from being like her, as it would not be like a human face, but rather a monster than a picture of nature . . . In short, magnifying glasses are like a high heel to a short leg, which if it be made too high, it is apt to make the wearer fall.[24]

This last Swiftian sally is not simply a complaint about illusion, the artificial distortion of the object; it is a worry about the effects of magnification and hyper-realization on the viewer. Cavendish's simile pivots between two constructions and depends on the movement between two answers to the question of whose size is extended. In one sense the "wearer" is the amplified microscopic object, but he or she is also of course the viewing human subject, using that instrument as a supplement to vision. The form-altering effects of the microscope are thus communicated from object to viewer. The "sensible paths" under scrutiny are now not the ways "From Words . . . To Things," as in the ode Cowley prefixed to Sprat's *History of the Royal Society*. In Cavendish, as the context makes clear, they point in the opposite direction, from things to ideas. Where Hooke craves closeness to the thing (closeness understood both as accuracy in representation and proximity), Cavendish harbors strong scruples about the propriety of the presentation.

Cavendish conceives the mutations produced by the microscope light-heartedly, as a fashion inconvenience, but elsewhere they are imagined with no little horror. Beginning with Locke's *Essay Concerning Human Understanding* and reverberating throughout the prose and poetry of the succeeding decades, there emerges a shared fantasy, summarized by the hypothesis of the microscopic eye. The epithet referred not only to the bulbous fly's eye viewed through the microscope (figure 2) but also – and more so – to the human eye suddenly endowed with microscopic powers, although all who employ the topos are aware of the possible double reference. It is as if that enlarged organ, once viewed through the microscope, now sheds its object status altogether, its enormity acquired by the viewing human subject. What would happen if exponentially sensitive vision were not acquired and dispensed with at will but were rather an innate and inescapable condition of unlimited sensory extension – a high-heeled shoe, as it were, that will not come off? Or, as Locke himself imagines it in the *Essay Concerning Human Understanding*:

But were our Senses alter'd, and made much quicker and acuter, the appearance and outward Scheme of things would have quite another Face to us; and I am apt to think, would be inconsistent with our Being, or at least well-being in this part of the Universe which we inhabit . . . If our Sense of Hearing were but

1000 times quicker than it is, how would a perpetual noise distract us. And we should in the quietest Retirement, be less able to sleep or meditate, than in the middle of a Sea-fight. Nay, if that most instructive of our Senses, Seeing, were in any man 1000, or 100000 times more acute than it is now by the best Microscope, several millions of times less than the smallest Object of his sight now, would then be visible to his naked Eyes, . . . But then he would be in a quite different World from other People: Nothing would appear the same to him, and others: the visible *Ideas* of every thing would be different. So that I doubt, Whether he, and the rest of Men, could discourse concerning the Objects of Sight; or have any Communication about Colours, their appearances being so wholly different . . . And if by the help of such Microscopical Eyes, (if I may so call them,) a Man could penetrate farther than ordinary into the secret Composition, and radical Texture of Bodies, he would not make any great advantage by the change, if such an acute Sight would not serve to conduct him to the Market and Exchange; If he could not see things, he was to avoid, at a convenient distance; nor distinguish things he had to do with, by those sensible Qualities others do.[25]

As the last sentence in particular indicates, sustained microscopic vision upsets depth perception, threatening the discourse of proportion that governs much discussion of the microscope, as in Power's assurance that "our Eyes were framed by providence in Analogie to the rest of our senses, and as might best manage this particular Engine we call the Body, and best agree with the place of our habitation."[26] George Berkeley's *An Essay Toward a New Theory of Vision* would formulate this reciprocity between touch and sight most fully: "the objects perceived by the eye alone have a certain connexion with tangible objects, whereby we are taught to foresee what will ensue upon the approach or application of distant objects to the parts of our own body," but "there is not the like connexion between things tangible and those visible objects that are perceived by help of a fine microscope."[27] Lacking the coordination between sight and touch that is requisite to what Berkeley calls "tangible vision,"[28] a "microscopical eye" would accordingly be not merely "unserviceable" but downright dangerous, for we could no longer regulate our actions and movements for our well-being, characteristically imagined by Locke as leading to "the Market and Exchange."

For many who entertain the hypothesis, acute sensitivity extends by analogy to each of the other senses in a veritable contagion of vulnerability. Pope's *Essay on Man*, which has left us one of the most famous instances of this extended figure – complete with smarting and agonizing pores, "aromatic pain," and stunned ears – tries to limit the danger by theodicy, celebrating the providential "bliss of Man . . . not to act or think beyond mankind," but theodicy does not stop the recurrence of the thought.[29]

I cite Richard Bentley's Boyle lecture to the Royal Society of 1693, again somewhat at length, as a remarkable example of the way that the surmise of the microscopic eye opens up into the nightmare of an uncontained physical and psychic "wound":

If the Eye were so acute as to rival the finest Microscopes, and to discern the smallest Hair upon the Leg of a Gnat, it would be a Curse and not a Blessing to us . . . Such a Faculty of Sight, so disproportioned to our other Senses and to the Objects about us, would be very little better than Blindness itself . . . So likewise if our Sense of Hearing were exalted proportionally to the former, what a miserable Condition would Mankind be in? What Whisper could be low enough, but many would over-hear it? What Affairs, that most require it, could be transacted with Secrecy? And whither could we retire from perpetual Humming and Buzzing? Every Breath of Wind would incommode and disturb us; we should have not Quiet or Sleep in the silentest Nights and most solitary Places; and we must inevitably be struck Deaf or Dead with the Noise of a Clap of Thunder. And the like Inconveniences would follow if the Sense of Feeling was advanced to such a Degree as the atheist requires. How could we sustain the Pressure of our very Clothes in such a Condition; much less carry Burdens, and provide for the conveniences of Life? We could not bear the Assault of an Insect, or a Feather, or a puff of Air without Pain. There are Examples now of wounded Persons, that have roared for Anguish and Torment at the Discharge of Ordnance, though at a very great Distance: What insupportable Torture then should we be under upon a like Concussion in the air, when all the whole Body would have the Tenderness of a Wound?[30]

John Milton had conceived his angels to be vital in every part ("All heart they live, all Head, all Eye, all Ear, / All Intellect, all Sense"[31]), but the end of the century evidences a rather different concern: for human understanding in a world "of experience," such radical and limitless vitality is considered a liability. We need to distinguish, then, between the microscope as it was put into cultural use, whether in the laboratory or in the parlor, and the imaginary but powerful construct of the "microscopic eye," whose implications shadow and exceed the polite promise of the actual instrument. The movement from microscope to microscopic eye points to an important paradox, perhaps not sufficiently emphasized in the histories that we have of late seventeenth-century scientifically influenced "experience" itself: increased power brings increased vulnerability.[32] What started as a conceit of the rational – Hooke's desire to remedy the defects of human sense and to "command things" by prosthetic extensions – turns into the irrational anticipation of wounded perception, the feared loss of command.

This turn should reconfigure or at least qualify the notion of subjectivity that we tend to ascribe to Locke and his contemporaries, and which finds its correlative in another popular technology and entertainment of the day: the camera obscura. So much has been said about the camera obscura as the central epistemological figure of the seventeenth and eighteenth centuries that we have to marvel at what a "different world" the microscopic eye presents. If, as Jonathan Crary has suggested, the "dark room" of the camera – a "closet wholly shut off from light, with only some little openings left" – encouraged an orderly and discernible cut between an interiorized observer and an exterior world, and therefore both represents and enforces a Cartesian dualism between subject and object, then the fantasy of the microscopic eye abolishes any nice metaphysics of interiority.[33] Viewer and object are almost always in danger of trading places or collapsing into each other, as the ambiguity of the phrase – the augmented vision that sees the fly or the fly's eye? – suggests. Jonathan Swift has this anamorphosis in mind when Gulliver, after encountering the minute Lilliputians, becomes, in the diegesis of *Gulliver's Travels*, the microscopic object viewed though the spectacles of the Brobdingnagians. What Swift accomplishes in narrative time, Pope tensely wards off in the taut pun of a couplet – "Why has not Man a microscopic eye? / For this plain reason, Man is not a Fly" – and Thomson, as we will see, imagines a remarkable turning of the optical tables.[34]

Microscopic eye and camera obscura are, then, dialectical consequences of each other. The world of the *Essay Concerning Human Understanding* is one in which all that are born are surrounded by bodies that perpetually affect them: "*Light* and *Colours*, are busie at hand every where, when the Eye is but open; *Sounds*, and some *tangible Qualities* fail not to solicite their proper Senses, and force an entrance to the Mind."[35] To read the *Essay*, now as at the moment of its initial reception, is to recognize that Locke's empiricism is never far from rendering us, if less happy in our habitat than Milton's angels, nonetheless very nearly all eye, all ear, all sense of touch. The mind cannot so easily post a sign stating (as it were): "No solicitors please." As a result, and in certain key ways like the ubiquitous blind man of the Enlightenment whom I will consider shortly, the microscopic eye haunts the camera obscura in many discussions in which the latter appears. Drawing on the intense interest after the Restoration in nerve and brain research, it offers instead of the camera's pristine inner space a sensory circuit, poignantly open and permeable to its environment. Susan Buck-Morss, by emphasizing in Locke an "aesthetic system of sense-consciousness," whose center (insofar as a network can be said to have a center) is located on the body's surface rather than bounded within its interior, offers an important corrective to the emphasis, in modern accounts of Enlightenment thought, on the supposed split between subject and object, and rightly restores the problem of permeability, and vulnerability, for which the camera obscura model provided one, but only one, answer.[36]

The question not yet addressed is why most scenarios of the microscopic eye involve a disruption not only to a closed, homeostatic economy of the mind but also to public communication, with consequences for economy in the literal sense ("such acute Sight would not serve to conduct him to Market and Exchange"). "Nothing would appear the same to him, and others," says Locke of the microscopically sighted man in the passage quoted at length above: "The visible *Ideas* of every thing would be different. So I that doubt, Whether he, and the rest of Men, could discourse concerning the Objects of Sight." Just what have language and communicability to do with this "science fiction" of unlimited sensation? To this question one might respond that the reason is not particularly remote, that the threat resides not in the microscopic eye itself but in the fact that not everyone possesses such an organ: the man-of-the-microscopic-eye has differing perceptions and forms singular ideas about everything, which he cannot convey to listeners. Give everyone a microscopic eye, according to this logic, and consensus would be restored; alternatively, like Gulliver among the people of Brobdingnag, the singularly sighted might in time learn the terms of his community even as he continues to see in finer ways.

This anxiety of singularity is certainly a factor, yet it just does not account for the extremity of the wounded perception that we see in Bentley, Pope, and other, largely conservative physico-theological thinkers – those agonized pores, the flooded sensory system. Nor does it take stock of the opening and unresolved schism, in this passage and others, between the organ of vision (which the microscopic eye enhances) and "visible *Ideas*," which it thwarts. The issue posed by the microscopic eye, I think, is not just the potential eccentricity of ideas, their deviation from consensual understanding, but also – perhaps more intriguingly, disturbingly – a feared impasse in idea-formation itself which haunts Lockean epistemology. To see why will require some further context in seventeenth-century optics.

When Kepler elucidated the dioptric properties of the eye – its reception, refraction, and resolution of emanations from external sources of light to produce the smaller, inverted, and reversed image or picture (*pictura*) on the retinal surface – he restricted his analysis to the physiological properties of the passive or "dead" eye, and he put to the side as a separate set of questions the animate body's coordination of these sensations (*passio*) received as well as any illumination (*actio*) it might have or actions it might take in consequence:

I leave it to natural philosophers to discuss the way in which this image or picture is put together by the spiritual principles of vision residing in the retina and in the nerves, and whether it is made to appear before the soul or tribunal of the faculty of vision by a spirit within the cerebral cavities, or the faculty of vision, like a magistrate sent by the soul, goes out from the council chamber of the brain to meet this image in the optic nerves and retina, as it were descending to a lower court.[37]

The world – as Donne put it with fitting metaphysical violence – might be contracted and driven into the glasses of the eye, but just what happened next Kepler's 1603 text tactfully declined to answer. The problem remained resistant to interpretation and would vex the work of Descartes, Malebranche, and others, including Locke. Descartes famously attempted to bridge the space between passive sensation and active or conscious vision by postulating a second set of eyes in the brain, which read objects symbolically through the motions they send up in the nervous system (thus "it is the soul that sense belongs to, not to the body"), and by arguing for an innate or "natural geometry" of the mind. And it is precisely against Descartes's assumption that the capacity to coordinate ocular information was part of human inheritance that Locke activated the famous "Molyneux question" in the *Essay*, answering with a firm negative the puzzle of whether a man, born blind, could upon suddenly recovering his sight distinguish shapes that he had hitherto known only by touch.[38]

Prompted by advances in cataract surgery, the Molyneux problem became, in Foucault's words, "one of the two great mythical experiences on which the philosophy of the eighteenth century wishe[d] to base its beginning"; without getting lost in its wandering woods, we need to consider it here because it negotiates a problem similar to the concerns that cluster around the hypothesis of the microscopic eye.[39] For Locke, as for Molyneux himself, the issue posed by the newly sighted man concerned the nature of the pathway leading from sensation and issuing in our "visible *Ideas*." For Locke and Molyneux as for Berkeley, these ideas are crucially not identical to Kepler's retinal image, nor are they the product of a second, inner, sense (as in Descartes), but they are acquired only over time by the coordination of visual with tactile experiences of spatial and temporal relations. The newly sighted man can perceive the play of light and obscurity, but he, too, does not have "tangible" vision – information about space, extension, distance, and motion that, from our early days, becomes entwined with our conception of light, colors, and shade. "To a man born blind and later made to see," Alenka Zupančič summarizes, "sight would not give any ideas of distance – he would see the most distant objects, as well as the closest ones, *as residing in his eye, or more exactly, in his mind.*"[40] For the newly sighted man suddenly flooded with light, in other words, sight – which like hearing normally functions across distance – approaches that one sense that does not act across space: touch. This compulsory and omnipresent touching presents a particular problem for the formation of what Locke calls "general ideas" (a process by which an idea is separated by abstraction from its original circumstances and then set up as a representative of similar ideas) *and for language* since, as Locke insists, names are annexed to our general ideas and not to immediate sensation.[41] Without "a constant connection between the Sound and the [general] Idea," Locke warns, very much like John Wilkins three decades earlier, words "are nothing but so much insignificant Noise" – mere "Sounds without Signification."[42] The blind man made to see thus exists somewhere beyond or before ideation and coherent language use, in a hypothetical place where no being can survive for long.[43]

Although different in certain respects, the possessor of the microscopic eye – call this individual the over-sighted man – resembles the newly sighted, dwelling in a similarly artificial but thoroughly uncomfortable flood land, touched by everything, unable to move about with safety, and hearing all discourse as "Noise," that common anathema linking Locke to the universal language schemes before him, in spite of their other differences.[44] The figure of the microscopic eye thus articulates an anxiety not only about receptivity but also about the transmission of understanding, conceived at two levels at once: the psycho-physiological and the social-semiotic. As peculiar as it might seem to us that issues of internal physical motion should be related to structures of social communication, we have to recall that such a correspondence would have been unquestioned by Locke and his contemporaries; "it was virtually impossible," John Rogers notes, "to discuss the interaction of physical bodies or mechanical parts without importing the vocabulary and values of the world of political relations, or vice versa."[45] Locke is not exceptional, then, when he brings the two levels together in a sustained metaphor describing the physiology of thought. This is a subject that he is as wary of specifying as Kepler was before him, in part for theological reasons, contenting himself with occasional allusions to the doctrine of animal spirits.[46] Yet what cannot enter the text directly *does* come in by way of metaphor, close to Kepler's evocation of a tribunal, at the moment when Locke confronts the possibility that, if the organs fail to communicate their material as information, then this matter may be lost entirely:

And if these Organs, or the Nerves which are the Conduits, to convey them [i.e., noises, sounds, tones, tastes, etc.] from without to their Audience in the Brain, the Mind's Presence-room (as I may so call it) are any of them so disordered, as not to perform their Functions, they have no Postern to be admitted by; no other way to bring themselves into view, and be perceived by the Understanding.[47]

In the course of this sentence, the materialist terminology of organs, nerves, and brains turns into a scene that subtly merges the legal, monarchical, and dramatic (a judge or a ruler would sit in the presence room to conduct hearings, although "audience" may also retain its association with the theater) – situations which have in common a concern for verbal representation.[48] This is a peculiar turn for the *Essay* to take, precisely because Locke elsewhere insists that ideas precede language, occupying an intermediate stage between sensory stimulants and the words that are attached to them; here, by contrast, he seems to imagine that the senses might speak to (find an "audience" in) the understanding.

To dismiss this as just a metaphor would be to miss the force of the unacknowledged problem in Locke's conception of experience: it is very difficult to find ideas that are entirely acquired by material and physiological channels or that we are able to prove true, with no overlay of belief or prejudice.[49] The Lockean conception of the idea pivots uneasily between things seen (unmediated sense-data) and things known more mediately. To put it somewhat differently: in the event of the failure or the unavailability of physical experience and physiological pathways, we do turn to linguistic channels. What cannot present itself by way of the nerves and the organs – either because it is too remote or (as in the microscopic eye) too close – can, as in a court of law or theater, get represented by the linguistic surrogate. This is a likelihood that Locke will not consider directly here, instead retaining it in a metaphorical scene which conceives those physiological "conduits" to be somehow already linguistic.

The relation of language to "experiment" is thus rather different from that advertised by Hooke and by Wilkins, who considered his "real character" to be ancillary to the advances in experimental science made possible by the microscope and other instruments. In Locke's *Essay*, the suggestion, which is addressed more directly when he turns to the problem "Of Naming" (Book 3), is that language can compensate for the limits or failures of sensory experience.[50] Yet if language is a "sensible path" – if it actively mediates rather than follows the conversion of sensation to idea – then what sort of pathway should it be? Should its representations aspire to the office of microscopic eye, which excludes nothing, magnifies everything, and has the capacity to turn all perception into the least mediated sense: touch? Or is it to exercise restraint, to regulate the entrance of information from the senses and, by limiting the touch of the real, maintain order (or, what amounts to the same thing for Locke, ideas) in the "Presence room"?

ADDISON'S "BY-WAYS": REPRISE

We have seen that this is precisely the question that Joseph Addison sought to answer, first in considering the pleasures of indirect information in his 1690s "Essay on The Georgics" and later in the texts that I argued were his elaboration of that early essay, "The Pleasures of the Imagination" (*Spectator* Nos. 411–21).[51] His "Principle of Pleasure" ensures, or attempts to ensure, order in the "presence room" by controlling how objects get presented there. In the last chapter, I discussed Addison's "principle of pleasure" in the broader context of the Restoration and early eighteenth-century reception of the *Georgics*, but now we can consider it as an intended solution for a specific problem: the attempt to offset the specter of disproportion inevitably conjured up by the "artificial" (technological) extension of the senses, the "entire problematic," in Hans Blumenberg's account, "of orientation in a reality for which standard measure, scope, and direction were almost entirely lacking."[52] "For there are several ways of conveying the same Truth to the mind of Man," Addison argues in the *Georgics* essay, and "to choose the pleasantest of these ways, is that which chiefly distinguishes Poetry from Prose." The "pleasantest" way is the least direct way: the "Byway" into the presence room. Unlike Hesiod or Varro, Addison continues, Virgil "loves to suggest a Truth indirectly, and without giving us a full and open view of it: To let us see just so much as will naturally lead the Imagination into all the parts that lie conceal'd. That is wonderfully diverting to the Understanding, thus to receive a Precept, that enters as it were through a Byway, and to apprehend an Idea that draws a whole train after it." If the "Mind . . . only takes the hint from the Poetry," "she" can "work out the rest by the strength of her own faculties."[53] Apprehending "Ideas" about objects, *The Spectator* will further suggest, is tantamount to owning them: a prospect can give a "Man of a Polite Imagination . . . a kind of Property in everything he sees"; presented through the "By-ways" of description, all objects, however disagreeable, can "administer to his Pleasures."[54] If, however, *The Spectator* continues, "the Object presses too close upon our

Senses" – exactly the dilemma of the microscopic eye – "it does not give us time or leisure to reflect on our selves."[55]

Addison's "Pleasures" thus emerge as an attempt to recenter the subject in the face of potential information overload. This danger the *Spectator* averts, as we have seen, by turning all modes of sensation into a version of reading printed text, which is exemplary for "the Reflection we make on our selves at the time of reading it," or into polite, articulate conversation. The description of a Man of Polite Imagination as one who "can *Converse* with a Picture" underlines this conversion of all interchange into verbal process – or at least the rare kind where the interlocutor does not misbehave, since "Sounds that have no Ideas annexed to them" represent some danger to Addison, as they did for Locke.[56] As long as all perception is rendered as a mode of quiet reading, unfolding in "time" (Addison, we saw, gestures to the temporality enabled by the "little Connexions of Speech"), then the senses will not be unduly solicited, "Ideas" will be duly turned over in the mind, and the world will become "conversable," a word whose scope and significance I discuss in some detail in the next chapter.

It is no surprise, then, that when Addison turns to the microscope in *Spectator* No. 420 and then at greater length in *Spectator* No. 519, he tries to accommodate its discoveries to the graduated principle of pleasure: "We are not a little pleased to find every green Leaf swarm with Millions of Animals, that at their largest Growth are not visible to the naked Eye."[57] *Spectator* No. 519 will develop this image into a full-blown version of the Great Chain of Being:

If we consider those Parts of the Material World which lie the nearest to us, and are therefore subject to our Observations and Enquiries, it is amazing to consider the Infinity of Animals with which it is stocked. Every part of Matter is peopled: Every green Leaf swarms with Inhabitants. There is scarce a single Humour in the Body of a Man, or of any other Animal, in which our Glasses do not discover Myriads of living Creatures. The Surface of Animals is also covered with other Animals, which are in the same manner the Basis of other Animals that live upon it; nay, we find in the most solid Bodies, as in Marble it self, innumerable Cells and Cavities that are crouded with such imperceptible Inhabitants, as are too little for the naked Eye to discover . . . We find every Mountain and Marsh, Wilderness and Wood, plentifully stocked with Birds and Beasts, and every part of Matter affording proper Necessaries and Conveniences for the Livelihood of Multitudes which inhabit it.[58]

Notwithstanding this pleasing prospect of Nature as a well-stocked pantry, the Spectator's poise is more precarious at moments like these, since they threaten to make him either as puny as a flea or as lumbering as an elephant:

> Let a Man try to conceive the different Bulk of an Animal, which is twenty, from another which is a hundred times less than a Mite, or to compare, in his Thoughts, a length of thousand Diameters of the Earth, with that of a Million, he will quickly find that he has no different Measures in his Mind, adjusted to such extraordinary Degrees of Grandeur or Minuteness . . . [T]he Imagination, after a few faint Efforts, is immediately at a stand, and finds her self swallowed up in the Immensity of Void that surrounds it: Our Reason can pursue a Particle of Matter through an infinite variety of Divisions, but the Fancy soon loses sight of it, and feels in it self a kind of Chasm.[59]

Such chasms Addison holds at bay with the sublime compensation of the thought that there are higher beings than man, whose imaginations can keep pace with their reason. The Great Chain of Being is designed to assuage the vertigo of the disoriented subject, who is suddenly "in a different World" (Locke's phrase, quoted above). It turns infinity into a system, as Catherine Wilson has noted, permitting one "to say what the divine view of things is even while admitting that it is beyond the reach of human perception or comprehension."[60] As a chain or scale, it also turns simultaneity into sequence, so that Nature becomes the "Book of Nature," amenable to the Addisonian "time of reading."

There is, however, the most delicate of balances between the celebration of plenitude, or Nature as a well-stocked pantry, and horror at the swarming infinitude of life, where Nature is instead a great food chain, in which sentient beings are endlessly consumed by larger sentient beings. The discord only intensifies because, as Addison's "peopled" matter might suggest, the hypothesis of a Great Chain of Being is uncomfortably homologous with the discourse of division of labor, whose unity is available to a similarly hypothetical "philosophic eye," never quite situated in an actual human body.[61] It also permeates the discourse of imperialism, where the "Chain indissoluble bound" binds a far-flung imperial system, one in which "generous commerce binds / The Round of Nations in a golden Chain" (*Su.*, 98, 138–39). At that point, however, the animals "affording proper Necessaries and Conveniences for the livelihood" of others are all human. Just what worlds, or to use Hooke's phrase, "*Terra-Incognita's*," confront the "microscopic eye" then?

THE NOISE OF NAMELESS NATIONS: *THE SEASONS*

As the introduction to this chapter has already suggested, the formation of the Lockean–Addisonian "idea" has governed much commentary on

The Seasons as well. In Thomson's poetry, John Barrell argued in his classic reading of the Hagley Park sequence (*Sp.*, 950–62), "an 'idea' of the landscape has been imposed, and this place has now become a landscape which we can compare with others."[62] Since then (1972), discerning the imposition of ideas that convert places to landscape has been the project of many significant studies; this approach has permitted the unmasking of what Ann Bermingham and others have called "the ideology of the landscape." This critical project has remained largely the same as Barrell's work on Thomson and others has been extended to include the British treatment of its colonial possessions. A number of critics have recognized, with W. J. T. Mitchell, that "the semiotic features of landscape . . . are tailor-made for the discourse of imperialism," which conceives of itself as an "expansion of 'culture' and 'civilization' into a 'natural' space that is itself narrated as 'natural' as empires move outward in space."[63] Laura Brown, Jill Campbell, Karen O'Brien and others have shown us just how this feat of "naturalization" is achieved rhetorically in Whig panegyric. The poet may adopt what Brown, discussing Pope, calls the "rhetoric of commodity fetishism" in which animated objects are the only reality: one of her examples is the famous toilet scene from *The Rape of the Lock*, where "Unnumber'd Treasures open at once, and here / The various Off'rings of the World appear; / . . . This Casket *India's* glowing Gems unlocks, / And all *Arabia* breathes from yonder Box."[64] Such rhetoric, as Campbell argues, is more ambivalently diagnosed as wish-fulfillment in Thomson's late *Castle of Indolence*, where the idle inhabitants of the castle "need but wish, and, Instantly obey'd / Fair-Ranged the Dishes rose, and thick the Glasses play'd" (*C. Ind.*, 1.305–06); in the end they receive the mild disenchantment of seeing "kind Hands" (as if unattached to any bodies) "attending Day and Night, / With tender Ministry, from Place to Place" (2.669–670).[65] Or the labor relations that produce such things may be eclipsed from the poem along with their products, in a heightened pastoralization by which the earth is seen to be spontaneously generous, as in Thomson's description of the "foodful Earth," "Life-sufficing Trees," and "*Ceres* void of Pain" in the tropical regions (*Su.*, 118, 836, 863).[66]

Yet Barrell had himself noted that when Thomson approaches his remarkable account of summer in the tropics "the eye cannot correctly compose the landscape."[67] Empire puts considerable stress on the effortful sonority of *The Seasons*, and the author perhaps best known for the anthem "Rule Britannia" becomes notably inconsistent as he tries to comprehend the realities of Britannia's rule in anything other than a vague imperative or wishful subjunctive mode. Although early in *Spring* he typically declares that the "superior boon" of Britain's "rich soil" is suited to pour "Nature's better Blessings . . . / O'er every Land, the naked Nations cloath, / And be th' exhaustless Granary of a World" (74–77), *The Seasons* are burdened by images of the horrified and blankly staring figures charged with the task of pouring such blessings.[68] Struck with the plague in the Spanish West Indies, for instance, Admiral Vernon's "blank assistants" are "fix'd / In sad Presage" (*Su.*, 1049–50), and Sir Hugh Willoughby's "hapless Crew" get frozen into statues – "to the Cordage glued / The Sailor, and the Pilot to the Helm" (*Wi.*, 932, 934–35).

It is, in fact, just before the narrator's imaginary flight to view "the wonders of the torrid zone" in the later editions of *Summer* that Thomson offers his version of the "microscopic eye" topos, which had already become something of a more benign fixture in georgic-descriptive verse from Philips's *Cyder* (1709) on. I quote at some length from this remarkable passage, whose striding verse at any rate does not lend itself to short units of quotation:

> GRADUAL from These [the willows] what numerous Kinds descend,
> Evading even the microscopic Eye!
> Full Nature swarms with Life; one wondrous Mass
> Of Animals, or Atoms organiz'd,
> Waiting the *vital breath* when PARENT-HEAVEN
> Shall bid his Spirit blow. The hoary Fen,
> In putrid Steams emits the living Cloud
> Of Pestilence. Thro' subterranean Cells,
> Where searching Sun-beams scarce can find a Way,
> Earth animated heaves. The flowery Leaf
> Wants not its soft Inhabitants. Secure,
> Within its winding Citadel the Stone
> Holds Multitudes. But chief the Forest Boughs,
> That dance unnumber'd to the playful Breeze,
> The downy Orchard, and the melting Pulp
> Of mellow Fruit, the nameless Nations feed
> Of evanescent Insects. Where the Pool
> Stands mantled o'er with Green, invisible,
> Amid the floating Verdure Millions stray.
> Each Liquid too, whether it pierces, sooths,
> Inflames, refreshes, or exalts the Taste,
> With various Forms abounds. Nor is the Stream
> Of purest Crystal, nor the lucid Air,
> Tho' one transparent Vacancy it seems,
> Void of their unseen People. These, conceal'd
> By the kind Art of forming HEAVEN, escape
> The grosser Eye of Man: for, if the Worlds

In Worlds inclos'd should on his Senses burst,
From Cates ambrosial and the nectar'd Bowl,
He would abhorrent turn; and in dead Night,
When Silence sleeps o'er all, be stun'd with Noise. (*Su.*, 287–316)

The passage then retreats to a normative evocation of the hierarchical mighty chain of beings and to the praise of that "kind Art of forming heaven" (in line 311 above). The critic who might want a microscopic eye has the tables turned on her (for "little haughty Ignorance" is female) so that she becomes the fly, and a myopic one at that: a "Critic-Fly, whose feeble Ray scarce spreads / An Inch around" (326–27). Yet that violent deflation comes late: the poem has already opened the aperture; before it closes we have exceeded the limits of immediate sensory perception – but not exactly the same limits imposed by vision and extended by the microscope. Joseph Trapp, we might recall from chapter 1, lamented that the advance of English poetry had not kept pace with the advance of scientific technology ("As Natural Philosophy has, by the Help of Experiments, been lately brought to much greater Perfection than ever; this kind of Poetry [e.g., didactic or preceptive], no doubt, would have made proportionable Advances, if the same age that had shew'd a Boyle, a Halley, and a Newton, had produced a Virgil"). But what has the poem-as-microscopic-eye *let in* that the actual instrument cannot?

Initially written for the 1730 edition of *Spring*, where it described the diseases that might afflict the early crops from arctic gales, this passage was modified in 1744 and moved to *Summer*, so that it could come into contact with the passage detailing the imperial imagination on its excursus into the landscapes of Africa, South America, and India.[69] In this final location it is hard not to hear, with Jill Campbell, this passage's "nameless Nations," "unseen People," and "winding Citadel" as a peculiar reentry of that evacuated imperial history.[70] The poem, but not the microscope (or more directly than the microscope), reinserts a human and political economy into the natural one. If in certain Royal Society endeavors, in polite company, and in the numbers of *The Spectator*, the microscope often functioned as an act of containment or celebration, this act of poetic seeing, working as microscopic eye, reverses direction and opens out to an influx of the historical world: "[I]f worlds / In Worlds inclosed should on his Senses Burst, / From Cates Ambrosial and the Nectared Bowl / He would abhorrent turn" (312–15). The food that the more complacent strand within Thomson would render as pastoral – pasteurized of its historicity – is full of impurities. And these are not (just) insects: Thomson's frequently mocked poetic diction – which less "Romantically" we can recognize as his remarkable attempt to create an English poetic idiom equivalent to Virgil's own periphrases (cf. *parvosque Quirites* ["small citizens"] for the bees at *Georgics* 4.201) – renders a weird human presence: "nameless nations," "unseen people," the "inhabitants" of the "winding citadel."[71] The microscopic eye momentarily runs the reification of commodities in reverse. There are people in that food.

In hinting at the human relations behind, or in this case within, the world of things, Thomson's passage is notably different from comparable moments in other Whig panegyric. In Philips's *Cyder*, the microscope's "small Convex / Enlarges to ten Millions of Degrees / The Mite, invisible else, of Nature's Hand / Least Animal; and shews, what Laws of Life / The Cheese-inhabitants observe"; when the narrator turns from cheese to apples, we are told that in its "well-dissected Kernels" and "narrow Seeds," an "inmate Orchat ev'ry Apple boasts." In *The Universe* – a poem best described as Henry Baker's 1734 attempt to offer his "microscope made easy" in verse – the topos more directly courts visions of empire, but in a far less troubled rhetoric of commodity fetishism of the sort Brown locates in Pope: "Thus, ev'ry single Berry that we find, / Has, really, in itself large Forests of its Kind. / Empire and Wealth one Acorn may dispense, / By Fleets to sail a thousand Ages hence."[72]

"Nameless nations" – Thomson's periphrasis deserves attention. As attempts to render an equivalent of Virgil's Latin, such instances of crafted circumlocution are never things indifferent. In the case of seventeenth- and early eighteenth-century translations of the *Georgics*, Virgil's epithets and periphrases tended to produce a veritable hive of politically inflected translations. So Dryden, supporter of late Stuart imperial ventures, had translated *parvosque Quirites* not as "small citizens" but as "trading Citizens," whereas the seventeenth-century parliamentarian Thomas May had rendered them as citizens of a republic or commonwealth ("They all elect their King"), and Addison discovers in them constitutional monarchy of "Laws and Statutes."[73] In Thomson's case, "nameless nations" brings us back to the society of Wilkins, Hooke, Power and the whole linguistic-scientific milieu centered in the Royal Society that, as we have seen, provided the original context for the "microscopic eye." This paradoxically compact circumlocution, that is, looks back to the anxiety about naming and the noisy sectarian Babel that, it was hoped, "real languages" and universal language schemes might hold in check. For such a purpose Wilkins had tried to name and chart nothing less than "all things and notions" in his *Essay*. If we keep in mind how central the operation of naming was to the imperial project as well – whether in the form of taxonomical schemes like Linnaeus's system (published in 1735, during the protracted writing of *The Seasons*) or in the cartography and narratives of exploration which sought to identify all native names and peoples so that voyagers and traders might know whom they were dealing with[74] – we realize what a curious epithet "nameless nations" is. It is a name that is not a name, a challenge to the ambition to "command things" (Hooke's phrase, once more). No wonder that *Summer* will conclude, some one thousand lines later, with an explosion of reassuring (English) names: Raleigh, Sidney, Hampden, Russell, Bacon, Shaftesbury, Locke, Milton, Spenser, and so on (1408–579).

The linguistic context emerges in greater detail when we recognize that Thomson is drawing not only on the microscopic eye topos, as it appeared in Locke, Bentley, Pope, and others, but also on a related passage, well-known and often contested in its time, in the *Essay Concerning Human Understanding*. Locke – and Locke as popularized by Addison – is a frequent presence in *The Seasons*, both in the numerous allusions to the *Essay Concerning Human Understanding* and in direct invocation, as in *Summer*'s praise of Locke "who made the whole internal world his own" (1559). In the microscopic eye sequence, the allusion to Locke is to one of the *Essay*'s descriptions of the chain of being, as it extends downward, "from INFINITE PERCEPTION to the Brink / Of dreary *Nothing*, desolate Abyss" (*Su.*, 335–36). The chain of being, as Lovejoy showed long ago, is a nearly ubiquitous commonplace, but Locke's *Essay* is distinctive for its placement of that hierarchy in the context of Book III's discussion: "Of Naming." We are deluded, Locke insists against upholders of organic language theories, if we think that the names we give to species refer to their "real essences." Such designations are rather "sensible marks of our ideas," "arbitrary impositions" reached by "tacit consent" – without which, as we have seen in my second section above, words are to Locke just so much "noise."[75] Moreover, as he continues:

[T]he ranking of Things into *Species*, which is nothing but sorting them under several Titles, is done by us, according to the *Ideas* that we have of them: which tho' sufficient to distinguish them by Names; so that we may be able to discourse of them, when we have them not present before us: yet if we suppose it to be done by their real internal Constitutions, and that Things existing are distinguished by Nature into Species, by real Essences . . . we shall be liable to great Mistakes.[76]

Namelessness presents a considerable danger in Locke's treatise, for it suggests that gray zone that eludes the Lockean "idea," a zone almost missing from the clean well-lighted place of the *Essay*. This passage suggests that if we name what is "not present before us" so that we can command it, then namelessness – very much like the wordlessness of the possessors of the microscopic eye in Locke's version of the topos – can result not just from distance or absence but from a terrifying, embedded proximity.

The "nameless nations" that burst on the senses, in other words, adumbrate that condition of touching or pressing "too close" that Addison had hoped that words would prevent by their singular appeal to the secondary pleasures of the imagination (to cite just once more *Spectator* No. 418: if "the Object presses too close upon our Senses . . . it does not give us time or leisure to reflect on our selves," and "description" is exemplary for its way of encouraging such spatial or temporal positioning). In Thomson, that is, the "By-ways" of meaning have strangely looped around into uncomfortable proximity – distancing the insects, perhaps, but for a moment bringing home (responsibility for) "nations."[77] In this case, the poetic diction does not, as in the rhetoric of pastoral spontaneity or commodity fetishism, "naturalize" the human relations and historical presentness; it magnifies them enough to bring them within range, denaturalizing the "landscape of Nature."

Here, as in passage after passage in *The Seasons*, allusion, too, works like the poem's dioptric glass. Or, to put the point more accurately, where the microscope was known to work by concentrating multiple rays of light, Thomson's poem often intensifies by crowding together multiple intertexts and subtexts, which can easily interfere with each other. It is important to emphasize the residual aural aspect, for the compulsive ubiquity of some form of near-quotation in almost every line of Thomson's poetry signals a return of the ear into the silent medium of print, even when the effect of this citational style is, as it usually is, merely subliminal. These are mostly remembered phrases and idioms, too many to be checked at every point against the book on the shelf, but ingrained by the practice of memorization and recitation that formed the backbone of Thomson's own education and the school-room training he assumed in his readers.[78]

Thomson's hold on the ear was apparent enough to his contemporaries, who were not necessarily pleased. Samuel Johnson, with characteristically back-handed praise, charged him with "filling the ear more than the mind" in the *Lives*, and *The British Journal* paid the poet the dubious compliment of describing his style as one "which, without fettering Words with Sense or Meaning, makes a sonorous, rumbling Noise."[79] Even Joseph Warton, who otherwise admired Thomson, felt that the diction of *The Seasons* was "turgid" and "obscure," and almost without exception, as Patricia Spacks has observed, the poet praised for his descriptive powers or "art of seeing" was damned for his language.[80] Obviously, there are differences between the Latinate sonorousness that contemporary critics called "noise" and an emphatically citational style, but from the perspective of Thomson's contemporary critics, both marked the same fault: the presence and pressure of something either in excess or in default of "idea" or "Meaning," which they then associate with some sort of aberrant or excessive (in contemporary terms, "impure" or "unchaste") sound.[81] These contemporary responses are, of course, logical contradictions – for how can verbal description be separable from language? – but we might recognize the contradiction as a version of Addison's wariness of "Sound": "It would be yet more strange, to represent visible Objects by Sounds that have no Ideas annexed to them, and to make something like a Description in *Musick*."[82] In other words, "noise" appears to be the name that Johnson and like-minded contemporaries gave to words on the page that either had "no Ideas annexed to them," or presented the possibility of ideas that were, in Johnson's words, suspiciously "adventitious."[83]

And it *is* the figure of "noise," non-ideational sound experienced as sensory *un*pleasure, that is evoked from the field of (extended) visuality at the end of the passage: if the eye of man could see what is in – or what labor goes into – those "Cates ambrosial" and that "nectar'd Bowl," then he would "in dead Night, / When silence sleeps o'er all, be stun'd with Noise" (*Su.*, 314–16, cited in full above). With the instant movement within the sentence between eye and ear, Thomson here joins and heightens what in Locke, Bentley, and Pope had remained separate hypotheses: "If our eye were so acute... So, likewise, if our Sense of Hearing were exalted proportionately . . ." (etc.). The result is to heighten sound over the other senses, and to grant it a strange, free-floating autonomy, for where *does* that noise come from? Slavoj Žižek's comment about the addition of voice-over soundtrack to silent film, "Ultimately we hear things because we cannot see everything,"[84] seems pertinent and accurate at least in this instance, for the figure of "noise" appears at the moment that the being endowed with the "microscope eye" becomes aware of existences, "nameless nations," "worlds in worlds inclosed," unavailable to sense-verification.

Whatever their differences, then, the painful cognitive noise emphasized at this moment in *The Seasons* and the "noise" that Johnson and others blamed as a departure from "meaning" and "idea" are both "noise" in the sense developed *from* seventeenth-century science by twentieth-century information theory. Or rather, to restore the proper historical sequence of influence, it is not an accident that in such theory, with its deep and acknowledged roots in classical science, the trope for communicative interference is "noise." "Let us call *noise* the set of these phenomena of interference that become obstacles to communication," writes Michel Serres, where the "communication" is not limited to any single medium.[85] For Serres, it is important to add, such instances of static in the flow of "information" are not really evils to be overcome. They are marks, or vital residues, of an observer's awareness of his or her participation in a larger system of forces, where the "observer" is not the contemplative, closed subject, aspiring to a "philosophic" eye," but an open, vulnerable and dependent being. If we perceived that larger system in full, says Serres, paraphrasing very closely Leibniz's *Monadology*:

We should hear this deafening clamor just as we hear the roar of the sea at the edge of the beach. It should deafen us, drown us. Leibniz said the following in his language: the cloud of minor perceptions, external and internal, should induce a state of discomfort and dizziness; it should prove intolerable. But, save for exceptional instances, we perceive almost nothing of this intense chaos which nonetheless exists and functions, as experiments have demonstrated conclusively... The attempt to understand this blindness, this deafness, or, as is often said, this unconsciousness thus seems of value to me. We have eyes in order not to see ourselves, ears in order not to hear ourselves. The observer observes nothing, or almost nothing.[86]

Almost nothing, that is, but noise, that residue of what George Eliot called "the roar on the other side of silence."

I have been arguing that in Thomson, this noise is the noise of history or, more accurately, the presentness of ongoing history beyond lived experience, or phenomenological verification. Thomson's "noise" brings within the middle range, somewhere between imperceptibility and "Idea," what is missing from the narrative of famous Britons, their literary accomplishments (Raleigh, Sidney, Bacon) or their military exploits (Hampden), that concludes *Summer* – missing precisely because they underwrite, or too intimately touch, those recorded accomplishments. I hope that it is clear that this unsettling "experience of the present" (Williams) or inchoate acknowledgment of "the problem of the present as a historical problem" (Lukács) is *not* unmediated (immediate), but results from a disturbance in mediation. More specifically, the problem of presentness manifests itself in *the failure of mediation to produce pleasure*, the principle that Addison had cannily identified with a purity or homogeneity of sensation, and with spatial or temporal distance from the pressure of the object world. If, as Lukács pointed out, immediacy is the false illusion of bourgeois thought as it confronts its own social and historical reality – false because it has been "illuminated and made transparent... by a multiplicity of mediations" – then the microscopic eye signals the failure of that comfortably familiar orientation.[87] What had appeared, in Thomson's words, a "transparent vacancy" dissolves to reveal multitudes of "unseen people" – not the famous *multum in parvo* of pastoral closure, but its inverse, *multa ex parvis*.

Serres, in the comment quoted above, wishes to understand and to value the disturbances of sense he identifies as noise, and so, in a different context, do I. But I also do not want to overvalue them. My goal has been relatively modest: to describe the evolution of an under-recognized mode of historical manifestation. The affect of discomfort and troubling of the Lockean idea, which I have tried to identify by means of the "microscopic eye" as historical presentness perceived *as a problem*, is in Thomson's own work too fleeting to result in any decisive program of action, in any sustained protest against the barbarism that adheres to the reverse side of the documents of imperial civilization. It is instructive and chastening to heed both the similarities and the differences between the microscopic eye passage and Walter Benjamin's famous description of the "horror" with which the historical materialist regards the cultural treasures of the past because they "owe their existence not only to the great minds and talents who have created them, but also to the anonymous toil of their contemporaries."[88] Thomson's text displays the horror, and for the same reasons, but with the obvious difference that the narrator will turn away from the thought of the anonymous toil, rather than from the cultural treasures. Or, insofar as the disturbance is admitted in any prolonged way in *The Seasons*, it issues in displays of stylized sentimental emotion. The alternatives that George Eliot's narrator would present us with – dying of the roar on the other side of silence or walking around well-wadded with stupidity – hardly make an attractive choice.

Is the choice as simple as suicide or stupor, though? If one were to turn from Thomson's microscopic eye to the rhetoric of the abolitionist cause later in the century, the later texts would acquire a new familiarity from the connection. To quote one hyperbolic pamphleteer cited in Charlotte Sussman's study of consumer protest and British slavery: "The inhabitants of Great Britain, who use soft sugar, either in Puddings, Pies, Tarts, Tea, or otherwise . . . literally and most certainly in so doing, eat large quantities of that last mentioned Fluid [blood], as it flows copiously from the Body of the laborious slave." With this and other instances of what Sussman aptly calls the "metaphoric equivalence between the producer and the thing produced," the logic of cannibalism almost acknowledged at the level of idea in *Summer* – or rather halted in the Lockean passage to the "presence room" – will fully be articulated.[89] In retrospect and only in retrospect, then, can we see Thomson's discovery and redirection of a charged semantic figure standing at the beginning of a movement of consumer protest, or at least providing what Lyotard would call the "idiom" for what "cannot yet be" phrased, but must be.[90] My hope has been to identify ground zero, the unprocessed material out of which such protests can (although there is no guarantee that they will) emerge.

CHAPTER III

Cowper's georgic of the news: the "loophole" in the retreat

Nor less amused have I quiescent watch'd
The sooty films that play upon the bars
Pendulous, and foreboding in the view
Of superstition prophesying still
Though still deceived, some stranger's near approach.
                    The Task, 4.291–95

> [The method with which historical materialism has broken] is a
> process of empathy whose origin is an indolence of the heart,
> acedia, which despairs of grasping and holding the genuine
> historical image as it flares up briefly.
>   Benjamin, "Theses on the Philosophy of History"

INTRODUCTION

"'Tis pleasant through the loop-holes of retreat / To peep at such a world"
(*Task*, 4.88–89): we are so accustomed to thinking of William Cowper as
a figure of retirement that the "loophole" in these famous lines from *The
Task* (1785) has often been read in its twentieth-century sense, as an escape
or retreat – an "out," as in tax law – as if the "of" is descriptive and the
phrase offers a mere redundancy (a retreat consisting of retreat).[1] So it is that,
discussing the poetry of William Cowper in 1949, Kenneth MacLean asked,
with reference to particular episodes in *The Task* and perhaps with a certain
distaste: "Aren't we shutting shutters on winter evenings, giving ourselves
occupational therapy with our books, our weavings of nets for fruit, our
twining of silken threads on ivory wheels? Peeping at the world through the
'loopholes of retreat' – the newspapers! The stricken deer is hiding in the
shade."[2] Not too much has changed in certain respects in the 1987 work of
historians Leonore Davidoff and Catherine Hall, whose acute assessment
of Cowper's centrality to late eighteenth- and nineteenth-century middle
class domestic ideology displays rather different methodology and interests,
but the same verdict: "The cosy fire, the close-fitting shutters keeping out

not only wind and rain but the social disorder of the 1780s and 1790s . . . ,
the convivial cups of tea, the comfy sofa . . . , the 'social converse' and
the family group were all celebrated."[3] To scholars interested specifically
in the late-century fate of the georgic, this apparent "flight from history"
has seemed an accelerated forfeiture of the genre's public vision.[4] Thus
Dustin Griffin observes that *The Task* shifts attention from the public
sphere to the private by redefining the georgic "theme" of labor as "virtually
spiritual activity," and, most recently (1999), John Barrell suggests that
after the disappearance of formal georgic, a version of georgic survives as
a "'discourse' . . . by attaching itself to the discourse of sentiment." For
Barrell, these sentimental affiliations involve, in the case of Cowper and
others, "a retreat to the domestic, the small scale, to something like the
little England of Dyer's map."[5]

But what about that detail, gingerly dropped and left pendant in
MacLean's exclamatory prose: " – the newspapers!"? For William Cowper
was indeed hooked on the newspaper: "I read Johnson's prefaces every night
[except] when the Newspaper calls me off, at a time [like the] present, what
Author can stand in competition with the Newspaper," the poet wrote
to William Unwin during the long winter of 1783–84, while "The Sofa"
stretched into *The Task*.[6] Both before and during the writing of *The Task*, the
poet subscribed to the prominent London daily, *The Morning Chronicle*, and
he regularly received and read the tri-weekly *General Evening Post*, as well
as the monthly *Gentleman's Magazine*.[7] As many contemporary accounts
testify, the years 1782–84 were a particularly intense time for "news." Their
eventfulness included the unpopular conclusion of the War of American
Independence, heated controversies in Parliament over the management of
the East India Company, and the dissolution of the Fox–North coalition,
resulting in new elections.[8] The editors of *The Gentleman's Magazine* complained that "the great and important events of 1782 have been so various
and diffused, and have crowded upon us so copiously and rapidly, that
though we have collected them with care, we were not able to arrange them
with precision. Where all could not be admitted, the chain was necessarily
broken; nor could it be resumed . . ."; in response they enlarged each issue –
and raised the price.[9] The popularity of *The Morning Chronicle* during this
period derived in large part from the prodigious memory of its editor,
William "Memory" Woodfall, who was able to deliver "Parliamentary intelligence" in the form of the debates held in the Commons, purportedly
verbatim, without taking notes in the gallery of the House, which was
prohibited.[10] Fox, North, Pitt, and others are regular presences and imagined interlocutors in Cowper's letters of the period, and both the letters

and *The Task* reflect not only the developments in America and India but also the immense available array of global and national information: the violent earthquake in Calabria and Sicily of February 1783, domestic food shortages during the summer of 1783, and other forms of wayward "intelligence" – the trade name for a piece of news or information – theatrical, military, commercial, and more.

It is the newspaper, after all, that in the passage alluded to by MacLean, Davidoff, and Hall provides the "loophole," but unlike the twentieth-century critics, Cowper is using the word in its original sense, as an "opening" or passageway, useful for both communication with and fortification against the outer world.[11] The place of retirement has an "out," it seems; that "of" is possessive, too. A "sensible path" (to recall Hooke's phrase from my first chapter), the newspaper linked the bodily and phenomenological life of the individual reader with the expanding imperial system. Cowper – who had earlier looked for some kind of collective identity in Methodism and the practice of congregational hymn-singing[12] – thus inhabits and animates both sides of the suggestive metaphor offered by Benedict Anderson:

The obsolescence of the newspaper on the morrow of its printing... nonetheless, for just this reason, creates this extraordinary mass ceremony: the almost precisely simultaneous consumption ("imagining") of the newspaper-as-fiction. We know that particular morning and evening editions will overwhelmingly be consumed between this hour and that, only on this day, not that... The significance of this mass ceremony – Hegel observed that newspapers serve modern man as a substitute for morning prayers – is paradoxical. It is performed in silent privacy, in the lair of the skull. Yet each communicant is well aware that the ceremony he performs is being replicated simultaneously by thousands (or millions) of others of whose existence he is confident, yet of whose identity he has not the slightest notion.[13]

The "lair of the skull" can be a crowded place. Like other scholars interested in the circulation of emotion (Homi Bhabha in the context of nationhood; Julie Ellison and Adela Pinch, studying the internationally oriented eighteenth century and Romantic culture of sensibility[14]), Anderson describes the historical and collective subjectivity engaged by the news as a permeable, open circuit of awareness – no fine and private place, like Marvell's grave, or the Cartesian ego. Nor is this circuit of consciousness particularly bounded by the "little England of Dyer's map," as Barrell suggests. In the words of Donald Lowe, writing before Anderson, the newspaper "expanded space to include anything from everywhere."[15] It is, if not a microscopic, then a globally telescopic eye, but with the same capacity to make "worlds... burst" on the senses.

There are really two issues intertwined in Anderson's description: where the first concerns the openness of this outward-oriented subjectivity engaged by the daily paper, the second is the altered perception of history invited by the rapid obsolescence of editions or installments of news. The newspaper's speeding up of communication renders ongoing history as a process in flux; time contracts such that "now" is always of the verge of expiring into "then."[16] Although Anderson suggests a connection between this sense of the fullness of the historical present and what Pinch calls the "extravagance" of feeling (its transindividual potential, its migrations, its contagiousness), he does not explore it; his own interest resides more in the modes of apprehension that enable ideas of the nation than in the historical changes that might drive a wedge between the history of the individual and the history of feeling, and he may also be limited by the Benjaminian term "*empty* homogeneous time," which does not comprehend the fullness and heterogeneity of the meanwhile.[17]

As we have seen, some such connection – between the complexity of the present and the occluded ways that its structure thereby gets expressed affectively, but not privately – was attempted by Raymond Williams. For Williams, "social experiences in solution" are misunderstood as "merely subjective" if and when our analytic categories treat the social as "fixed and explicit" and in a "habitual past tense." "If the social is always past, in the sense that it is always formed, we have indeed to find other terms for the undeniable experience of the present," he wrote, adding that he meant "not only the temporal present" but any moment conceived as an unfixed mixture of changing elements, "within which we may indeed discern and acknowledge institutions, formations, positions, but not always as fixed products, defining products."[18] For Williams, I have suggested in my introduction, "feeling" – by which he always meant the unpleasurable sensations of "disturbance, blockage, tension" – marked the uncertainty principle of history-on-the-move and the irreducibility of "present being" to recorded articulations and received ideology. Although he insisted that "there cannot be a direct and unmediated contact with reality," he resisted what he considered the "appalling parody" of that position, "the claim that all experience is ideology." To his critics, however, he just seemed to fall back into a naive faith in experiential immediacy, particularly since his discussion of "feeling" and "experience" remained largely separate from his work on communications media.

Both in my introduction and in the analysis attempted in chapter II, I have argued that we can recognize certain kinds of feeling or consciousness as collective and significant modes of engagement with history understood as an ongoing inchoate present by watching their emergence, not from some kind of immediate contact with the real (that questionable "lived experience"), but rather from the clash between rival mediations of the social field. This chapter continues the strategy of the last one: I am interested in the georgic's competition with other, contemporary "artificial organs" of perception and communication, and I treat as significant sites for interpretation those moments in which the poem's attempt to contain and "remediate" (mediate and remedy, or outdo) rival sensory extensions fails to produce the Lockean currency of the "Idea" and fails, equally, to obey the Addisonian mandate of "Pleasure." In this way, I try to heed the Althusserian insight that the overall structure of any historical moment is an "absent cause" ("immanent in its effects" and "nothing outside of its effects"), but where a more properly Althusserian critic might turn to reconstruct the overall structure, I try to attend to an effect that rarely comes under Althusserian scrutiny: the presence of the structure in *a*ffect. If the structure of the present is not available at the moment to thought, does it nonetheless lodge, at least in part, in modes of perception and representation that elude both "idea" and direct articulation?

This chapter leaves the field of optics for the news culture of the eighteenth century, with a particular emphasis on the rivalry that took shape during the early 1780s between the newspaper and the didactic, georgic-inflected poetry of William Cowper as distinct vehicles of "intelligence." This competition was occasioned by Cowper's habit, which finds its most famous instance in Book 4 of *The Task*, of turning the contents of the daily news into poetry, so that the newspapers streaming into Olney and the poems going out of it formed a two-way paper channel between that town and London. Should the turn from microscopes to newsprint seem an errant analytic procedure, I would recall that the connection between the two had already been made in the title of Addison's and Steele's periodical, *The Spectator*. Here I have found most helpful Joanna Picciotto's argument that, as "professional observers" who modeled their efforts on the experiments of late seventeenth-century virtuosi, Addison and Steele "tried to recreate through writing the technology of the lens" and to make their readers "'virtual witnesses' – using *The Spectator* as a pair of spectacles" in order to "restore" (in the words of Addison as Mr. Spectator) "the proper Ideas of Things." In light of the last two chapters, however, we might be more suspicious of Addison's faith in the "proper Ideas of Things," or the transparency of the newspaper's intervention.[19]

In converting the daily newsprint into poetry, we will see, Cowper exploits Virgil's pun on *vertere* to the fullest: his intentional strategy might be summarized as a "georgic of the news," an attempt to "turn" the random or dissociated particles of news into conversation. He hopes thereby to establish poetry not only as a distinctive *genre* for the sifting of the present but also as a distinctive *medium* – one bearing a superior relation to the sound of "proper" intercourse than other print forms. Versification is thus an attempt at a domesticating cultivation of the teeming flux of foreign and local events rendered daily by the papers. Yet this "noisy" present in part represented and in part suggested by the newspapers cannot be made fully "conversable" in the linked contemporary senses of that word: communicable and comprehensible, admissible to polite discourse and available to easy understanding. Therefore the second half of this chapter explores the way that the poem, burdened with silence as much as noise in its attempt to simulate the moderate tones of polite conversation, renders elements of Cowper's "unconversable" present; these are available to a mode of affective perception that the poet called "indolent vacuity of thought" (in order to describe the interstices between ideas) and are palpable in the poem at the level of figure rather than articulated as direct statement. This paradoxically full but non-ideational vacuity, I want to suggest, is itself an unlikely mode of historical knowledge. Others besides Cowper associated this condition with the distinctive experience of the present as a flux of news, and I conclude by examining the semantic shift – in which Cowper played a significant part – that redefines such vacuities as the play of aesthetic perception.

THE NEWS AND THE "NOT YET" HISTORY

The reading of the news provides an opportune site for examining the feeling or affective consciousness of ongoing historical presentness because, as our dismissive colloquial coinage ("That's history!" or "She's history!") suggests, what is news is precisely what is not yet – although some of it may become – history. The kind of representation that newspapers or, as they were often called, "diurnal histories" offered was thus different both from the *grands récits* of historiography and from the anecdotal collection of minor or marginal happenings. They limited themselves neither to the fall of empires nor to the fall of a sparrow, but presented both (so to speak) juxtaposed and falling together. Nor was it entirely clear, from the point of view of the daily reader, how these categories, or any other of our most favored headings (public and private, foreign and domestic) would be differentiated in time.

Consider, for example, an issue of *The Morning Chronicle*, in this case one of the pages that we know Cowper read at the start of what would become the long winter featured in the titles to Books 4 through 6 of *The Task*.[20] The front page for September 30, 1783 (see figure 4) displays, at left,

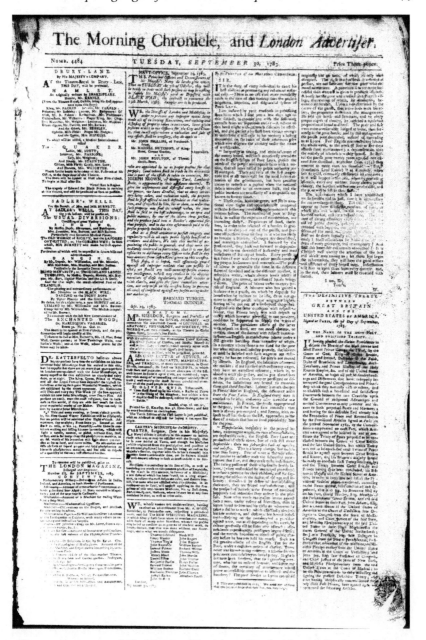

Figure 4 Front page of *The Morning Chronicle, and Daily Advertiser* for September 30, 1783; cf. William Cowper, *The Task*, 4.73–87 (reprint of microfilm, Library of Congress, Washington, DC).

theatrical intelligence from Drury Lane and Sadler's Wells; below that an advertisement for the "great Wonderful Wonders" of the conjurer Gustavus Katterfelto, who does make it into *The Task* ("And Katterfelto with his hair on end / At his own wonders, wond'ring for his bread" [4.86–87]); then, slightly to the left, some notices for an anatomy lesson performed by one Mr. Sheldon and for "Carter's Medicine for Dropsy"; moving right, a letter about the Poor Laws; and lastly, farthest to the right and bottom, the text of the treaty between Great Britain and that fledgling entity about to be recognized – the United States of America. Some of this material (the spoils of the victor) will persist in the main headings of historical narrative; some will remain a footnote (poor Katterfelto "with his hair on end"); some, like Mr. Sheldon and Dr. Carter, will vanish.

Far more than *The New York Times* or another paper of our own era, with its regular sections (international, domestic, entertainment, arts, real estate, and classifieds), the eighteenth-century newspaper exhibited an extraordinary collision of undifferentiated items. Most contemporary dailies did not distinguish between foreign and domestic intelligence, or they did not do so consistently; most mixed news items together with stray notices and advertisements, and all generally consisted of what one 1757 commentator called "a chaos of confused matter promiscuously jumbled together."[21] Writing his poem "The Newspaper" in the same year that Cowper's *Task* was published (1785), George Crabbe sought to comprehend "that variety of dissociating articles which are huddled together in our Daily Papers." Such "dissociating articles" staged, as Crabbe noted critically, a deliberate narrative incoherence such that readers (and poets writing about the news) "cannot slide from theme to theme in an easy and graceful succession; but, on quitting one thought, there will be an unavoidable hiatus, and in general an awkward transition into that which follows."[22] This anti-narrative tendency was in part a function of the multiple columns and several possible points of entry (a feature often noted and turned into a game by readers), and it was intensified by the eminence given to "foreign intelligence" from Europe, the Americas, India and beyond, since editors could not wait for confirmation before going to print, and later posts often superseded or contradicted earlier ones.[23] And if the newspaper worked to counter narrative continuity and coherence, it also worked (in spite of its uses to the later historian) against memory and against what Walter Benjamin would call *Erfahrung*, or transmissable experience.[24] "When you have once perused the four pages of unconnected occurrences, and miscellaneous advertisements," wrote one contributor to *The London Magazine* in 1766, "the abrupt transitions from article to article, without the smallest connection between one paragraph and another, overload and confuse the memory so much, that, when you are questioned, you can never give a tolerable account of what you have been reading."[25] (The point still holds today: do you remember what you read in the paper yesterday? But the day before – or before that?)

Some eighteenth-century onlookers, like Crabbe, found this chaotic, inchoate array of discrete and discontinuous items appalling. Others felt an exciting frisson: a letter sent to the editor of *The London Magazine* in 1780 – and suggestively signed "W. C." – offers a more tolerant, amused appreciation:

It has been often observed, that there is not so inconsistent, so incoherent, so heterogeneous, although so useful and agreeable a thing, as a publick News-paper: the very ludicrous contrast in advertisements, the contradictory substance of foreign and domestick paragraphs, the opposite opinions and observations of contending essayists, with premature deaths, spurious marriages, births, bankruptcies, &c &c. form a fund of entertainment for a world, of which it is in itself no bad epitome.[26]

The verifiable William Cowper wrote William Unwin in similar terms in 1782, referring to a page of *The Morning Chronicle* published two days earlier: "What a medley are our public prints. Half the page filled with the ruin of the country, and the other half with the vices and pleasures of it! Here an Island taken, and there a new comedy, here an Empire lost, and there an Italian Opera, or the Duke of Gloucester's rout on a Sunday!" (*Letters*, 2:33). And he kept on reading, avidly.

The "dissociating articles" of newspaper prose thus rendered contemporary reality as pliant, the moment as unstable or metamorphic, and therefore, or so it seemed, open to intervention. Readers could quickly become writers, and vice versa; consumers and advertisers also changed roles. If, as Crabbe put it, "here, compressed within a single sheet, / Great things and small, the mean and mighty meet,"[27] just how they were to meet appeared open to a playful negotiation, thanks to the distinctive layout of the newsprint (usually four folio pages of four columns each). The entry from *The London Magazine* of 1766 cited earlier offered the following "improvement of the newspapers," and one can find in other accounts variations on this method: "After we read the Public Advertiser in the old trite vulgar way[,] i.e., each column by itself *downwards*, we next read two columns together *onwards*; and by this *new method* found much more entertainment than in the *common* way of reading, with a greater variety of articles curiously blended, or strikingly contrasted." Then follow three pages of examples, of which the following "improvements" on the usual way of reading are representative:

> Yesterday Dr. Jones preached at St. James's,
> and performed it with ease in less than sixteen minutes.
>
> The sword of state was carried –
> before Sir John Fielding, and committed to Newgate.
>
> There was a numerous and brilliant court;
> a down-look, and cast with one eye.
>
> Last night, the princess royal was baptised;
> Mary, alias Moll Hacket, alias Black Moll.
> . . .
> At noon, her R. H. the princess dowager was
> married to Mr Jenkins, an eminent taylor.
> . . .
> Sunday a poor woman was suddenly taken in labour,
> the contents where of have not yet transpired. . . . [Etc.][28]

Although this is all in fun – only in print do princess dowagers marry tailors – the turn from vertical reading by column to horizontal scanning anticipates, in peculiarly literal form, the conceptual terms used by Terry Eagleton, Jon Klancher, and other scholars of the eighteenth-century public sphere. In Eagleton's words, "cultural discourse and the realm of social power are closely related but not homologous: the former cuts across the latter and suspends the distinctions of the latter, . . . temporarily transposing its 'vertical' gradations onto a 'horizontal' plane."[29] Of course, as Eagleton and Klancher intimate, not too much should be made of the radical or leveling potential of the newspaper in and of itself; for while it makes apparent the dissonances and inequities within the social realm, it does not necessarily create the expectation that these will be altered, let alone guarantee the opportunity for such change. Yet there does emerge, in the accounts of contemporary news practitioner–readers, an important illusion of present malleability and, with that, a degree of historical agency which, however circumscribed it now seems, was not trivial. By inserting one's own advertisement ("'Tis this which makes all Europe's business known, / Yet here a private man may place his own; / And where he reads of Lords and Commons, he / May tell their Honours that he sells rappee" ["The Newspaper," 247–50]), by subscribing to a publication or a petition, or just by dying, one might make news.[30] And by responding to the implicit demand to join together those dissociating articles – that is, to *articulate* them (in one of the several significant contemporary senses of the word) – any reader could "make" history.

In trying to render the newspaper's teeming presentness, and the resulting sense of ongoing history as a flexible, absorbing, or oppressive "now," I am not claiming that a paper like *The Morning Chronicle* offered some sort of pristine contact between the subject and the reality in which he or she was immersed (the sort of claim sometimes attributed to Raymond Williams). Although the news is relatively undifferentiated in comparison with historiographical narrative, it too undergoes a process of selection – even *The New York Times*, with all the modern advantages of cheap paper and the advanced printing technology that permits variously sized editions, advertises its contents as "All the news that's fit to print." Something presumably does not fit, or is not "fit," for publication, a point I will explore later. While less carefully organized and packaged, the late eighteenth-century press operated under considerable restraints, some similar to, others different from, those today. These included the confines of space, since, because of the Stamp Duty on paper and the limited capacity of each printing unit, most daily newspapers could not easily exceed four folio pages, no matter the volume of incoming correspondence, although weeklies and monthlies had more flexibility. There were also strong commercial considerations (such as paid advertising, in part to offset the cost of publication, in part because of the appeal of the goods advertised), while political partisanship vied with what was at best a nascent ideal of journalistic objectivity.[31]

Yet I would stress that where it fell short of transmitting "reality" to the moment, the newspaper created a significant reality *effect*. Its very busyness or "hypermediacy" – the separate columns, differently sized types, and several points of entry; the various possible combinations and recombinations of its "dissociating articles" as well as the ephemerality of their "intelligence" – all generated the *illusion* of immediacy. The paradox of the newspaper, Richard Terdiman nicely observes, is that in it "form *denies form*."[32] The paper thus testified obliquely to the contradictions and complexities of ongoing events not by mapping them faithfully but by miming them with its own incoherences or dissociations.[33] As the 1766 *London Magazine* entry cited above suggests, by observing that the "unconnected occurrences . . . confuse and overload the memory" such that it cannot "give a tolerable account of what" it has read, the feeling of presentness created by the news is less cognitive than it is sensory and affective. Following Fredric Jameson, we might say that it resists cognitive mapping.[34] This consciousness we might call a virtual historicity, and we will see that it includes the desire for – but also desire's counterpart, an anxiety about – historical participation.

THE "TASK" OF CONVERSATION: ARTICULATING THE NEWS

I burn to set th' imprison'd wranglers free,
And give them voice and utt'rance once again.
Cowper, *Task*, 4.34–35

> But talking is not always to converse...
> Cowper, "Conversation"

With the spread of daily print publication all readers are potentially writers, of course, but some engage in the habit more sedulously than others. William Cowper, as I noted, had his own peculiar way of making news: he translated its prose "articles" into verse, reassembling them as his poetry. We see this practice emerging before *The Task* when, writing William Unwin at the height of the war with France and America, Cowper records the effect produced on him by a distressing surmise, printed in *The General Evening Post* during June 1780, accusing the French of plotting the recent riots in London: the delicate poet falls into poetry, composing this unsettling news into a set of Latin verses. "Whatever has at any time moved my Passions," Cowper tells Unwin in the 1780 letter, has had a similar effect: "Were I to express what I feel upon such Occasions in Prose, it would be Verbose, inflated, and disgusting, I therefore have recourse to Verse, as a suitable Vehicle for the most vehement Expressions my Thoughts suggest to me" (*Letters*, 1:353). The peculiar "pleasure in poetic pains," the *Task* would soon maintain, lies in "[t]he shifts and turns, / Th'expedients and inventions multiform / To which the mind resorts, in chace of terms / Though apt, yet coy, and difficult to win" – all technical occupations for the mind which "steal away the thought" and prevent it from becoming too preoccupied with "themes of sad import" (*Task*, 2.285–304). This calculated hydraulic model of poetic action and stress-reduction, which would in time influence Wordsworth's claims for the effect of metrical composition in the "Preface" to *Lyrical Ballads*, prepares us for the intentional strategy of Cowper's full-scale representation of the newsprint (largely issues of *The Morning Chronicle* for September 1783) in Book 4 of *The Task*.

Like Thomson's *Seasons*, whose "microscopic eye" rendered and recoiled from the pressure of those "nameless nations" on the ear, *The Task* at first represents the discordant contemporaneity of the historical world as *noise* which needs to be managed if it is not to become too insistent. The postboy who arrives bearing "News from all nations lumb'ring at his back" is the "herald of a noisy world," and his arrival is announced appropriately by "the twanging horn" heard across the bridge leading over the Ouse into Olney (see *Task*, 4.1–7). (It is worth recalling here Cowper's description of the Gordon riots of 1780: "I never suspected till the Newspaper inform'd me of it a few Days since, that the barbarous Uproar had reached Great Queen Street"; the same letter congratulated Joseph Hill "upon a gentle Relapse into the customary Sounds of a great City, which, though we Rustics abhorr them as Noisy & dissonant, are a Musical & sweet Murmur compared with what you have lately heard" [*Letters*, 1:362].) The first 119 lines of Book 4, which center around the newspaper, are accordingly saturated with images of sound. As Julie Ellison notes in her excellent discussion of Cowper's use of the news as a remedy for "the blues," Cowper selects, from *The Morning Chronicle*'s coverage of the parliamentary debates leading up to the fall of the Fox–North ministry, Woodfall's description of Pitt's "loud laugh" while handling and dismissing an opponent (*Morning Chronicle*, November 12, 1783; *Task*, 4.33).[35] Then, after Pitt's laugh, followed by the "heart-shaking music" of the budget, and even the "Snore" of the British troops in America, we are launched into full range of the cacophony of news, from which I quote a part:

> Here runs the mountainous and craggy ridge
> That tempts ambition. On the summit, see,
> The seals of office glitter in his eyes;
> He climbs, he pants, he grasps them. At his heels,
> Close at his heels a demagogue ascends,
> And with a dext'rous jerk soon twists him down
> And wins them, but to lose them in his turn.
> Here rills of oily eloquence in soft
> Mæanders lubricate the course they take;
> The modest speaker is ashamed and grieved
> T' engross a moment's notice, and yet begs,
> Begs a propitious ear for his poor thoughts,
> However trivial all that he conceives.
> Sweet bashfulness! it claims, at least, this praise,
> The dearth of information and good sense
> That it foretells us, always comes to pass.
> Cataracts of declamation thunder here,
> There forests of no-meaning spread the page
> In which all comprehension wanders lost;
> While fields of pleasantry amuse us there,
> With merry descants on a nation's woes. (*Task*, 4.57–77)

The passage offers a remarkable anatomy of the reading habit that Cowper desires to cultivate in himself and, since he is simultaneously outlining his own practice of poetic composition, in those who read the news in (and through) his verses. As Ellison observes, the newspaper reader and poet strives to organize undifferentiated noise into space, as "a map of busy life" (*Task*, 4.55).[36] If successful, he can see, instead of Crabbe's "dissociating articles in print," the conventional landscape of a prospect piece: "*rills* of oily eloquence . . . lubricate the course they take," while "*cataracts* of declamation thunder" and "*forests* of no-meaning spread the page" (4.64–65, 73–74, emphasis added). This spatial or perspectival reshaping of the flat nonsense of sound inserts a saving distance between the cacophony of the world and the reader, who is now able to "see the stir / Of the great Babel and not feel the crowd. / To hear the roar she sends through all her gates / At a safe distance, where the dying sound / Falls a soft murmur on th' uninjured ear" (*Task*, 4.89–93). Sound heard at a distance, as Ellison remarks, provides Cowper (and his audience) with a favorite figure for a mediated contact with the political and commercial life of the world's metropolitan hubs. Hearing the "murmur" is thus a way of maintaining an affective connection to these vital centers without sustaining their mortal injuries.[37]

If noise offers one threatening extreme, the inert muteness of the printed page offers another. "Stillness accompanied by sounds so soft / Charms more than silence" (as Book 6 of *The Task* puts it), and the burden of so much of Cowper's poetry is that utter silence does not charm at all. Cowper seems to fear that too much privacy might become a form of privation, and in spite of its corruptions, public life offers at least a version of the "revolvency," "restless undulation" and "fresh'ning impulse" that he celebrates in nature (see *Task*, 1.367–82). Although the news reader is "[f]ast bound in chains of silence" (4.53), he seeks to liberate the fixed print figures from similar chains: "I burn to set th' imprison'd wranglers free, / And give them voice and utt'rance once again" (*Task*, 4.34–45). This liberation of stilled speech, like the toning down of loud wrangling, is presumably accomplished by the act of reading to oneself or perhaps, as Cowper often did, aloud to the domestic circle.

The Task, moreover, is staging not only an account of a news consumption (the emphasis of Ellison's discussion) but also an elaborate rearticulation of the news for a similar readership. In other words, Cowper is simultaneously offering the public his own "sound" in competition with the disordered sound – the opposed but complementary possibilities of noise and silence – presented by *The Morning Chronicle* and similar papers. Although he humorously announces his own indolent role as consumer-drone (the news correspondent "sucks intelligence in ev'ry clime, / And spreads the honey of his deep research / At his return, a rich repast for me" [4.111–13]), he is also aware of himself as a professional author and georgic producer. He generates not merely hothouse cucumbers – that "prickly and green-coated gourd" famously celebrated in the mock-georgic of *Task* 3 (446–565), the poem's most explicit allusion to Virgil – but rather the poem that would become the most popular text in middle-class households of the 1780s and 1790s, at least in the areas surveyed in Davidoff and Hall's statistical research.[38] Hence the marked deictics in the long passage quoted above ("*Here* runs the mountainous and craggy ridge . . . / *Here* rills of oily eloquence . . . cataracts of declamation thunder *here* / *There* forests of no meaning spread the page") point self-mockingly to the page of *The Task* as well as to the news item. With the "modest speaker" who "begs, / Begs a propitious ear for his poor thoughts," Cowper is presumably satirizing the sort of letter to the editor as the obsequious example concerning the Poor Laws, printed in the September 30 issue of the *Chronicle*, with its formulaic opening apology,[39] but that mock-modest guise also belongs to the author who, as the headnote to *The Task* explains, sat down to answer a request from a lady and "brought forth at length, instead of the trifle which he at first intended, a serious affair – a Volume."

The rival "sound" that Cowper is offering is, I think, best explicated by his famous letter to William Unwin on the familiar style in verse-writing, whose context was Cowper's combative reading of Samuel Johnson's *Lives* (those same "prefaces" that were apparently unable to compete with the arrival of the newspaper). Taking exception to Johnson's criticism of Matthew Prior for the "constraint" of Prior's verses, Cowper responds indignantly, "By your leave, most learned Doctor, this is the most disingenuous remark I ever met with":

Every man conversant with verse-writing, knows, and knows by painful experience, that the familiar stile, is of all stiles the most difficult to succeed in. *To make verse speak the language of prose, without being prosaic,* to marshall the words of it in such an order, as they might naturally take in falling from the lips of an extempory speaker, yet without meanness; harmoniously, elegantly, and without seeming to displace a syllable for the sake of the rhyme, is one of the most arduous tasks a poet can undertake. He that could accomplish this task was Prior. (*Letters*, 2:10, emphasis added)

The statement is more often cited in order to place Cowper on a literary-historical trajectory bound for Wordsworth's promotion of the "language of prose" in the "Preface" to *Lyrical Ballads* than it is examined for its real complexity. Since Book 4 of *The Task* offers a very pointed example of "mak[ing] verse speak the language of prose," it would seem important in its context to define Cowper's concerns in this letter, the closest approximation of a defense of poetry that he ever wrote. These concerns are at once nuanced and distinct from those later set forth by Wordsworth's "Preface."

The first, signaled by that catch-phrase heard so often in literary criticism from Gray and Johnson through Wordsworth, "the *language* of prose," is a question of diction, or levels of *written* speech ("prose," as *Le Bourgeois Gentilhomme*'s M. Jourdain famously fails to realize, is always written). Drawing on the work of Donald Davie and A. D. Harvey, John Guillory has convincingly argued that what seemed to be local skirmishes over the proper relation between "the language of prose" and "the language of poetry" were in fact debates, with considerable sociological consequences, over whether poetry was to maintain a "cultural capital" akin to the prestige formerly held by classical learning. Would – and should – poetry retain a "distinction," in Pierre Bourdieu's freighted sense of the word, from the multiplying prose genres at the moment that a new category, vernacular "literature," was coming to include both poetry and prose? This question is acute precisely because by mid-century the homogenizing pressure of standard English – that is, the polite, urban language forged in the metropolis and its letters, or what Davie (following Matthew Arnold) called "the tone of the centre" – is fast eroding any distinction between poetic and prose *diction*.[40] Both Gray and Wordsworth, as Guillory wryly shows, react with limited success against this threat of indifference by apparently opposite but fully complementary strategies. Where Gray attempts to replicate, *within* the vernacular of the 1740s, a distinction like the outdated one between classical and vernacular literacy by promoting a specialized "poetic diction" (only to be disappointed by the immense popular appeal of his "Elegy Written in a Country Churchyard" to a prose-consuming audience), Wordsworth later attempts not to complicate but to simplify, insisting on, in the 1800 "Preface" to *Lyrical Ballads*, the suitability of the "real language" of "low and rustic life" for poetry (only to suffer Coleridge's correction that what he really achieved was neither rustic nor "real" but the *lingua communis* of the educated citizen of the capital, that "tone of the centre").[41]

Cowper's omission from Guillory's masterful account would seem a strange one, since so many of Wordsworth and Coleridge's later comments on the proper language of poetry are forged in relation to *The Task*, and particularly because Cowper's assertive engagement with Samuel

Johnson just at the moment he is writing his poem (together with his simultaneous immersion in contemporary handbooks on rhetoric and belles-lettres, notably Hugh Blair's version of the New Rhetoric) makes clear his own investment in the "cultural capital" of vernacular literature, and his none-too-modest desire to insert his own poetry into its rising course. If we insert Cowper into the context offered by Guillory, different emphases emerge. In comparison with Gray's aristocratic archaism or Wordsworth's equally learned experiments in ordinariness, Cowper is remarkably undisturbed by the confluence, into one polite language, of the *diction* of poetry and prose. Such language should *not* be "prosaic," he notes frankly, in a version of Addison's dictum that the georgic writer should "fling the dung with grace."[42] However, this relative insouciance about levels of diction hardly means that he does not harbor a desire for the distinctiveness of poetry in relation to its rival – it is just that this desire does not emerge in terms of levels of written English, *genera dicendi*, or diction at all. Where it does manifest itself begins to be apparent if we shift Guillory's emphasis ("the *language* of prose") two words earlier in Cowper's version of the phrase ("to make verse *speak* the language of prose"). Cowper's commitment to the specificity of poetry appears as a nostalgia for the speaking voice – for a sound ("syllables" undisplaced "for the sake of the rhyme") threatened *not* by linguistic homogeneity but by the silence of the page.

Cowper, in other words, understands quite well the point that Wordsworth's "Preface" may have slyly or polemically glossed in calling the "real language" of men the "language of prose": prose does not speak. Forged in the letters of the era, beginning with Addison and triumphing in Hume, Boswell and others, the conversational style is the supreme invention of a particular stage in the age of print, declaring familiarity yet bearing little resemblance to actual interchange, which depends on a range of non-verbal signifiers and is riddled with colloquialisms, malapropisms, and fractures. As Walter Ong pointed out long ago in illustratively informal prose, "typographic folk believe that oral exchange should normally be informal (oral folk believe it should normally be formal)."[43] Earlier stages of print culture, moreover, had little patience for the simulation of orality – in 1589, for example, George Puttenham displays contempt for writing that tries to be "ordinary talke, then which nothing can be more unsauourie and farre from all ciuility," and one would still be hard pressed to find any pretense to conversation in the prose of Burton or Browne.[44] Of course, poetry no less than prose needs to adjust to the mediacy, the writtenness, of the printed page; but while it must "accept its place in the world of the written,"[45] it can aspire to outflank prose by asserting its relative proximity to spoken language, its superiority at conjuring balanced sound effects out of paper and ink. In the handbooks and lectures that Cowper was reading, that claim was based on poetry's "numbers" (meter, syllable length, and, where present, rhyme), a residue of its presumed early association with music; Blair unites in one lecture a standard account of the origin and progress of poetry, the invention of writing and its correlate, prose, and then, to distinguish the two, a survey of versification. Guillory's account dismisses the importance of metrical "numbers," but Cowper, whose poetic skills were honed in the writing of hymns for congregational song, does have a considerable investment in the superior sound effects of poetry in comparison with prose, praising *Paradise Lost* for its music ("It is like that of a fine organ") and urging William Unwin's school-age son to recite parts of Milton's poem – "The sooner the ear is formed, and the organs of speech are accustomed to the various inflections of the voice, which the rehearsal of those passages demands, the better" (*Letters*, 2:11). And so, while we do need to see his comment to Unwin as a masked defense against the pressure of prose forms, as in the cases of Gray and Wordsworth, it is a defense that does not take refuge in an argument about a distinctive language or diction (and so does not enter Guillory's analysis). Cowper realizes, I think, that the distinction, if it is to be claimed, is a question of the difference within and between the modes of sense perception, a difference that bears on the question of media.[46]

What is interesting about Cowper, then, is not his choice of a conversational style – the "divine Chit chat" for which he was famed[47] – but his determination to pursue that prose phenomenon (publicly, at least) in verse. At first consideration, this might seem an unduly circuitous choice, since poetry is presumably even further than polite prose from "actual" talk. But unlike Wordsworth, Cowper makes no claims to render "the real language of men," nor does he celebrate it. His own poem on the subject, "Conversation" (1781), reads far more like a perverse (if brilliant) list of conversational offenders, from the wranglers to the reticent, than a celebration of "colloquial happiness," which the poem locates among the apostles, an unconsolingly remote example.[48] If poetry, as I believe Cowper wants to claim, offers a superior way of getting sound out of a page, it is not "superior" by virtue of its faithfulness to real conversation, full as that is with moments of expropriation and appropriation, but for its capacity to simulate a politer, gentler interchange – an improved or "secondary orality," which Ong has described as a "more deliberate and self-conscious" entity than whatever may have preexisted writing and print.[49]

Perhaps we should understand Cowper's heated defense of Prior, other-wise an unlikely candidate for heroics against the formidable Dr. Johnson, in connection with this claim for poetry. When the poet of *Task* 4 evokes the "chains of silence" and "th' imprison'd wranglers," he is appealing in part to the metaphor of the fetters, chains, and bonds of language that preoccupied poetics. Milton's defiance of the "troublesome and modern bondage of rhyming" is of course the most famous example, but a more sustained one was available in the preface to the work that Cowper calls Prior's "best poem" – and faults Johnson for not "noticing" (see *Letters*, 2:4) – *Solomon on the Vanity of the World* (1708):

I would say one Word of the Measure, in which This, and most Poems of the Age are written. *Heroic* with continued Rhime, as DONNE and his Contemporaries used it, carrying the Sense of one Verse most commonly into another, was found too dissolute and wild, and came very often too near Prose. As DAVENANT and WALLER corrected, and DRYDEN perfected it; It is too confined: It cuts off the Sense at the end of every first Line, which must always rhime to the next following; and consequently produces too frequent an Identity in the Sound, and brings every Couplet to the Point of an Epigram. . . . If striking out into *Blank Verse*, as MILTON did (and in this kind Mr PHILIPPS, had He lived, would have excelled) or running the Thought into *Alternate* and *Stanza* . . . as SPENSER and FAIRFAX have done . . . be a proper Remedy for my Poetical Complaint, or if any other may be found, I dare not determine: I am only enquiring, in order to be better informed . . . . He that writes in Rhimes, dances in Fetters: And as his Chain is more extended, he may certainly take larger Steps.⁵⁰

Although Cowper associates dissolution and wildness not with prose, which had become more self-conscious and styled in the intervening seventy-five years, but with the "noisy world," and although he sometimes made different metrical choices than Prior (who does not use the blank verse dear to Cowper's heart in *The Task*), Cowper's "poetical complaint" or "enquiry" is still essentially the same: what *sort* of sound to conjure up out of the page.⁵¹ And it is an enterprise that is as difficult – a "task" as "arduous" – for him as it was for the author of *Solomon*. For while the poet in *Task* 4 "burns to set th' imprison'd wranglers free," he certainly does not want them to wrangle. At the same time, because the deictics "here" and "there" inevitably call attention to places on a page rather than by hearth, table, or pulpit (the poet's favorite spots), "Cowper," the living source of chit chat, is in danger of getting pulled back into the silent page, and *The Task* itself turned into a commodity like the consumer goods and publications advertised in *The Morning Chronicle* (see *Task*, 4.78–87).⁵²

His "poetical complaint" is in fact a more acute dilemma than Prior's, because sound is never just sound for Cowper but has distinct epistemological consequences. Different ways of hearing are, for him, different ways of knowing. By attempting to create the resonant space of a simulated conversational voice, Cowper hopes to make the dangerously "noisy world" – or, alternately, the equally intractable silent "map" – "conversable" in the full, extended sense of that master word of the period. As it emerged in Addison's comments on the man of polite imagination (he who can "converse with a Picture"), or in Hume's treatment of the "conversable world," and elsewhere, conversability is not just a matter of style in literary or social conduct but a far-ranging cognitive ideal.[53] Cowper's name for conversation was "sacred interpreter of human thought" ("Conversation," 23), and his epithet derives from Henry Fielding's assertion that conversation is "the only Guide to Knowledge." Fielding had offered, in support of that claim, the following, expansive definition, which develops an etymological line from *vertere* (to turn) to con*versa*tion, as way of revolving ideas in discussion:

The primitive and literal Sense of this Word is ... to *Turn round together*; and in its more copious Usage we intend by it, that reciprocal Interchange of Ideas, by which Truth is examined, Things are, in a manner, *turned round*, and sifted, and all our Knowledge communicated to each other.[54]

Nicely "sifted" and decorous, "conversable" knowledge demands only what Hume called the "easier and more gentle exercises of the understanding."[55] It is a longing for such a dream of orderly apprehension that the poet's momentary, Lucretian perspective on the newspaper expresses, in the lines that follow its "map of busy life":

> Thus sitting and surveying thus at ease
> The globe and its concerns, I seem advanced
> To some secure and more than mortal height,
> That lib'rates and exempts me from them all.
> It *turns* submitted to my view, *turns* round
> With all its generations; I behold
> The tumult and am still. (*Task*, 4.94–100, emphasis added)

By adopting (however fitfully) a mode of georgic for his speaking *versus*, Cowper is neatly exploiting Fielding's etymological pun to its fullest.

We can thus complete an account of the *intentional* strategy of *The Task*. The ostensible work of Cowper's georgic of the news is to "articulate" those dissociating bits of prose in both senses of that verb at once. To utter them as if in well-cultivated conversation is, the poet hopes, to join or joint them together, to construct the nation – indeed the globe – in the image of the parlor's conversable world.

That is the *hope*, at any rate. Yet, as the poet pithily observed in "Conversation" three years earlier, "to talk is not always to converse" (8), and Cowper is more aware than most that "the conversable world" is constructed on the shaky ground of its exclusions, both of topics and people.[56] Shortly after the description of the newspaper, *The Task* will lose its way, its speaker exclaiming, in some distraction: "Roving as I rove, / Where shall I find an end, or how proceed?" (4.232–33). *The Task* as a whole, or read at any length, seems a desperate attempt to keep up the conversation – any conversation. Well before Michel Serres, whose work he anticipates in certain surprising ways, Cowper seems to recognize that "to hold a dialogue is to suppose a third man and seek to exclude him."[57] This third man and dialectical challenge Serres calls "the *demon*, the prosopopeia of noise," although in *The Task* one is never quite sure whether the greater threat is the noise of the hordes at the door or just the pressure of a terrible, isolating silence – each lurks at different moments. Such sensitivity to the precariousness of any conversation is temperamental, certainly, but it is also has a historical specificity. The potentially vertiginous image of the turning globe in the passage above – as opposed, for example, to a rural or urban prospect available to a single, fixed view – is not accidental, given the premium set on foreign intelligence in the newspapers of the later eighteenth century. While many a citizen had imagined, like Addison weeping at the Royal Exchange in 1711, the possibility of "mutual Intercourse and Traffick among Mankind" (*Spectator*, 1:294), global table-talk, always a tenuous fiction, seemed increasingly so in the national crises of 1782–84, with the loss of America and the questions about the British management of India.

Therefore, while I have so far been suggesting that the newspaper enters *The Task* as a test case for Cowper's desire to "make verse *speak*," to "sift" through in a conversable manner what the newspaper prose offers either too silently (and as too remote for understanding) or with too much dissociating noise (too nearly invasive), I want now to propose that it also appears as the *limit* of conversability, in all the aural, moral, and epistemological senses. With its advertisements for exotic "nectareous essences, Olympian dews" as well as its unreliable foreign intelligence, the newspaper offered a confused reminder of the dependence of any individual's bodily existence on far-flung conditions; this is a contradiction that Fredric Jameson describes by remarking that "the truth" (a key word of Fielding's definition of conversation) of any local "experience no longer coincides with the place in which it takes place . . . [but] lies, rather, in India or Jamaica or Hong Kong; it is bound up with the whole colonial system" and is therefore not fully "conceptualizable" for most people.[58] Yet what is not available as a concept – what is not "conversable" – is not therefore beyond the poem's representation. As the next section of this chapter will argue, we do *The Task* better justice if we attend not only to the defenses it mounts against challenges to the conversational ideal but also to the way that it admits them. To talk is indeed not always to converse. I turn, then, to the poem's animation of what I want to call (neologism notwithstanding) the unconversable world, Cowper's version of something like the Althusserian absent cause alluded to in Jameson's comment. This world will make its presentness felt, we will see, not exactly as Serres's noise but as its dialectical twin: a silence which is emphatically not an absence, and an effect that takes the structure of a particular kind of affect.

THE UNCONVERSABLE WORLD: WAITING FOR STRANGERS

Cowper had hoped that *The Task* would be read as whole piece, writing Unwin, "If the work cannot boast a regular plan (in which respect however I do not think it altogether indefensible) it may yet boast, that the reflections are naturally suggested always by the preceding passage" (*Letters*, 2:285). Yet the passage that immediately succeeds the account of reading the newspaper has proved particularly attractive to the excerpting practices of anthologists. Also those of poets: in his meditative lyric "Frost at Midnight" (1798), Coleridge would preserve Cowper's lines largely intact – but moved quite some distance from the "map of busy life" and its wordly context.[59] The result is that Cowper's original has had the inevitable fate of being treated as a set piece which is then recognized, and interpreted, by its famous Romantic progeny. I will return briefly to Coleridge at the end of this section, but I want to put Cowper's passage back into its original textual and contextual settings. This sequence will occupy the place of fulcrum in this section, and I will frequently be referring back to it, by the name Cowper modestly gave it in the Argument to *Task* 4, a "Brown Study":

> Not undelightful is an hour to me
> So spent in parlour twilight; such a gloom
> Suits well the thoughtfull or unthinking mind,
>
> . . .
>
> Laugh ye, who boast your more mercurial pow'rs
> That never feel a stupor, know no pause

Nor need one. I am conscious, and confess
Fearless, a soul that does not always think.
Me oft has fancy ludicrous and wild
Sooth'd with a waking dream of houses, tow'rs,
Trees, churches, and strange visages express'd
In the red cinders, while with poring eye
I gazed, myself creating what I saw.
Nor less amused have I quiescent watch'd
The sooty films that play upon the bars
Pendulous, and foreboding in the view
Of superstition prophesying still
Though still deceived, some stranger's near approach.
'Tis thus the understanding takes repose
In indolent vacuity of thought,
And sleeps and is refresh'd. Meanwhile the face
Conceals the mood lethargic with a mask
Of deep deliberation, as the man
Were task'd to his full strength, absorb'd and lost.
Thus oft reclin'd at ease, I lose an hour
At evening, till at length the freezing blast
That sweeps the bolted shutter, summons home
The recollected powers, and snapping short
The glassy threads with which the fancy weaves
Her brittle toys, restores me to myself. (*Task*, 4.277–307)

With the lines, "I am conscious, and confess / Fearless, a soul that does not always think" (284–85), Cowper ignites, as with Ithuriel's spear, a familiar century-long controversy waged from Locke on, concerning the relationship of consciousness to thought and the basis of personal identity. As in a letter to John Newton several months later that takes up the same subject (*Letters*, 2.281–82), Cowper is quoting loosely from Locke's *Essay Concerning Human Understanding*. In its polemical, anti-Cartesian context, Locke had been intent on denying the existence of an immaterial substance that can exist independently of the body and its "twin fountains" of knowledge, sensation and reflection. He therefore insists at the beginning of the second book of the *Essay* that it is impossible for a man to think without being "conscious to himself, That he thinks"; "consciousness," which depends on physical embodiment, "is inseparable from thinking, and . . . essential to it."[60] If we imagine that thought might occur apart from bodily consciousness, Locke protests, "then it will be hard to know wherein to place personal Identity," a concern that the *Essay* supports with a series of bizarre experiments on the logic of the Cartesian *cogito*, imagining the soul of sleeping Castor choosing for its scene of thinking the body of waking

Pollux and meditating the resulting conundrum of personal identity. It is, however, possible not to think at all: as Locke writes in the lines that Cowper quotes roughly, "I confess my self, to have one of those dull Souls, that doth not perceive it self always to contemplate *Ideas,* nor can conceive it any more necessary for the *Soul always to think.*"[61] Just what happens in those conscious gaps or syncopes of thought is not Locke's concern – nor is the possibility that one might be conscious without thinking – he mentions the unconsciousness of sleep and leaves it at that, hoping to have located in consciousness a continuous principle of "self." In retrospect, as we know, he did just the opposite: the *Essay* was followed by a chorus of voices, as Christopher Fox and Jean Hagstrum have shown, that cried out, like Thomas Reid, that "if personal identity consisted in consciousness, it would certainly follow, that *no man is the same person any two moments of his life.*"[62]

Cowper enters the debate in order to probe the very vacant spaces in thought that the *Essay* had suggested but not explored, to imagine at some length the "unthinking mind" (281) that is not just a sleeping mind. His innovation, as Marshall Brown has suggested in an important, extended reading of *The Task,* is the way that he renders "the divorce of consciousness from attention." Yet I would part from Brown's conclusion – which separates the passage from its context and makes Cowper more of an imminent Kant than perhaps he is – namely, that here, for the first time, "consciousness becomes autonomous, independent of the world in which the conscious being lives."[63] For while that may at some level be Cowper's hope, what is striking is how much this "unthinking" consciousness which eludes the Lockean idea – this "indolent vacuity of [i.e., in] thought" (297) – in fact offers a curious reprise or précis of some of the most worldly moments of the poem, including the newspaper sequence that precedes it. Within the rifts of identity or personhood move other persons, as we will see. Cowper's unthinking of the Lockean idea coincides with a moment in which the poem's pattern of figuration is acutely open to context, so that the affective consciousness represented is not a recess or retreat but an aperture, a medium – a loophole – through which the world's strangeness enters.

In the "Brown Study," the physiognomical sign or figure for the "vacuity of thought" and accompanying remission of Lockean identity is the "mask / Of deep deliberation" (299–300), which makes of the first-person speaker a third person, that seemingly "task'd" man of lines 300–01. The speaker suddenly seems foreign or at least inscrutable to his domestic circle, where, of course, strangers are promptly multiplied: the masked, tasked man apprehends "some stranger's near approach" (295) presaged in that sooty film (292), which also contains, *inter alia*, "strange visages" (288) – the film, of course would later be anthropomorphized fully by Coleridge as a "fluttering stranger."[64] Moreover, the "fancy ludicrous" and "poring eye" activated during this seeming deliberation and absorbed with what Lord Kames would have called the "ideal presence" of a simulated object are recurrent, even compulsive figures throughout *The Task*.[65] We should recognize them, to begin with, as versions of the fancy and the "peering eye" that have just been engaged by the reading of the newspaper. In that sequence, as I noted earlier, Cowper had tried to assimilate the reading of the newspaper to the Lucretian paradigm for exempt spectatorship; the claim that reading offers "some secure and more than mortal height, / That lib'rates and exempts me from them all" (4.96–97) offers a version of *De Rerum Natura*'s depiction of a shipwreck viewed from dry land by a spectator (*De Rerum*, 2.1–13). As Cowper's exploration of the classical topos in a modern guise unfolds, however, it becomes clear that the newspaper reader is not entirely the spectator *ab extra*, sublimely contemplating the swirl of events from afar, but on both dry land and ship at once, immersed in virtual travel. Of the newspaper correspondent (or the subject of his "foreign intelligence"), Cowper writes:

> He travels and I too. I tread his deck,
> Ascend his topmast, though his peering eyes
> Discover countries, with a kindred heart
> Suffer his woes and share in his escapes,
> While fancy, like the finger of a clock,
> Runs the great circuit, and is still at home. (*Task*, 4.114–19)

If the newspaper, in that first chiastic line, places the reader on the topmast without quite removing him from the sofa (distributing the fancy between domestic Castor and nautical Pollux, to extend Locke's surmise), then the brown study immediately following enacts a similar, but inverted and more pronounced, chiasmus. There, as we just saw, under the sway of "fancy ludicrous," the "I" becomes "he" (the "task'd" man) until the shutter, swept by the wind, "summons home / The recollected powers, and . . . restores me to myself" (286, 304–07). This second, fuller exchange absents the "I" altogether, but rather than putting him on the ship instead brings the stranger in. The result is similar to the influx of "worlds / In worlds" upon the microscopic eye in *The Seasons*. The space that we have seen laboriously cultivated between *The Task*'s reader and the world – first in the landscape topography fashioned out of news prose, then in the more attenuated "finger of a clock" in the passage just quoted (and to which I later return) – suddenly contracts, so that, for a moment, it is as if not only the newspaper itself but a foreign intelligence has entered the home.

When I suggest that Cowper's Englishman, engaged in sofa-travel through the participatory medium of the news, has so absented himself that he resembles a stranger in his home, I am not just using that vocabulary for effect, for if we were to ask whom in the poem this poring, absorbed mask most resembles, we would have to point to certain haunted strangers that wander through it, each of them dispossessed or vagrant subjects touched by the effects of imperial expansion or exploration. Cowper had a life-long fascination for the Lucretian paradigm, although not the version promulgated by Lucretius himself but its anti-type, which Hans Blumenberg has located in Pascal, Nietzsche, and others: the spectator who has lost his foothold or else dived into the wreck entirely. Blumenberg argues that by Hegel and the nineteenth century, the figure of the spectator drawn perilously to the shore "anticipate[s] the concept of 'historicity' . . . the indissoluble interrelation of subject and historical process,"[66] but Cowper's preoccupation with the tableau – not only in *The Task* but also in the letters and in the notoriously bathetic final lines of "The Castaway" – suggests that it is already fully operative as such in later eighteenth-century Britain, where it is activated by, and associated specifically with, the risks, gains, and culpabilities of transoceanic conquest.[67]

The Task is peopled with such anti-Lucretian spectators, caught up in the flux of historical, and specifically imperial, process. There is first the sentimentalized stock figure of Crazy Kate in *Task* 1. Kate is inundated with the presence of an absence: seized by a version (and etymological cognate) of "fancy *ludi*crous," her "de*lus*ive fancy," she gazes intently out after a long-estranged, dead lover:

> Her fancy followed him through foaming waves
> To distant shores, and she would sit and weep
> At what a sailor suffers; fancy too
> Delusive most where warmest wishes are,
> Would oft anticipate his glad return,
> And dream of transports she was not to know. (*Task*, 1.539–44)

There are also the several mariners who crave the sight of land and "Nature in her green array," like the one who stands "Upon the ship's tall side . . . possess'd / With visions prompted by intense desire; / Fair fields appear below, such as he left / Far distant, such as he would die to find – / He seeks them headlong, and is seen no more" (*Task*, 1.449–54; cf. 1.520–23).

This version – the wrecked spectator from the ship – we can recognize as an extension of Thomson's horrified colonial explorers in *The Seasons*.

Drawn as well by an uncertain form of desire to stare across watery wastes is the strange figure of "gentle Omai," the South Seas visitor first brought to England in 1774, who in *Task* I provides the most extended instance of these wishful, anxious gazers – anticipatory figures, in Blumenberg's terms, of historicity. Omai was returned in 1776 on Captain Cook's final voyage to Tahiti and did not long survive his artificial repatriation, but since the news of his death had not yet reached Britain by 1784, Cowper images Omai in the poem's present, standing on the shores of his native island. Out of place in what was once his home, but ambivalent about another capture (for such his initial departure was, in some sense), he gazes out to sea. The speaker asks:

> . . . And have thy joys
> Lost nothing by comparison with ours?
>   . . .
> Methinks I see thee straying on the beach,
> And asking of the surge that bathes thy foot
> If ever it has wash'd our distant shore.
> I see thee weep, and thine are honest tears,
> A patriot's for his country. Thou art sad
> At thought of her forlorn and abject state,
> From which no power of thine can raise her up.
> Thus fancy paints thee, and though apt to err,
> Perhaps errs little, when she paints thee thus.
> She tells me too that duly ev'ry morn
> Thou climb'st the mountain top, with eager eye
> Exploring far and wide the watr'y waste
> For sight of ship from England. Ev'ry speck
> Seen in the dim horizon turns thee pale
> With conflict of contending hopes and fears.
>   . . .
> Alas! expect it not. (*Task*, 1.647–48, 654–68, 672)

At first glance, Omai appears as an exfoliation of ideal Englishness, a "patriot" weeping over his country's internal corruptions. The poet, groping for an understanding of an inaccessible other, supplies a version of himself, so that Omai appears here as a mirror image of the sentimental speaker gazing out at him; the erring fancy of the "I" meets Omai's similarly deluded fancy returning across a horizontal, watery space. This doubling movement seems a familiar one, described from Levi-Strauss through Homi Bhabha as typical of the ethnographic imagination: "the ethnographic object is constituted 'by dint of the subject's capacity for self-objectification . . . for projecting outside itself ever-diminishing fragments of itself'" – an elaboration, in international space, of the logic of Adam Smith's impartial spectator.[68] Yet if we look more closely, such a complacent image of sentimental patriotism seems troubled by the figure "pale / With conflict of contending hopes and fears" and that "eager eye" futilely scanning the horizon for moving specks. Like Kate earlier in the poem, like the speaker later on in his brown study, Omai is also waiting, expectantly, for – "some stranger's near approach." Or, as in the uncanny logic of the superstition that intrigued Cowper and Coleridge, he is anticipating a stranger who may be a friend – the categories of stranger and friend are as fluid as the seas that connect Britain to Tahiti (the ocean that "bathes thy foot" and may have "wash'd our distant shore" as well as its correlative, the sentimental wash of tears). Kate, Omai, and the speaker by the hearth are all in the impossibly frozen situation of apprehending something without knowing when, who, or what it will be.

For my purposes, Omai offers an interesting way of interpreting this recurrent figure, not because he provides the comforting ballast of an historical referent – indeed, we find the complex of rumors that constitute the English version of his history terribly weightless – but because, as one of the biggest and most confused public events of his time, his story provides an opportunity for seeing how an incoherent "article" of news enters into contemporary public consciousness and representation, including poetic representation, which tries, unsuccessfully, to make sense of it. From the moment of his arrival, Omai had been followed avidly by the newspapers, which offered vastly conflicting accounts of his parade of visits to Court, Parliament, Cambridge, and other notable sites, while watching his indoctrination in English language and customs – and notably his inoculation with the smallpox vaccine – with minute interest.[69] Injection was indeed one unspoken metaphor of the visit as relayed by the papers, for Omai became a human laboratory for testing what Englishness was by studying what someone else would find strange. How would he greet the King? With a comically informal and automatic "How d'ye do," reported *The Morning Chronicle*; not so, according to *The General Evening Post* four days later. And in a custom equally close to news readers' hearts: how would he sit on a sofa? ("He threw himself at full length," said *The Morning Chronicle*; not so, replied the *Post*, "for how can it be believed that during a voyage of so many months, on board a King's ship, he had not learned the art of sitting on a chair"?[70]) How would he like cherries? ("Too much like blood.") And Handel? ("Wild amazement.")[71] These and other painful instances suggest that, as in the case of the four "Iroquois" Kings who came to London earlier in 1711 or like the more nearly parallel example of the Tahitian Aorturoo, who accompanied Bougainville to France during the 1760s, part of what is at stake in such highly publicized visits is an attempt at what Joseph Roach (in the context of the 1711 visit) calls a process of "[self-definition] by staging contrasts with other races, cultures, ethnicities."[72]

Staging, of course, was the other, more explicit metaphor, since everywhere Omai went, including the theater, he became theater. Such ritual performances fumbled compulsively to fill the void of understanding, attempting to grapple with open questions about the consequences of British expansion and exploration overseas, the newest phase of which was inaugurated by the opening of the South Seas in the early 1770s.[73] What is Englishness and what will it be in a quickly expanding empire? To what extent is any life lived at home ineradicably intertwined with far-flung existences, among which this visitor from the South Pacific offered just one, unusually visible, example? What burdens are carried, or should be, by such incompletely known but extensive interdependencies?[74] This is, in the terms I introduced earlier, an anxious uncertainty about the boundaries of the "conversable world" in both senses of Hume's resonant phrase: not only the world made up of polite conversationalists but also the world as knowable at all. Does the "globe . . . tur[n] submitted to view," as we have seen Cowper briefly fantasizing in the newspaper sequence? Or is it no longer possible to comprehend a global reality that can be, as Fielding hoped it could, "turned round, sifted, and . . . communicated to each other"? It is not accidental that the question perhaps most often renewed with respect to Omai concerned the visitor's skills of communication and conversation. He was sometimes reported to speak remarkably well, as in *The London Chronicle*'s improbable report that "Omiah, the native of Otaheite, we are informed can read and write English well enough to hold a correspondence," a rumor whose next sentence makes clear the proximity between conversation and other more intimate minglings: "It is still said he is going to be married to a young Lady of about 22 years of age, who will go with him to his own country."[75] But more often he was said to speak poorly, a source of some entertainment to his hosts, who found that their desire to make Omai "conversable" had turned into a considerable task.

Interspersed among other news that had nothing to do with him, Omai was thus an instance of what the *London Magazine* entry (cited earlier) called "the contradictory substance of foreign and domestick paragraphs" – but one in which the possibility and the contradiction of positing substance distinctively "foreign" or "domestic" was precisely the issue. Although he was returned by Captain Cook in 1776 – left on Huahine with a stock of goats, horses, and European clothes – such uncertainties about the implication of transoceanic expansion did not much abate but took a new, even more unanswerable form: what had happened to Omai, now injected with a measure of English culture (plus the livestock and gratuitous clothes), once reinstalled in his native context? The posthumous publication of Cook's official *Voyage to the Pacific Ocean* in 1784 and the sally of rival, spurious accounts of Omai's return which between 1781 and 1784 preceded and sought to scoop the authorized version did much to keep the question alive but little to answer it, since Cook had died before reaching England and no one successfully followed his path back until 1789.[76] All *The General Evening Post* could do – as late as 1784 and while Cowper was still working on *The Task* – was to reprint portions of Cook's narrative of the return voyage in an attempt to "satisfy our readers who will no doubt be anxious with regard to the fate of Omai."[77] We can now see that Cowper's representation of Omai in *Task* I is attempting to perform the same work as the *Evening Post*: to satisfy an anxiety both personal and collective about the fate of this enigmatic, briefly befriended stranger – token of the new fluidity of relations across space – by trying to fill in the interstices of what the press could only render as "dissociating articles," both because of the dearth in intelligence and the narrative incoherence we have seen described by Crabbe ("on quitting one thought, there will be an unavoidable hiatus, and in general an awkward transition into that which follows").[78]

I earlier cited Fredric Jameson's account of the contradiction, under imperialism, between any lived experience and the structures (social and economic) which inflect that experience with the force of an absent cause, immanent in its effects: a full account of any such experience can no longer be rendered from the home "in which it takes place [but] lies, rather, in India or Jamaica or Hong Kong. . . ."[79] In the Freudian terms that Jameson for the most part avoids, we can add that in such a situation all that is familiar necessarily includes the strange, so that everyday experience is uncanny. There is a "roar that lies on the other side of silence," to return to George Eliot's marvelous phrase (epigraph to my chapter 2) – the noise of nameless nations. "Yet," Jameson continues, "this absent cause can find figures through which to express itself in distorted or symbolic ways." In this regard Jameson's Althusserian understanding of history is close to the formulation of Raymond Williams, defending his position that "there are cases where the structure of feeling . . . tangible in a particular set of works is undoubtedly an articulation of an area of experience which lies beyond them." One recognizes such moments, Williams claimed, with the appearance of a "semantic figure" or new kind of work that "produces a sudden shock of *recognition*" (*Politics and Letters*, 164). Mindful of the impact that it had on its readers,[80] I would suggest that the peering, poring, scanning eye that collapses space by dwelling intently on such distant objects felt as almost-but-not-quite present – as the brown study puts it, the stranger in "*near* approach" – offers just such a figure, although it is in certain respects misleading to say that it "articulates" an experience, since it is a figure of expressive inarticulateness, and of the limits of lived experience. A gesture shot through with contradiction, because it is both desire and apprehension for both stranger and friend, this uneasy stare marks the point at which the conversable world's attempts at polite articulation (in both senses of the word that designated the acts of joining and uttering) come up against a world system too large to sustain them, a system that introduces and imbricates "strangers" among "friends."

As such, the expectant, fixed stare of fear and desire offers the antithesis of the mobile, visual "command," the "equal, wide survey," that John Barrell has so nicely explicated in Thomson, Dyer, and eighteenth-century georgic-topographical verse – and which the transformation of the newspaper as conventional landscape ("cataracts of declamation"; "forests of no-meaning") attempts at first to accomplish. It qualifies, although it does not refute, Suvir Kaul's contention that the author of the long poem in the eighteenth century, Cowper included, "imagined poetry to be a unique and privileged literary form for the enunciation of a puissant (and plastic) vocabulary of nation, particularly one of a Britain proving itself (in fits and starts, to be sure) great at home and abroad."[81] For it acknowledges (as may Kaul's own penchant for parentheses) a teeming historical present that is not, cannot be, enunciated in the anthems of empire, for it is not conversable in the various senses of that term.

However, what interests me in particular is not just the fact of this darker apprehension of historicity but the conditions for its involuntary return in the poem. The brown study in *Task* 4 with its Janus-faced speaker helps us understand that fixation on this pending strangeness and "indolent vacuity of thought" are the two faces of each other. In attempting to specify their relationship we could call the vacuity of thought a protective defense against those imminent strangers or, less figuratively, the as-yet-unknown implications of overseas intimacy dramatized so pathologically in episodes like Omai's visit with its baffled news coverage and lurking more mundanely in any issue of the daily news. It is, after all, an "*indolent* vacuity of thought," and indolence in one of its incarnations is boredom – that state often associated with the eighteenth century and described nicely by

Adam Phillips as a state of "suspended animation." Boredom, Phillips writes movingly, "makes tolerable the impossible experience of waiting for something without knowing what it could be," the terrible fixity of desiring an object and fearing that desire at the same time.[82] However, the significance of that vacuity of thought is more than just as defense, or, if it is one, we need to recognize that it admits the threat it parries. Like a loophole in fortification, it is both an aperture and shield at once. For I have been suggesting that this lapse in Lockean ideation and identity, this interstitial moment of unthinking consciousness that is both described in the brown study and enacted by the pattern of figure in the poem more generally, is the *condition* for the entry of ongoing history's absent but immanent force. This apperception cannot enter as idea or articulation (direct narrative statement, recognition of explicit structure) because it is not – not yet or not acceptable as – one. But its potent sign or effect is the peculiar *a*ffect of muted risk, that register of waiting "with conflict of contending hopes and fears." For that reason it would be precisely the wrong question to ask, as one may still be tempted to do, whether Cowper "intends" the poring eye and mask of the speaker to recall Omai and other staring spectators, inundated with the imminence of their history. To put the question in those terms is to miss Williams's and Jameson's separate insights about the work that figure can do in excess of intention, particularly when the history one is part of lies beyond lived experience and sense perception. It is to miss the critique of the Lockean idea that Cowper's poem itself mounts.

THE FLICKER OF HISTORY: COWPER AND WALTER BENJAMIN

At the center of the brown study sequence and as its synecdoche, Cowper's flickering film of fire thus functions like a muted version of the brief flare of history in the image that constitutes the second of my two chapter epigraphs, from Walter Benjamin's "Theses on the Philosophy of History." Benjamin provides a necessary theoretical frame of reference, at any rate, because his work offers one of the most sustained meditations on the relationship between a culture of news, or "information," and involuntary consciousness as a distinctively open, historical medium, "imprint[ed]," as he wrote in "A Berlin Chronicle," with "the collision between a larger collective and [the self]."[83] Taking aim at the "dissociating articles" of news very much as we have seen Crabbe and others doing, Benjamin argued in his essay on Baudelaire that with their "lack of connection between the individual news items," "newspapers constitute one of the many evidences" of modern man's "inability to assimilate the data of the world around him by way of experience" (*Erfahrung*, by which Benjamin designates collective "tradition," embodied and transmitted from generation to generation by storytelling, rather than "experience" in the British empirical tradition). Not solely the newspaper itself but more generally the "replacement of the older narration by information, of information by sensation, reflects the increasing atrophy of experience." Yet just because the news, with its privileging of the "happening" isolated from narrative tradition, eludes *Erfahrung*, it is not therefore unavailable. Its content just becomes available in a different way: in the form of *Erlebnis*, the lived event, which "tend[s] to remain in a certain hour of one's life" and is therefore subject to compulsive recurrence, or "involuntary memory." Like shock in the model of trauma that Benjamin takes over from Freud's *Beyond the Pleasure Principle*, the momentary and dissociated "happening" is "parried by consciousness," understood not as an impermeable "barricade" to social experience but as its unpredictable medium.[84]

Although Benjamin seems to expect this shock-like encounter to "sterilize the incident for poetic yield," the achievement of Baudelaire, he argues, is to make poetry out of such fragmentary lived moments, which stand like blank spaces in the calendar, dropped from tradition (*Erfahrung*): Baudelaire "envisioned blank spaces which he filled in with his poems," Benjamin writes enigmatically: "His work cannot be categorized as historical, like anyone else's, but it intended to be so and understood itself as such."[85] Baudelairean lyric is *peculiarly* historical (historical not "like anyone else's"), that is, because of its capacity both to parry and to lodge within it "heterogeneous, conspicuous fragments," resistant to chronological connection with other days; such heterogenous articles, nonetheless, are "the fragments of genuine historical experience." In spite of all his poignant plaints for lost *Erfahrung*, Benjamin does not nostalgically hope for its restoration – he doubted, as Martin Jay has shown, that such a return was possible in the modern, capitalist world – and, with his later work, he began to look forward to a dialectically recovered likeness of *Erlebnis*, as in the "Theses," with their flame image and their emphasis on "time of the now . . . blasted out of the continuum of history."[86] A posthumously published fragment adds: "History in the strict sense is an image from involuntary memory, an image which suddenly occurs to the subject in a moment of danger. . . . Historiography has to test its presence of mind in grasping fleeting images."[87]

Short of making William Cowper into a Benjaminian historical materialist (which he certainly was not) or into Baudelaire (with whom he did indeed have certain social and splenetic affinities), I hope to have suggested a similar, complex relationship between his poetry and the news, or, more aptly, the sense of the historical present that is fostered by a nascent news culture. At a level that differs quite sharply from all the overt statements for or against empire, and for or against the imperiled condition of Britain in 1784 (and *The Task* contains many, of each kind, particularly in Books 1 and 2), Cowper's poetry is more interestingly and involuntarily "historical" – although not just "like anyone else's" – for the ways it captures, lodged in the interstices of thought, those figures and flickering recognitions of historicity that do not answer to the pleasure principle of narration, and cannot be assimilated into polite conversation or the equally polite interchange of ideas. Benjamin's understanding of the way such recognitions "tend to remain in a certain hour of one's life" helps us interpret Cowper's insight into the temporal quality of Fancy both in the brown study passage and in the newspaper sequence leading up to it. Under the sway of fancy, as we have seen, the poet in his reverie "lose[s] an hour / At evening" (4.302–03); reading the newspaper just before that – and now we can return to the most striking aspect of the passage discussed earlier – "fancy, like the finger of a clock, / Runs the great circuit, and is still at home" (4.118–19). Cowper, I think, invokes the image of a clock that goes around and around repetitively not as a reminder of chronology, as one might expect, but for its relative stasis; it cannot mark progression as can a calendar, but rather the hour, over and over again.

But Cowper, it must be interjected at this point, is not writing lyric but a version of georgic, whereas historiography is, for Benjamin (and Benjamin's Baudelaire), distinctively lyrical and anti-narrative. It is Coleridge who would make lyric out of *The Task*, fifteen years later in "Frost at Midnight," and now we can see that he does so precisely by excising the "indolent vacuity of thought" sequence from its narrative surroundings, moving what "Frost at Midnight" renders as "the interspersed vacancies / And momentary pauses of the thought" (46–47) far, far from the newspaper's "map of busy life." The memory that flares up in response to *Coleridge's* "film, which fluttered on the grate, . . . the sole unquiet thing" (15–16) is involuntary but personal, the dream "of my sweet birth-place" (28) – a phrase which would in turn migrate one year later into the opening of the 1799 *Prelude*, rightly called by Clifford Siskin a mixture of lyric and georgic.[88] The stranger that materializes in Coleridge's poem, for all its near-gothic elements, is reassuringly "townsman, or aunt, or sister more beloved"; the thematization of historical strangeness and the actuality of strangers is gone or at least muted. What seems to me so interesting about Cowper's choice not to separate consciousness from the world of information that imprints it – which in modal terms appears in the choice not to submerge the georgic in lyric – is that *The Task* thereby makes palpable the connection between the pressure of historical presentness and sensory consciousness that is less discernible in "greater Romantic lyric." This is not merely a point about literary history or the genealogy of form, although it is not uninteresting as such. More provocatively, it begins to suggest a curious relationship between the eighteenth-century culture (and perceived over-load) of news, the georgic attempt to offer a rival medium of knowledge, and Romantic *aisthesis* – which in Kant's *Critique of Judgment* also takes as one of its images "the sight of the changing shape of fire on the hearth" as contemplated by the fancying subject.[89] That relationship now needs to be defined.

"VACUITY OF THOUGHT": BETWEEN ACEDIA AND AISTHESIS

At this point a skeptical questioner might rightly ask whether I am granting too much to Cowper's claims for the significance of textual contiguity in *The Task* – in this case, the poem's juxtaposition of the newspaper's na-tional and international map with the "vacuity of thought" which comes right after it. While association may indeed be the organizational princi-ple of the baggy, paratactical monster that is *The Task*, on what basis can one claim that this particular one transcends the train of thought – the "ludicrous" imagination – of William Cowper, or articulates an impor-tant cultural connection? In addition to the "feeling" of history "in solu-tion," in other words, where is the collective "structure," that other half of Raymond Williams's deliberately paradoxical phrase? In fact, the associ-ation between news reading and "vacuity of thought" was not Cowper's quirk. In order to understand its wider currency – while remaining mind-ful that *association* within a shared structure is not simple causation or Marshall McLuhanite determination – I move out again (as a complement to this chapter's second section, above) to consider the relationship be-tween "vacuity" and the news as those two phenomena were treated by the eighteenth-century periodical press. A review of this discourse may also clarify the relationship between the involuntary influx of historical pre-sentness (the information "overload" treated in *The London Magazine*) and aesthetic perception, as well as Cowper's intervening role as a pivot between their two flames.

We have seen that, in the wake of Locke's admission that the soul does not always think, the problem of the "vacuities of thought" vexed moral-philosophical and proto-psychological discourse with the fault lines, and hence the fictionality, of any integrated "personal identity." At the same time, however, vacant spaces were making news of sorts in a different arena: within the discussions of the periodical press. These two conversations were not discontinuous, of course, since *The Spectator* promised to bring "Philosophy out of Closets and Libraries, Schools and Colleges, to dwell in Clubs and Assemblies, Tea-Tables, and in Coffee-Houses," but neither were they identical.[90] The concerns grouped under such frequently employed phrases as "vacant of thought," "vacuity of the mind," "interstitial vacancies," or "the blanks of society" took, in journalistic discussions, a slightly different but no less anxious turn, displaying worries about what kind of characters magazine and newspaper writing both catered to and constructed.[91]

In one of its contemporary senses, a vacancy was a temporary interval of leisure or unoccupied time. Addressing men and women affluent enough to have such freedom, periodical publications made it their work to recommend, as Addison wrote, "certain Methods for filling up their empty Spaces of Life."[92] No one was more worried about the productive management of free time than Samuel Johnson, who kept an equally stern eye on his own wayward propensities for melancholic idling, and the Rambler accordingly advised a strict regimen of improving hobbies: "He that should steadily and resolutely assign to any science or language those interstitial vacancies which intervene in the most crouded variety of diversion or employment, would find every day new irradiations of knowledge."[93] But this sense of vacancy as vacation was active alongside another, which designated not a certain kind of free time but a certain kind of empty mind. "There is a Creature," wrote Steele in *The Spectator*, "who has all the Organs of Speech, a tollerable good Capacity for conceiving what is said to it, together with a pretty proper Behaviour in all the Occurrences of Common Life; but naturally very vacant of Thought in it self, and therefore forced to apply it self to foreign Assistances."[94] To these "Blanks of Society," as they were frequently called, the periodical writer and news writer happily offered such assistance: "It is incredible to think how empty I have in this Time observ'd some Part of the Species to be," wrote Addison, "what mere Blanks they are when they first come abroad in the Morning, how utterly they are at a Stand till they are set a going by some Paragraph in a News-paper." To this "Set of Men . . . altogether unfurnish'd with Ideas," Addison added several days later, "I must likewise lay Claim."[95]

These dicta of Mr. Spectator begin to suggest the complex dialectic taking shape between the news as a cultural phenomenon and vacuity of mind as a social as well as psychological problem; it also indicates the nascent rivalry between the periodical essayist (whether Addison, Steele, Johnson, or even the contributors to miscellanies like the rival *Gentleman's Magazine* and *London Magazine*) and the newspaper writer, author of those "dissociating articles" of prose later lampooned by Crabbe. Although the idle man could turn to the papers to "fill the vacuity of his mind with the news of the day," as *The Idler* put it, the phenomena of "news" also tended to empty the same minds it was designed to fill. Johnson himself, seeking in part to distinguish himself from the daily hack, provides a particularly trenchant diagnosis of this circular movement of effects, criticizing the "rivulets of intelligence" that streamed from the daily newspaper as "information sufficient to elate vanity, and stiffen obstinacy, but too little to enlarge the mind into complete skill for full comprehension."[96] Such foreshortened comprehension was exacerbated by two seemingly contradictory aspects of news writing, according to Johnson: its tendency to encourage "reading without the fatigue of close attention,"[97] but also its redundancy, which paradoxically caused rather than spared mental exhaustion. "The tale of the morning paper is told again in the evening, and the narratives of the evening are bought again in the morning," and so even "[t]he most eager peruser of news is tired before he has completed his labour"; the result, Johnson grimly concluded, is that "journals are daily multiplied without increase of knowledge."[98] As a playful remedy, Johnson in the person of the Idler proposed the slowing down, or gradation, of the news: if all news writers agreed to confederate, "the morning and evening authors might divide an event between them; a single action, and that not of much importance, might be gradually discovered so as to vary a whole week with joy, anxiety, and conjecture." If the news could be rendered in slow motion it might give more time for thought, or so the fictional example of such slow-motion-news provided (at some length) suggests. What the Idler does not acknowledge, although Johnson knows it perfectly well, is that any event, presented ever so gradually over time, stops being "news."

The Idler in 1758 thus corroborates the contributor to *The London Magazine* of 1766, quoted earlier, who noted that the "abrupt transitions from article to article, without the smallest connection between one paragraph and another, overload and confuse the memory." Johnson, however, provides the more sophisticated social analysis, free of any hint of technological determinism, which has been nicely criticized for our own times by Michael Warner for its artificial separation of the logic of print technology from the culture of which it is a part.[99] News does not cause the overload by itself, Johnson recognizes; rather news writers are only "necessary in a nation where much wealth produces much leisure, and one part of the people has nothing to do but to observe the lives and fortunes of the other."[100]

Both world spectator and "castaway" of history, representing himself both as the consumer of the "rich repast" proffered from around the globe in the newspaper advertisements of *Task* 4 and as the assiduous producer of the poem-as-luxury item – *The Task* as giant cucumber – William Cowper, like Johnson, is poised uneasily in both of these worlds.[101] What is distinctive about *The Task* is the way that, while Cowper was immersed in contemporary discussions about the effects of newspaper reading (he could be our "W. C." from above; certainly he made very similar pronouncements in his letters), and while he was well read in Lockean and post-Lockean philosophy (either in its original sources or through the press's popularizing mediation), his poem nonetheless tilts both discourses about vacancies in thought in a new direction – one decisive in retrospect, as it turned out, because of *The Task*'s influence on the next generation of writers. Johnson had construed mental "vacuity" in the most negative terms, as an unproductivity verging on spiritual sloth, or what an earlier age had called *acedia*. Cowper, prone as he was to cyclical melancholy and loss of faith, is by no means free of such associations. Yet in the brown study passage and *The Task* at large, we see him uncertainly edging this state toward a creative "repose" (4.296), a movement perhaps best glossed by his central revision of the *Georgics*' phrase, *studiis florentem ignobilis oti* (*Georgics*, 4.564): Virgil's "studious of the arts of inglorious ease" becomes Cowper's "studious of laborious ease, / Not slothful" (*Task*, 3.361–62).[102] "Laborious ease" might cause us to assimilate Cowper's revision of the torpid indolence of *The Spectator*'s empty-headed "Blanks of society," Johnson's melancholic idler, and Locke's sleeper to the "majestic indolence" of aesthetic experience that Willard Spiegelman has recently traced in Romantic poetry and philosophy. Kant, as Spiegelman points out, describes the poet as "conducting the free play of the imagination as if it were a serious business of the understanding."[103] But Cowper's "indolent vacuity of thought" is not (yet) Kantian free play either. Far more unstable, weaving precariously "brittle toys" (4.307), it may be play of sorts – ludic or ludicrous – but we have seen that it is not free. That image of the "bars" hemming in the "sooty flames" might stand nicely for the embeddedness, textual and cultural, of this interstitial consciousness, a vacuity replete with contemporaneity's "dissociating articles" and news.

Spiegelman has lucidly surveyed the historical and qualitative shift whereby a pathological torpor (*acedia*, "wanhope," Burtonian melancholy) gradually became a more genial recreation (aesthetic suspension, Wordsworthian wise passiveness); he does not seek to account for its cause. Moving straight from Johnson to the canonical Romantics (Wordsworth,

Coleridge, Keats, Shelley, and their later American cousins), his task is simply to make the case that indolence in its negative incarnation "was transformed and elevated by the Romantic poets in their individual efforts to legitimate their innovations in poetic forms and genres."[104] Just "what caused" such a notable epistemic and semantic drift is certainly overdetermined, but the example of Cowper points to one form a partial answer might take. At the position of pivot between the emptiness of *acedia* and the fullness of aesthetic experience, Cowper's teeming vacuity of thought, I have tried to suggest, is an unlikely, involuntary mode of knowledge that responds to the pressure of an eventful and information-laden present, one shaped by technological and territorial extension. The relationship between the later eighteenth-century culture of news and the affective, proto-aesthetic consciousness that starts to emerge out of the georgic attempt to offer a rival medium of information is not just the "displacement" or "negation" of contemporaneity by the "self," as in the forceful historicist arguments of the later 1980s and 1990s. Instead, it defines this consciousness as the heir, a crucial if residual carrier, of a world of information-in-flux, that teeming historical presentness that is "not yet" fully formed as knowledge, but presses insistently, insinuating itself at the level of recurrent figure. This genealogy might remind us as well of the element of external risk and historical inundation that intervenes at the genesis of a full-fledged account of aesthetic perception. "[T]o analyze the element of *comfort* in beauty, without false emphasis," Kenneth Burke reminds us, "we must be . . . more 'dialectical,' in that we include also, as an important aspect of the recipe, the element of *discomfort* (actual or threatened) for which poetry is 'medicine,' therapeutic or prophylactic." (Burke's other term is "equipment," which better suits the characteristic, didactic thrust of the georgic, as it tries to define a use-value for poetry.[105]) To render my argument in the most provocative or playful terms: I am turning the tables on our plaint that the postmodern condition of information supersedes a Romantic idea of the literary and asking whether the reverse is not also true. Recalling the impulse of so many biblical and post-biblical accounts to provide a narrative of the events leading up to Genesis 1:1's "In the beginning," I have proposed that if, according to a narrative of the genesis of Kantian or Schillerian aesthetics, "in the beginning" was the first free play of the imagination, then "before the beginning" but strongly contributing to it was – the news.

CHAPTER IV

"Passages of Life": aural histories in The Excursion

> Intricate labyrinth, more dread for thought
> To enter than oracular cave;
> Strict passage . . .
> Wordsworth, "On the Power of Sound"

INTRODUCTION

In the fifth book of William Wordsworth's *The Excursion*, the fantasy of perception heightened to a pitch of vulnerability that we have seen figured in the "microscopic eye" of earlier eighteenth-century verse returns in the form of the Solitary's protest among the sepulchral monuments of the country church:

> If this mute earth
> Of what it holds could speak, and every grave
> Were as a volume, shut, yet capable
> Of yielding its contents to eye and ear,
> We should recoil, stricken with sorrow and shame,
> To see disclosed, by such dread proof, how ill
> That which is done accords with what is known
> To reason, and by conscience is enjoined;
> How idly, how perversely, life's whole course,
> To this conclusion, deviates from the line,
> Or of the end stops short, proposed to all
> At her aspiring outset. (*Excursion*, 5.250–61)[1]

The Solitary's aversion to sensory extension is a terror directed not at invisible or distant presences but downwards (into the earth) and backwards (in time): what if our senses were so acute that we could feel, as with "eye and ear," the animate presence of the dead, whose lives – at least to the "wounded spirt" of the Solitary (*Exc.*, 9.786) – would read like a catalogue of deviations, defaults, and disappointments? Against the Solitary's antipathy to the immediacy or virtuality of such a past, one might contrast a number of contemporary texts that thirst for history not as textual representation but as sense-presentation, not as a "then" but as "now": these could include Wordsworth's own Sarum Plain episode in *The Prelude*, Helen Maria Williams's *Letters from France* (1790), and certainly another sepulchral meditation – William Godwin's *Essays on Sepulchres* (1809). "I love to dwell in a country," Godwin muses, "where, on whichever side I turn, I find some object connected with a heart-moving tale, or some scene where the deepest interests of a nation for ages to succeed, have been strenuously agitated, and emphatically decided":

> I never understood the annals of chivalry so well, as when I walked among the ruins of Kenilworth Castle. I no longer trusted to the tale of the historian, the cold and uncertain record of words formed upon paper, I beheld the queen "of lion port . . . uprear her starry front." The subtle, the audacious and murder-dealing Leicester stood before me. I heard the trampling of horses, and the clangour of trumpets. The aspiring and lofty-minded men of former times were seen by me as I passed along, and stood in review before me.[2]

Godwin's worry in this essay is not that the earth might speak too much, or that it might say anything unwelcome if it did; the concern is rather that it might be too mute, and, moreover, that the historian's "cold and uncertain record of words formed upon paper" might add to the silence.[3]

A number of questions are implied: can the past be felt, as if by "eye and ear," in the present? What prompts such responses? To what extent is such sensory immediacy – "virtual history" – desirable? To what extent is it adequate? How distanced, or close, should the past be? Many of these concerns already reside, at least incipiently, in that representative tableau which concludes the first of Virgil's *Georgics*, and with which I introduced this book. At that moment, we recall, Virgil's representation of cultivation turns into an explicit image of excavation, and his *agricola* becomes an unlikely agent of historical discovery. Where Wordsworth's Solitary recoils, Virgil's unpremeditating farmer just marvels (*mirabitur*):

> *scilicet et tempus veniet, cum finibus illis*
> *agricola incurvo terram molitus aratro*
> *exesa inveniet scabra robigine pila,*
> *aut gravibus rastris galeas pulsabit inanis,*
> *grandiaque effossis mirabitur ossa sepulcris.*

> [Yea, and a time shall come when in those lands, as the farmer toils
> at the soil with crooked plough, he shall find javelins eaten up
> with rusty mould, or with his heavy hoes shall strike on empty
> helms, and marvel at the giant bones in the upturned graves.]
> (*Georgics*, 1.493–97)

Prompted by such artifacts, *mirabitur* is, of course, a distinctively aesthetic response: powerful, but also limited. Although Plato and Aristotle praised *admiratio* as the only beginning of knowledge, Virgil's more ambiguously marveling ploughman suggests that such preconceptual or "particular" judgment is, by the same token, *only* the beginning.[4] The particulate elements (Plato's *aistheta*) are inexplicable until they enter discourse (*logos*); they await analysis. Virgil's astonished *agricola* – here unflatteringly diminished in size and elsewhere called *ignarosque viae*, or "ignorant of the way" (*Georgics*, 1.41) – points to other outcomes beside philosophy or conceptual knowledge. These include, if not actual recoil or resistance to knowing, then at least the failure of articulation, and therefore a communicative gap between generations. That the concern about transmission weighs heavily on Virgil at this moment is apparent in the complex temporal structure of the *Georgics* 1 passage: turning from an account of the blood-soaked Emathian plains (1.490–92), the poet imagines his own war-torn present as the future's past, and he conceives of that future as ignorant of its heroic but treacherous history. But is such ignorance really bliss – or, at the undecided moment of Roman history which Virgil inhabited, costly?[5]

This book has so far explored the ways that georgic encourages within eighteenth-century poetry an intensified medium-consciousness, by which I have hoped to suggest both the poetry's concern for its specificity as a rival to contemporary visual, auditory, and print channels of perception and communication (microscope, conversation, newspaper) and, as a result, its corollary attentiveness to the receptive consciousness *as* a medium, a "sensible path" for a circumambient, historical presentness. I have argued that certain kinds of uncomfortable sensation and emotion – stunned horror at cognitive or suprasensory noise, a vacant suspension between thoughts – can present a significant register of historical knowledge, one important precisely by virtue of its elusive resistance to the ideology of the "idea" and the "principle of pleasure." Yet we have also seen some of the limitations of merely dwelling with that roar on the other side of silence: the narrator of *The Seasons* turns away from the "noise" that accompanies the sight of "nameless nations" in his food, and the alternative suggested by George Eliot to "walking around well-wadded with stupidity" – namely, dying of the roar in an excess of sensitivity – is hardly more auspicious. Moreover, the apperception of ongoing history as an excess that "remains to be phrased" (Lyotard) has a short shelf-life. "Half-knowledge," as David Simpson has skeptically labeled the Lyotardian distrust of grand narratives, does not last over generations.[6] This final section of my argument acknowledges the real limitations of "unconversable" knowledge (in the terms offered by chapter 3, which discussed conversation as an epistemological as well as stylistic ideal), particularly in communications that take place over time.

But if we think of history as transmitted knowledge, as a relationship to the past, is there a way of rendering the unconversable world as anything other than a failure of phrasing? How is that past to pass through language without being reduced or betrayed by claims to total or totalizing representation? What work of words does not avoid what remains elusive about the past but also refuses to disclaim historical knowledge altogether, with the excuse that history is, after all, unknowable? These dialectical, sometimes irreconcilable imperatives have obviously exerted particular pressure on the historiography of the last quarter-century. Fredric Jameson writes that "history – Althusser's 'absent cause,' Lacan's 'Real' – is *not* a text, for it is fundamentally non-narrative and nonrepresentational; what can be added, however, is the proviso that history is inaccessible to us except in textual form," and Jameson cautions against two ideological traps of studies in historical mediation: overestimating the way a text reorganizes its social ground, or reifying that ground as some given that the text thereby inertly "reflects." Jean-Luc Nancy outlines a related Hobson's choice: "It is as if we were suspended between both: either something happens that we cannot grasp in our representation, or nothing happens but the production of historico-fictitious narratives."[7] Where Jameson and Nancy are both pointing to the loss of the elusive or "absent" Real that inheres in any epistemological claim, particularly ones we make about the present, Michel de Certeau doubles that loss by adding to it the erosion that occurs because of the passage of time. Hence de Certeau's *The Writing of History* is explicitly elegiac in its observation that historiography is an "odd procedure that posits death, a breakage everywhere reiterated in discourse, and that yet denies loss by appropriating to the present the privilege of recapitulating the past as a form of knowledge. A labor of death and a labor against death."[8] It is a "labor against death" because the historiographer claims the epistemological compensation of knowledge and the aesthetic reward of historical form, but "of death" because de Certeau recognizes that this recompense is always compromised, that conveying the past is also betraying it, and that the epistemological and narrative gain remains fragmentary. De Certeau's historian moves, as it were, between the compensatory and anti-compensatory poles that have marked elegiac writing at least since the Renaissance, between the impulse to "find in loss a gain to match" (Tennyson) and the antithetical movement which, as in Baroque *Trauerspiel* or much twentieth-century poetry, resists turning loss into gain, a completed "work," a *Trauerarbeit*.[9] The more extreme the event to come under the historian's scrutiny the more urgent the double imperative both to resist ideological closure and to refuse simple proclamations about the unknowability of the past, celebrations of aporia.[10]

The problem, however, did not begin with postmodernism. It might be said to reside implicitly in Virgil's rendition of the unexpectedly uncovered residues of violence. The furrows themselves may spark *admiratio* in the unprepared farmer, but is that enough, and what sort of communication across time resides in the poet's own *versus*? It is both explicit and central in this chapter's focal text, *The Excursion*, Wordsworth's most explicitly georgic poem, where Virgil's tableau appears not in the form of an isolated or occasional tag – as in Philips's *Cyder* and subsequent eighteenth-century imitations of the *Georgics* – but as an organizational principle, a pervasive rhizomatic presence that is far more disturbing than in Philips or in other celebratory verse. Obviously then this chapter, like much of my argument so far with respect to earlier poetry, attempts to reverse the tenacious account of the georgic as the mode which turns history into nature. As I noted in my introduction, Virgil's tableau suggests that the problem is not that the plough or the pen buries in furrows or in verses what should be disclosed; this paradigmatic scene points rather to a failure of reception and recognition, a problematic inability – sometimes refusal – to know what has been turned up *as* history.

The last two chapters have considered the question of access to the historical present, to the shifting structures extending spatially beyond the limits of "lived experience" and unaided sense perception, and therefore necessarily to unresolved grappling with the process of imperial expansion. I have tried to set forth the paradox of georgic mediation, whereby the poem can become an aperture or lodging for a reality that lies beyond it – beyond its narration but not beyond its representation. Such sites, we have seen, cluster at moments of disturbed sensation and idea-formation; they are signaled by disturbances of place, unsettling any fixity of "here" and "there" (imperial center and periphery, subject and object), and these dislocations in turn often coincide with the moment that noise or silence cuts across the visual field or into the pleasurable ebb and flow of the conversational, didactic voice. They disrupt the bid, which Heidegger considered constitutive of the modern age, to conceive the "world as picture," thereby pointing to elements that we take to be "postmodern" at work within the longer tradition of modernity.

This chapter brings all of the questions explored in earlier chapters to bear on extension backward in time rather than outward in space, and it therefore moves us closer to the realm of historiography proper, the problem of access to the past. To consider extension backwards in time rather than outwards in space is to move away from the international present, whose impact on Wordsworth's poetry has been well studied to date. I hope to have suggested the genealogy behind the apprehension of the "local as global" that Saree Makdisi, for example, has found in Book 7 of *The Prelude*, where London appears "a space in which the familiar distinctions between 'here' and 'there,' between metropolis and colony, between east and west and north and south, become confused and blurred."[11] Such representations are deeply indebted to Wordsworth's understanding of eighteenth-century georgic, and they make a more interesting legacy than just the didacticism that he is usually assumed to have taken from Thomson and Cowper. I am not, however, abandoning the problem of presentness identified by Williams as a particular challenge to our analytic categories; for Williams this was not, as I noted in my introduction, limited to the representation of the present "age" – the past, too, has pockets of history that never reached or just exceeded coherent articulation. The histories of *The Excursion's* mute inglorious Miltons belong to this category; they differ sharply from Godwin's imagined encounter with Elizabeth, Leicester, or Sidney, and from the buried epic uncovered by Virgil's farmer. Lives of unfulfilled desire, they ended, but never found their "end"; their contents in normative terms are nearly contentless, full of discontent. In this sense they remained for their duration "in solution," never precipitating out into annals or written records, nor even – as in the "Lives of Infamous Men" collected by Michel Foucault, a project similar in some other respects to Wordsworth's – undergoing a brush with Foucauldian "power."[12] How to find a fit form for such formlessness, and how to do without one?

By examining – with a thoroughness and complexity we have not yet measured – the relationship between epistemological or affective com-pensations and a historiography attentive to the muteness of the dead, Wordsworth's *The Excursion* anticipates this dilemma of historical proce-dure. But it does not just replay it before our already-knowing analytic scrutiny. This chapter turns the tables and seeks to read *The Excursion* as an experiment in the historiography of the past. As such the poem is related in certain respects to the contemporary practice of anecdotal historiography, which characterized itself as a kind of news bulletin from the past, full of "incidents . . . of a volatile and evanescent sort, such as soon escape the memory, and are rarely transmitted by tradition," although in other ways crucially different.[13] Odd as it may seem at first, the historical anecdote occupies a similar position in *The Excursion* – which seeks both to emu-late and to rival its practice – as the microscope and the newspaper do in

The Seasons and *The Task*. Wordsworth's poem shows us, I think, that although historiography may start with the willingness to accept the compensation of narrative form, it does not stop at that principle of pleasure. At a certain point, the history of the muted lives buried in the earth exposes the partiality of the compensatory drive. We will see that this point coincides with the places in which the poem itself exceeds its own treatment of elegiac form (anecdote, epitaph) and instead displays disturbances in spatial and temporal perception, as well as conflicts among the senses and their modes of perception; these are problems that I have suggested are better understood in terms of media and mediation.[14]

THE HUSBANDRY OF THE PAST AND THE PASSIONS IN THE *GEORGICS*

First: where did it begin, this conflation of the elegiac (including the melancholic or anti-elegiac) and the historiographical that one hears in Michel de Certeau, as in Jules Michelet, de Certeau's muse, and more widely across postmodern historicisms? Thus Stephen Greenblatt – perhaps with Michelet's "strange dialogues" in mind – also began the 1988 *Shakespearean Negotiations* "with the desire to speak with the dead."[15] A distinctly anti-consolatory strain of elegy has been a main theme in the Romantic new historicism, whose project, as Alan Liu has summarized it, consists primarily in "verifying the 'lostness' of the lost object."[16] My answer, perhaps less whimsical than it first appears, would be that the conflation began in Virgil – or, to put the case less hyperbolically, that it is thoroughly conceived and given generic form in the *Georgics*.

For the farmer at the end of the first *Georgic* is not the only figure in Virgil's poem to turn up the past and its dead from beneath the earth. The carefully executed symmetry of the poem places at the end of the fourth *Georgic* another such figure: Orpheus, whose story (the first of our two classical accounts; Ovid provides the other) is placed as an inset narrative offered by Proteus to the arch-husbandman, Aristaeus. Proteus describes Orpheus's descent to Tartarus to reclaim Eurydice, then the reascent with its famous climax:

And now as [Orpheus] retraced his steps he had escaped every mischance, and the regained Eurydice was nearing the upper world, following behind . . . when a sudden frenzy seized Orpheus, unwary in his love. . . . He stopped, and on the very verge of light, unmindful, alas! and vanquished in purpose, on Eurydice, now his own [*suam iam*], looked back [*respexit*]! In that moment all his toil was spent [*ibi omnis / effusus labor*], the ruthless tyrant's pact was broken, and thrice a crash was heard amid the pools of Avernus. (*Georgics*, 4.485–93)

Orpheus's impatient attempt to make Eurydice "his own" too quickly causes him to lose her, and his exertions and sufferings in the underworld are dissolved. They are "*effusus labor*" (labor wasted, spent, or literally "poured out"):

She cried: "What madness, Orpheus, what dreadful madness [*quis tantus furor*] hath ruined my unhappy self and thee? Lo, again the cruel Fates call me back and sleep veils my swimming eyes. And now farewell! I am swept off, wrapped in uttermost night, and stretching out to thee strengthless hands, thine, alas! no more." She spake, and straightway from his sight, like smoke mingling with thin air [*fumus in auras / commixtus tenuis*], vanished afar, and, vainly as he clutched at the shadows and yearned to say much, never saw him more. . . . What could he do? Whither turn himself, twice robbed of his wife? (4.494–502)

Orpheus is more than twice robbed, as it turns out, for he is doomed to repeat his loss over and over in song ("month in, month out . . . he wept, and, deep in icy caverns, unfolded this his tale") and even after his violent death: as the Hebrus carries his dismembered head down its current, "the bare voice and death-cold tongue, with fleeting breath, called Eurydice – ah, hapless Eurydice! 'Eurydice' the banks re-echoed, all adown the stream" (4.507–27).

We are so used to thinking of the *Georgics* as a celebration of productivity and the "dignity of man's labor" that Orpheus has often been viewed as an aberration in the georgic cycle.[17] It is easy to underestimate the pattern that links his fruitlessly expended labor to a network of image and echo that consistently defines *labor* as fundamentally reparative or restitutive, precarious, and subject to lapse. Virgil loves to pun on *labor* and *lapsus* (from the verb meaning to slide or fall away), so that labor is always called forth to redress a lapse and just as often occasions it. The image of Eurydice swept backwards across the Styx pointedly and poignantly recalls the first *Georgic's* admonition against the cessation of effort in the production of corn (itself an attempt to counteract that initial falling-off from an age in which "Earth yielded all, of herself, more freely" [1.127–28]):

I have seen seeds, though picked long and tested with much pains [*multo . . . labore*], yet degenerate, if human toil, year after year, culled not the largest by hand. Thus by law of fate all things speed towards the worst, and slipping away fall back [*sic omnia fatis / in peius ruere ac retro sublapsa referri*]; even as if one, whose oars can scarce force his skiff against the stream, should by chance slacken his arms, and lo! headlong down the current the channel sweeps it away. (*Georgics*, 1.197–203)

No other set of lines or even critical commentary better captures Virgil's understanding of *labor*, which is not defined in terms of any one kind of pursuit or skill (*ars*), but provides a more general word for the force expended and burden sustained in any pursuit.[18] "*Labor*" in the *Georgics* is precisely this – rowing against an adverse current, the attempt to counteract the entropic forces of physical or human nature. And the stream that the poet narrating the *Georgics* rows against is the flux of time itself, as in this passage from the third *Georgic*, where he catches himself slackening his pace in an erotic account of the amorous passions among the herds:

But time meanwhile is flying, flying beyond recall, while we, charmed with love of our theme, linger around each detail! [*Sed fugit interea, fugit inreparabile tempus, / singula dum capti circumvectamur amore.*] Enough this for the herds; there remains the second part of my task, to tend the fleecy flocks and shaggy goats. (*Georgics*, 3.284–88)

The scene and its characteristic rhythms are the same: slackening, pause, and the disappearance or waste of the object sought. As in the case of Orpheus, the threat to labor is *amor*, as captured in Virgil's enigmatic phrase "charmed with the love of our theme" (*capti . . . amore*), where the theme has been love itself.

The *Georgics*, then, represent Orpheus's mourning *as* labor within a spectrum of labors joining cultivation to exhumation and therefore including the historiographer, whether that historiographer is unwitting, like the plowman of Book 1, or like the Maecenas-commissioned writer of the poem, self-consciously, if uneasily, promoting a program for the reclamation of a land and a history torn by civil disorder.[19] Between Orpheus and the plowman, there are, of course, differences-within-similarity. Orpheus loses Eurydice when he tries to take hold of her too soon (*respexit*, as Harry Berger showed some time ago, can indicate just this kind of impatient and unguarded looking-back[20]) and when he treats her as a loved *object*, a possession that he can make "his own." Virgil's *suam iam* ("now [or suddenly] his own") captures both aspects of this double error with remarkably precise compression. For the marveling farmer at his *versus*, by contrast, the past is too remote. If Eurydice is too meaningful for objectification, the relics that provoke the farmer's *admiratio* are objects without meaning or context. They are therefore not sufficiently his own, at least not "now," or no longer. But in the case of *both* extremes of distance (affective and temporal) and proximity, the result is *effusus labor*, a labor against death that becomes a labor of death.

The *Georgics* thus establish the premise that recuperation of what has been lost to time or entropy as something at once distinct from the laborer against death yet bearing vitally on him depends on the husbandry of passion – and the management of distance – at the site of the production of the past. That insight, and the intersection of elegy and historiography that enables it, is one that we will see Wordsworth, careful reader and translator of Virgil's poem that he was, finding there and developing.

WORDSWORTH: THE OPEN HEART

Let us then return to the Solitary, whom we left recoiling from the disclosures contained in the volumes of the graves beneath his feet. Readers of *The Excursion* have variously diagnosed that poem's despondent character, attributing his insistent malady to causes ranging from a failure of imagination to a specifically political malaise.[21] The poem itself multiplies causes rapidly: the Solitary loses first his daughter, then his son, then his wife, then a succession of ideal surrogates for family: first "Society . . . my glittering bride / And airy hopes my children" (*Exc.*, 3.735–36), and then Lady Liberty ("humbled Liberty grew weak / And mortal sickness on her face appeared" [2.275–76]). The overdetermined repetition of loss after loss (would not any one have been sufficient cause for despondency?), especially where each of these heterogeneous events remarkably resembles the last *descriptively*, is itself of interest. It suggests that whether one takes the personal bereavement as a displacement secondary to an ultimately political deprivation, or vice versa, a feature common to both is the unreadiness or unpreparedness for loss ("with such brief time . . . With even as brief a warning – and how soon," as the Solitary describes the successive deaths of his children [3.639–45]). In both the personal and the political casualties, a hastiness of desire for a surrogate object undermines the Solitary's ability to understand as distinct each person or thing that he has lost, and this inability is in part manifested by his description of each in terms of an earlier event. Wordsworth seems interested in suggesting a character who suffers the perils of his wish for immediacy, the consequences of the bid to recover and repossess too soon which leads to another, then another loss: the fate, in other words, of Orpheus. And as if to confirm that predicament, Wordsworth supplies – perhaps from his own youthful apprenticeship as a translator of the *Georgics*, including the Orpheus sequence (an aspect of his career not often recalled) – fairly pointed allusions to that figure: "And, so consumed, she melted from my arms; / And left me, on this earth, disconsolate," says the Solitary of his wife. Of another vanishing "glittering bride," he cries, reproachfully: " 'Liberty, / I worshiped thee, and find thee but a Shade!' " (3.678–79, 776–77).[22] Like Eurydice, depicted, as we have seen, *fumus in auras commixtus tenuis*, the Solitary's family and his civic ideals recede like a puff of smoke in thin air – in spite of (or is it because of?) his clutching at shadows.

In the Solitary's case, unlike Orpheus's, too many rapid experiences of death have produced languid apathy – for he is still "to private interest dead, and public care" (*Exc.*, 2.209) – and its corollary, the turn away from the dead and their history, articulated in the opening quotation of this chapter. It is against this anti-historical, not merely ahistorical, apathy that the several characters in the poem, chiefly the Wanderer and the Pastor, address their own labors, which take the form of "communion," a conversation meandering excursively in large part but focused by the exchange of stories among the characters. *The Excursion* turns storytelling or "storytilling," as Alison Hickey nicely dubs it, into a form of rural, georgic husbandry, substituting for the plow the instrumental exchange of "tragic facts / Of rural history" (*1799 Prelude*, 1.282–83).[23] It thereby conceives of listening and responsiveness as the ground of cultivation, as in the Poet's claim that the Wanderer offers "a skillful distribution of sweet sounds . . . imbibed / As cool refreshing water, by the care / Of the industrious husbandman, diffused / Through a parched meadow-ground, in time of drought" (*Exc.*, 1.68–72). And it is in the context of this construction of georgic labor that a version of the *Georgics* 1 topos recurs, one that hovers between mining and grave-digging. In often-quoted lines, the Wanderer, whose "eloquent harangue" (4.1276) has overshot its mark and failed to sway the Solitary, requests the Pastor to make the churchyard furrows, the graves, disclose their buried content:[24]

> The mine of real life
> Dig for us; and present us, in the shape
> Of virgin ore, that gold which we, by pains
> Fruitless as those of aery alchemists,
> Seek from the torturing crucible. There lies
> Around us a domain where you have long
> Watched both the outward course and inner heart:
> Give us, for our abstractions, solid facts;
> For our disputes, plain pictures.
>   . . .
> . . . [A]s we stand on holy earth,
> And have the dead around us, take from them
> Your instances; for they are both best known,
> And by frail man most equitably judged.
> Epitomise the life; pronounce, you can,
> Authentic epitaphs on some of these
> Who, from their lowly mansions hither brought,
> Beneath this turf lie mouldering at our feet. (*Exc.*, 5.630–38, 646–53)

I will return in the second half of this chapter to discuss this passage, especially the curious combination of speech and writing implied in the command to "pronounce . . . epitaphs." For now I want to point out the oddity of this proposal as a fulcrum between the poem's synchronic or horizontal communications between the living (the storytellers in the country churchyard) and their diachronic dialogues with the dead, lying vertically below their feet. If the Solitary recoils from the prospect of "every grave . . . a volume, shut yet capable of yielding its contents to eye and ear," why open so many such volumes to his eye and his ear? And if he is horrified by the anticipation of how the lives thus disclosed would reveal how much their ends "deviate" from the promise of their "aspiring outset," why recount – as in fact the Pastor does for more than two books – life after life of abandoned promise and deviation, lives if not of quiet desperation then certainly of disappointed aspiration: refugees from politics and polite urban society, abandoned lovers, serving maids, futile seekers after fortune? Wordsworth's first *Essay upon Epitaphs* worries that, in the absence of a prior confidence in the "sense of immortality," it is "inconceivable, that the sympathies of love towards each other . . . could ever attain any new strength, or even preserve the old, after we had received from the outward senses the impression of death, and were in the habit of having that impression daily renewed and its accompanying feeling brought home to ourselves."[25] Why, then, try to cultivate both sympathy and the absent intimations of immortality in the Solitary by bringing such impressions home and home again to his senses? Strange cure for the horror of death and disappointment, for the weight of dead generations on the brain of the living.

Esther Schor addresses some of these questions by treating the poem as an instance of "the social diffusion of grief through sympathy, . . . a force that constitutes communities and makes it possible to conceptualize history." Her project is to move away from a "psychological account [of] mourning as a discourse between the living and the dead" toward a "cultural approach," which reconceives mourning as a largely consolatory "discourse among the living," and she thereby extends into the Enlightenment the work of such scholars as G. W. Pigman on Renaissance attitudes toward grief, while implicitly correcting the tendency in studies of cultural memory to apply, perhaps too freely, vocabularies developed for the analysis of individual psyches to collectivities.[26] Yet in setting her cultural approach resolutely against psychological and especially psychoanalytical considerations (Freud is exorcized after the first page), Schor may rule out too much.[27] The title of her important study is *Bearing the Dead*, but there is also the possibility that the dead may not be bearable (endurable), that they may infiltrate or vex the discourse among the living. When and if they do, then we need to understand how such unendurability shapes and limits historiographical practice. And, for that matter, the living might not be so bearable either: as

Wordsworth's *Essay* suggests, the impressions of death may themselves vitiate the capacity for sympathy, which *Bearing the Dead*, notwithstanding its rich account of sentimental culture in Hume, Smith, Burke, and others, tends to regard as largely unproblematic and ethical.

The psychological and the cultural determinants of mourning as of historiographical practices, in other words, are neither independent nor separable. Accordingly, this section examines the affective constraints that inflect and trouble the intercourse among the living and therefore their conceptualization of, or interest in, the dead. Fredric Jameson's often-cited slogan – "*Always* historicize!" – is intriguingly ahistorical, setting aside, as it does, the possibility that certain conditions of affect or apathy may threaten the historicizing principle itself. However, I do not assume, or want to intimate here, that simple restoration of the capacity for sympathy – among the living, for the dead – insures the successful negotiation of the historiographical dilemma outlined at the outset of this chapter. For surely by the end of the poem, when the Solitary walks off, singular and singularly unconvinced by what Schor calls the "calm commerce of condolence," the "cure" has fallen short.[28] It falls short as cure, that is – but not as historiography, whose most interesting aspect, I will then argue, emerges when it exceeds the therapeutic drive.

As a number of critics have already pointed out, well before *The Excursion* Wordsworth had been experimenting with the uses of georgic; in particular the Virgilian model provided him with a flexible language for exploring and justifying closely interwined concerns about professional ethics and personal psychology. Uneasily invoking but reversing Virgil's own modesty topos – the ironic self-rebuke at the end of the *Georgics* that he, Virgil, has only been practicing the arts of "ignoble ease" (*Vergilium me . . . studiis florentem ignobilis oti* [*Georgics*, 4.564]) – Wordsworth claims that *he* engages in the art of "honorable toil" and is preparing for "some work / Of glory": "the history of a poet's mind / Is labour not unworthy of regard"; so, too, "the work shall justify itself," and so on (*1805 Prelude*, 1.653, 1.86–87, 13.408–10). The anxiety of indolence haunts *The Prelude* so strongly that readers have found in it "the oldest of bourgeois scruples" (Geoffrey Hartman) and "the most extraordinary résumé in English literary history," a "vita-like detailing that turns maturation into a preoccupation with occupation."[29] Presumably in order to quiet the unease about ignoble ease, *The Prelude* adapts the language of georgic to advocate what John Stuart Mill, speaking of Wordsworth, would call "the very culture of the feelings." "I was a chosen son," writes Wordsworth recalling his vocational qualms at Cambridge,

"For hither I had come with holy powers / And faculties, whether to work or to feel" (*1805*, 3.82–84), and it is crucial to his self-fashioning as a professional poet that "whether to work or to feel" be maintained as an apposition rather than an opposition. This poet's "work" *is* "to feel," according to that narrative, and the Two-Part *Prelude* (later the first two books of *1805* and *1850*) outlines the qualifications and training for that task. It is structured, as Bruce Graver has shown, very much like a calendar poem after Virgil and Hesiod, except that where the classical model assigned agricultural labors to each season – each work, each crop, has its appointed day – Wordsworth associates them with a kind of play: boating in summer, skating in winter, trapping woodcocks in autumn, stealing birds' eggs in spring.[30] (Wordsworth's notion of exercise, which he uses in the original Latin sense of *exercere*, to train or discipline, links the boy's experience in "every change / Of exercise and sport" with the husbandman's, who "exercises his fields" [cf. *Georgics*, 1.99].) As a result of the "fair seed-time" of his soul – according to this georgic vocational narrative – *puer ludens* will become *homo faber*, a poet who is assigned the specific task of "widening the sphere of sensibility," as the "Essay, Supplementary" to the *Poems* of 1815 would put it.[31]

If left at that, one would just be reiterating the Mill–Arnoldian narrative about Wordsworth, which all but invites (and has invited) the urge to turn against Wordsworth the notorious lines describing the Wanderer in "The Ruined Cottage" and later *The Excursion* – "he could *afford* to suffer / With those whom he saw suffer" (*Exc.*, 1.370) – along with a nod toward the Calvert legacy and other economic advantages which made such a professional narrative possible.[32] To leave it at that, moreover, would not address the problem of why feeling and sensibility might be conceived to require work – effort, Virgil's *labor*, that struggle against an adverse stream, a matter of physics which in turn evokes the poet's self-credentialing professional narrative. And one would be faced with the further problem of *The Excursion*, underway at the same time as *The Prelude* and participating in the textual import–export trade that sometimes existed between the two poems: for in *The Excursion* both the training and the task of "widening the sphere of sensibility" are reassigned to a retired peddler, who is at least as eager to restrict the display of sensibility as to widen it ("Enough to sorrow you have given . . ." is a directive repeated in some form throughout the poem) and who sometimes seems to edge toward insensibility ("Supine the Wanderer lay, / His eyes as if in drowsiness half shut" [1.932, 438–39]).

The description of the "seed-time" of the peddler's soul, laboriously revised by Wordsworth and often cited in critical discussions, is a useful place to begin to address the question of why feeling might require tending to begin with, particularly because of its combination of georgic topoi with the language of sensibility literature. "In the woods," Wordsworth wrote in the final version of this sequence:

> Spontaneously had his affections thriven
> Amid the bounties of the year, the peace
> And liberty of nature; there he kept
> In solitude and solitary thought
> His mind in a just equipoise of love.
> Serene it was, unclouded by the cares
> Of ordinary life; unvexed, unwarped
> By partial bondage. In his steady course,
> No piteous revolutions had he felt,
> No wild varieties of joy and grief.
> Unoccupied by sorrow of its own,
> His heart lay open; and, by nature tuned
> And constant disposition of his thoughts
> To sympathy with man, he was alive
> To all that was enjoyed where'er he went,
> And all that was endured; for, in himself
> Happy, and quiet in his cheerfulness,
> He had no painful pressure from within
> That made him turn aside from wretchedness
> With coward fears. He could *afford* to suffer
> With those whom he saw suffer. (*Exc.*, 1.347–71)

The Wanderer is presented as the self-sufficing *fortunatus* or "happy man" of Virgilian and Horatian descent; his affections have grown with an apparent natural spontaneity tempered by the careful discipline of a frugal mind ("he kept his mind"; "by constant disposition of his thoughts").[33] The pointed revision of Shakespeare alludes, as many have pointed out, to Miranda's anti-Lucretian cry in *The Tempest* ("O I have suffered / With those that I saw suffer"[34]), but where Miranda suffers from a "piteous heart," the Wanderer undergoes "no piteous revolutions." Thomas Gray, in "The Progress of Poesy," had given Shakespeare the golden keys to the storehouse of the passions so that he might "ope the source of sympathetic tears," but the Wanderer, as befits his training as peddler *cum* Stoic sage, keeps up a careful watch against the depletion of its reserves.

The image of the source of sympathetic tears remains, however altered, in the figure of the peddler's open heart: "Unoccupied by any sorrow of its own, / His heart lay open ... / To sympathy with man." Wordsworth's development of the metaphor of a psychic economy – derived from a number of eighteenth-century men of feeling and notably from Adam Smith – is quite precise. As Christopher Herbert, Marshall Brown, and others have noted, Smith's model in *The Wealth of Nations* for a system that attempts to maintain its own equilibrium by dividing its resources was, for Smith, originally a psychological one; one hears it, for example, in *The Theory of Moral Sentiments'* praise for the quasi-occult figure of "Nature," who "when she loaded us *with our own sorrows*, thought *that they were enough* and therefore did not command us to take any further *share* in those of others, than what was necessary to prompt us to relieve them."[35] As his motto ("Enough to sorrow have you given" [*Exc.*, 1.932]) indicates, *The Excursion's* retired peddler belongs to just such a restricted economy of sentiments, founded on the Smithian premise that the resources of sympathy are not inexhaustible (passion can be easily "spent," a *labor effusus*), and Wordsworth suggests that his character makes his energies available to the outer world because – and insofar as – they are not too divided by defending calm of mind from within. Hence the heart, in this passage's physiological and ergonomic conception of it, can be vulnerable only to so many pressures at once, and this happy husbandman "had no painful pressure from within / Which made him turn aside from wretchedness / With coward fears." For the poet ever inclined to weigh all "in the balance of feeling," as Wordsworth's note on "The Thorn" put it, sympathetic responsiveness depends on some minimal surplus of pleasure over pain.

We have, of course, a later-day version of this calculus of pleasure and pain, which can prove productive as an intertext precisely because it descends from eighteenth-century moral philosophy and inherits some of the problems that mark *The Excursion* as well. Compare with the idealized equilibrium of the Wanderer's heart the psychic apparatus conceived in Freud's *Beyond the Pleasure Principle*. There, with an odd blend of scientific literal-mindedness and lyricism, Freud imagined the human creature as a vulnerable "little fragment of living substance . . . suspended in the middle of an external world charged with the most powerful energies" and, to make matters worse, challenged by turbulence from within. Against the external world it develops a "protective shield," but toward the inner excitations there can be no such shield. The devious human creature of this early twentieth-century Leibnizian *Monadology*, however, has a particular way of dealing with these internal disturbances: by projection, it treats them as though they were acting from the outside, "so that it may be possible to bring the shield against stimuli into operation as a means of defense against them." One frontier may be treated as though it were the other, but a defense against both at once is not possible in a system whose resources are not inexhaustible.[36] In the case of *The Excursion*, projection works similarly but in the opposite direction: the Wanderer treats the disturbances of the external world, those "moving spectacles" caused by vagrancy, crop failure, and war, as if they were just coming from inside – as "restless thoughts" (*Exc.*, 1.604). For against such "piteous revolutions" from within the Wanderer, Wordsworth's most sustained attempt to imagine a being "from all internal injury exempt" (*1805 Prelude*, 5.67), is well shielded.

However, such compromises are neither easily achieved nor guaranteed in Wordsworth's poetry (or anywhere else, for that matter). The equilibrium established in the phrase, "Unoccupied by any sorrow of its own, / His heart lay open . . . / To sympathy with man," is at best precarious. If the heart is truly open to sympathy – if the barriers and partitions of the self are permeable – can it remain unoccupied for any extended period of time? Can one be at once sensitive to being touched and yet essentially untouched? We know that Keats, one of the more appreciative contemporary readers of *The Excursion*, thought not:

When I am in a room with People if I am ever free from speculating on creations of my own brain, then not myself goes home to myself: but the identity of every one in the room begins [so] to press upon me that, I am in a very little time an[ni]hilated – not only among Men; it would be the same in a Nursery of children.[37]

Momentary freedom from internal preoccupation leads to a penetration from without which acts with the force of an injury, annihilating the poet as here, or as in *The Fall of Hyperion*, lying "ponderous upon [the] senses."[38] In the poems that preceded *The Excursion*, Wordsworth treated the paradox of the open heart delicately, without resolving it absolutely. The Boy of Winander (initially identified as "I" in early draft manuscripts) has had "carried far into his heart the voice / Of mountain torrents," but we are next told that he dies. The mute adult poet stands "a full half-hour together" looking at his grave, but we do not know how that gap between them is to be crossed, and how one develops from the Boy of Winander to a Poet of Grasmere (*1805 Prelude*, 5.404–22).[39] Wordsworth simply asserts a degree of continuity by textual contiguity: the poet somehow survived. Elsewhere, the open heart is more nearly the dead heart. In the satiric "A Poet's Epitaph," the poet is at once already *in* the grave and – in his younger incarnation, who is so very "open" that all experience, in a strange, disturbing phrase, "broods and sleeps on his own heart" – being lured by force of sympathy *to* the grave: "Come . . . stretch thy body at full length; / Or build thy house upon this grave."[40]

In the full nine-book expanse of *The Excursion*, Wordsworth was not able to sustain the tension between the two poles (literally, the two ends) of the phrase "Unoccupied by any sorrow of his own, / His heart lay open." As the character of the Wanderer developed both during the years of composition and over the course of the poem, openness succumbed to the imperative of maintaining an unoccupied existence. Even in the passage as it was drafted over and over again, as "The Ruined Cottage" became "The Pedlar" and then Book 1 of *The Excursion*, Wordsworth struggles over the nature of his character's immunity: manuscript variants show that he wrote, "He had no painful pressure from *without* / Which made him turn aside from wretchedness," and then crossed it out, restoring "within" – hardly an inconsequential substitution.[41] In the later books of *The Excursion* it is as if Wordsworth once more substituted "without," for the Wanderer's "sympathy with man" is very nearly replaced by the achievement of a Stoic *apatheia*, an existence above and free from passion.[42] To sit, with the Wanderer, "disencumbered from the press / Of near obstructions," freed from the notes "by which the finer passages of sense / Are occupied," and thus able to "hear the mighty stream of tendency," ultimately involves a "severing" from the human and natural world (see *Exc.*, 9.69–92). For such loss, the Wanderer would believe, the Lucretian heights provide abundant recompense, but the poem as a whole seems less sure. The Wanderer may be made altogether too still by the power of harmony; as the Pastor's wife says of his meditations, "Combinations so serene and bright / Cannot be lasting in a world like ours" (*Exc.*, 9.468–69). Perhaps the more potent challenge to the validity of the Wanderer's "equipoise" comes from his ironic resemblance to the Solitary, to whom Wordsworth assigns the lengthy defense of Stoic ethics in Book 3 (359–410). In the Solitary, who is called the "pensive Sceptic of this lowly vale" (8.1), we see the faintness of the line between "uncomplaining apathy" (2.206) and a wisely passive *apatheia* like the Wanderer's. Notwithstanding their apparent opposition, the Stoic and the Skeptic are inseparably correlative.[43]

The willed control of *apatheia*, the apathetic loss of emotion, and the premature death of those liminal Wordsworthian figures whose hearts are too unshielded are, then, all radical but perilous solutions to the dilemma of the open, or feeling, heart in a world where sympathetic resources can be exhausted. Freud's allegory of the open heart – sense-consciousness as a vulnerable living vesicle defending itself with one shield against influxes arriving from two directions – is proposed in the context of *Beyond the*

Pleasure Principle's discussion of trauma, which that text defines as a break-down or failure of mediation: "We describe as 'traumatic' any excitations from the outside which are powerful enough to break through the protective shield."[44] To recognize Wordsworth's understanding of the "open heart" susceptible to pressures from "within" and "without" as an earlier version of this narrative is not to equate, facilely, these two instances in which the outside can go in. Unlike trauma, sympathy is volitional and not pathological. Nonetheless, for Wordsworth, it can, at a certain extreme, become wounding, an influx like Keats's sense of annihilation. The paradox of sympathetic openness, in other words, is that as this state verges upon traumatic exposure, sympathy becomes impossible, and sensibility turns into insensibility. The heart seals itself off, as in the case of the Solitary's disappointed romantic and philanthropic zeal, "to private interest dead and public care" (*Exc.*, 2.209).

Such indifference, *The Excursion* suggests, *may include the care for history, the interest in historical narrative.* The poem tries to address it with a peculiar, meandering form of talk, markedly different, as we will see, from Cowper's "chit chat" or from Fielding's ideal of an orderly "sifting" of ideas, and not ultimately consoling. Why the turn to telling? Here is where the complexity of the Freudian intertext begins to be helpful and not merely adventitious. The image of a "breach" in the protective skin of the psyche, along with the etymological burden of Freud's term (*trauma* as the Greek for wound), might suggest that the disturbance Freud has in mind is primarily a rupture of space and spatial mediation, an apparent recursion to his early, simpler emphasis on shock and mechanical violence in the "Project for a Scientific Psychology." Yet it quickly becomes apparent in *Beyond the Pleasure Principle* that Freud's spatial model has become intertwined with, even ancillary to, another, more sophisticated model, which holds that trauma is caused by a "lack of preparedness for anxiety" – a collapse, that is, not of physical space but of time. For unlike a literal bodily membrane, as Cathy Caruth puts it, "the barrier of consciousness is a barrier of sensation and knowledge that protects the organism by placing stimulation within the ordered experience of time."[45] Freudian trauma, then, is a break in the mind's experience of time and not a simple matter of quantity, not just the amount of "painful pressure" from without. Hence the limitations of deliberating whether an event is or is not "powerful" enough to be traumatic: for Freud, it is not only the nature and severity of the event which decides the trauma but also the "lack of preparedness" for it.

Why, then, bring *Beyond the Pleasure Principle* to bear on the problems of the open heart and the recoil from the volume of the grave in

Wordsworth's *Excursion*? Again I would emphasize that I do not seek to hold the Freudian text as a kind of interpretive "truth" or grid by which to interpret the poem. Freud's account of consciousness as a "little fragment of substance . . . suspended in the middle of an external world charged with the most powerful energies" and his account of trauma as a breach in a protective shield of spatial and temporal experience are, in his own cheerful phrase, "far-fetched speculation," and I take his "protective shield" (*Reizschutz*) not as science but as (science-)fiction. The point is that it is a speculation *we have seen*, when writers take up the georgic and encounter the limits of empiricism.[46] We have met the spatial dimension in Thomson's construction of the subject as "microscopic eye" at the moment in *The Seasons* that "worlds and worlds enclosed burst on the senses," as well as in the fine ambiguity of that phrase itself, which referred at once to the eye looking through the microscope and the tiny eye seen by it. We have encountered both the spatial and temporal models in combination when studying the relationship between the rapid "dissociating articles" of news and consciousness's "vacuity of thought" in *The Task*; there I argued that such vacancies, *because* they elude the temporal succession of Lockean ideas, are paradoxically replete with the unparsed figures of contemporaneity. They are loopholes (openings) in the retreat, which let "the stranger" in. Freud, in other words, is writing a version of georgic, a point that becomes more transparent when he declares that psychoanalysis had been intended as "a work of culture – not unlike the draining of the Zuider Zee,"[47] or in the interest of *Civilization and Its Discontents* in excavating an earlier Rome.

Or, to put it slightly differently: if *The Seasons, The Task,* and *The Excursion* return to ruptures, ripples, or static within media of perception and communication, if they come back to instances in which the outside goes inside without mediation such that they often image a permeable subject of sensory experience, it is because the georgic as a mode both courts the pleasures of mediated information and, at the same time, draws ambivalently beyond them, resisting the consoling patterns of idea, aesthetic delight, even historical progress. "The principle of pleasure" is Addison's phrase before it is Freud's – and it is a principle posited *in* his "Essay on the *Georgics*," then elaborated more fully under the tributary influence of Locke in the *Spectator* papers on the "Pleasures of the Imagination." Where Addison found pleasure and diversion in the Virgilian "By-ways" – pleasure, that is, in the ideational mastery made possible by spatio-temporal mediation – I have tried to suggest a more complicated story for Thomson and Cowper, arguing that their poetry, self-conscious as it is about the transmission of worldly data, is paradoxically textual shield *and* aperture (wound, loophole, sensible path). Their georgics, attempting to assert the principle of pleasure – whether gleaned in the timely utterances of conversation or the equanimous, panoramic survey, also gesture beyond it.

Thus considered as an heir to the problems posed by the georgic mode in its conflicted relationship to empiricism, Freud's version of georgic suggests a way of interpreting *The Excursion*'s tactics of grave-digging as a paradoxical means of counteracting the Solitary's aversion to unearthing the dead, while also pointing to certain problems in the Wanderer's proposal for historiographical practice. The Freudian intertext suggests that the middle books constitute a retrospective bid to place death and disappointment *in time* so that they can be confronted without "recoil." The "storytillings" are attempts to overcome the resistance to the volume of the grave – both the aversion to the stories the dead might disclose and the antipathy to putting their suffering into a "volume" (that is, narrative) at all. Such recoil threatens, if not history itself, whose forward march exceeds individual desire and action, then certainly its retention and transmission over time. The poem addresses the Solitary's Orpheus-like "lack of preparedness" for loss not by skirting the facts of death and defaulted promise but by returning to them, and again to them. It attempts, as it were, to dose out death homeopathically, or "thanatotically,"[48] and thereby to extend what the poem's narrator calls – in a phrase I take to be absolutely crucial to the poem – "the prolongation of some still response" (*Exc.*, 7.895), whose prior absence or disabling has contributed to that character's death-seeking aversion to historical retrospect or future promise.

At the same time, all versions of georgic that we have met so far should warn us that the untroubled assertion of the "principle of pleasure," particularly the compensatory pleasures of narration, threaten to deny the "hurt" of history unless they also incorporate the unpleasure that calls them forth. The question then becomes: what kind of communication of the past is capable of keeping the heart "open" enough for non-reductive responsiveness to historical pain, without becoming so invasive, so quickly touching, that the receptive heart becomes the wounded heart, or just closes down, and turns away, "to private interest dead and public care"? The stakes of such a question are high; we live with them still. In this particular case, an answer requires a fuller inquiry into *The Excursion*'s own husbandry of distance and sense at the site of the production of the past.

While the fate of the word "medium" as a term in nineteenth-century spiritualism for one who animates the dead is several decades off, one can detect
Wordsworth tilting it in that direction during his discussion of epitaphic
practice. The first *Essay upon Epitaphs* adapts the "in-between" or *to metaxu*
of Aristotelian and seventeenth-century natural science for its account of
graveyard inscriptions: the character of the dead should be presented "as a
tree through a tender haze or luminous mist," and the departed "object being looked at through this medium, parts and proportions are brought into
distinct view which before had only been imperfectly or unconsciously
seen."[49] Because the Wanderer requests epitaphs, or "epitomized" lives,
from the Pastor, and particularly because the first *Essay* originally appeared
as an extended note to Book 5, many excellent readings of *The Excursion*
have treated the *Essays* and the poem as mutual exegeses of each other.[50]
Yet this intertextual calibration does not entirely work. As the Wanderer's
actual request ("*pronounce . . . /* Authentic epitaphs") might remind us, and
as James Chandler and Esther Schor have noted, Wordsworth's framing of
the Pastor's forays into the "mine of real life" attempts to deliver within
writing the content and effect of oral narrative, while the *Essays* for the
most part maintain the dependence of epitaphic practice on writing.[51] An
oral epitaph – an oral epitaph published in the "Books" of *The Excursion*,
no less – offers a considerable contradiction in terms, to say nothing of
a "distressed genre" (Susan Stewart's justly celebrated phrase for the phenomenon of the eighteenth-century "new antique").[52] The problem of the
"open heart" posed at the end of the last section – the constraints that a
closed economy of emotion places on channels of historical transmission –
now comes together with the problem of "mediums" or media, both as
they are more narrowly construed today as a difference between orality
and literacy, and as they raise larger questions about spatial and temporal
perception.

   As it happens, the poem offers us another epithet for the Pastor's tales,
somewhat different from the "authentic epitaph." Just at the point that the
Pastor finishes the history of the Sympson family in Book 7 (38–310), we
come upon one of many signal instances in the poem of "the prolongation
of some still response." The Reverend Sympson's life offers, as Kenneth
Johnston has observed, a version of Wordsworth's dream biography, repeated in many of the characters set forth by *The Excursion*: a man "by
books unsteadied," this priest gives up a dubious, glittering public career

and resigns himself to the "doubtful choice" of a bare secluded Cure; here he is gradually converted to virtue and "punctual labor," supported by "his gentle Mate / And three fair children."[53] The oldest but the last to die of his family, he lingers, according the Pastor:

> '. . . Yet a little while,
> And this Survivor, with his cheerful throng
> Of open projects, and his inward hoard
> Of unsunned griefs, too many and too keen,
> Was overcome by unexpected sleep,
> In one blest moment. Like a shadow thrown
> Softly and lightly from a passing cloud,
> Death fell on him, while reclined he lay
> For noontide solace on the summer grass,
> The warm lap of his mother earth: and so,
> Their lenient term of separation past,
> That family (whose graves you there behold)
> By yet a higher privilege once more
> Were gathered to each other.'
>   Calm of mind
> And silence waited on these closing words;
> Until the Wanderer (whether moved by fear
> Lest in those passages of life were some
> That might have touched the sick heart of his Friend
> Too nearly, or intent to reinforce
> His own firm spirit in degree deprest
> By tender sorrow for our mortal state)
> Thus silence broke. . . .   (*Exc.*, 7. 278–99)

There will be many elements of this passage that require attention, but let us start with those "passages of life." It is such an overdetermined phrase, in part because its other occurrence in Wordsworth's poetry, as a description of the "spots of time" in *The Prelude*, has been such a touchstone for his modern readers. "There are in our existence spots of time," Wordsworth famously writes in *The Prelude*, which "retain / A renovating virtue," and "this efficacious spirit chiefly lurks / Among those passages of life in which / We have the deepest feeling that the mind / Is lord and master, and that outward sense / Is but the obedient servant of her will" (*1805*, 11.257–59, 269–72; cf. *1850*, 12.208–10, 219–23).[54] Even in the autobiographical poem, as Thomas Weiskel noted some time ago, the phrase is complex: "'Passages' refers presumably to events that involved a passing from one state to another (as in a *rite* of passage) and also to the passing back and through of retrospection. . . . But a passage is also a text; one reads these texts or signifiers by passing into and through them."[55] In *The Excursion*, these possibilities receive a different inflection; the "passage of life" refers to the transmission of "Lives" (albeit of infamous rather than famous men) between characters – orally within the text, as well as between the published poem and its readers – and it nicely summarizes the company's desire to animate the languid Solitary, to pass or transfuse some life into him, paradoxically from the dead.

Contemporary readers of *The Excursion* would not themselves have heard the reference to *The Prelude* and the poet's autobiography, but I think it might have prompted them to place the work in a different context. "A minute passage of private life" was how Samuel Johnson's *Dictionary of the English Language* characterized the biographical or historical anecdote – that popular, chatty eighteenth-century subgenre, whose name (*an-ekdota*, or something unpublished) derived from Procopius's unpublished manuscript account of the private lives of the court of Justinian.[56] (It has since, needless to say, become celebrated or notorious as the signature of the new historicism.[57]) Isaac D'Israeli, whose *Dissertation on Anecdotes* offered a major early theorization of the literary form in 1793, cites the *Dictionary's* authority – "Johnson has imperfectly defined the word, by saying, that, 'It is now used after the French for a *biographical incident*; a minute passage of private life'" – and D'Israeli then quarrels with the "private":

This confines its signification merely to *biography*; but anecdotes are susceptible of a more enlarged application. This word is more justly defined in the *Cyclopædia*, "a term which (now) denotes a relation of detached and interesting particulars." We give *anecdotes* of the art as well as the Artist; of the war as well as the General; of the nation as well as of the Monarch.[58]

The Excursion – with its "passages of life," its "mine of real life" – is, I venture, an "experiment" no less than *Lyrical Ballads*, but an exercise in historiography that is both like and – critically – unlike the anecdotal histories flourishing during the later eighteenth and early nineteenth centuries in ways we have yet to analyze. I will focus on D'Israeli, but other comparable projects would include such massive endeavors as the nine volume collection of *Anecdotes, Biographical and Literary*, compiled by John Nichols from 1782 on; the final volume in this series, published in the same year as *The Excursion* of 1815, promoted itself in these (I hope resonant) terms: "it is not a regular History – it is not a Romantic Tale – nor a Work of Fancy . . . it is a Mine of literary materials, whence future Biographers and Historians will readily and unsparingly collect what may suit their several purposes."[59]

D'Israeli's rejection of "vague theory" for "certain experiment" and his definition of "experience" as the "slow accession of multiplied facts" identify his *Dissertation* as an attempt to adapt the methods of Baconian induction and experimental philosophy – that vexed sensible and epistemological pathway from observed, singular instances and minute particulars to general, systematic knowledge – for the purposes of historiography.[60] The anecdote here emerges as the historian's version of scientific "experiment," by which he or she can, by slow accretion ("accession"), come to conclusions about human nature and history; it thereby offers to conjectural or national history a form, and a display, of reality testing. In the case of the reader of anecdotes, for whom that movement from minute circumstance to generalized knowledge is repeated in the act of reading, the experiment is very much a controlled one. If Wordsworth's Wanderer is imagined, by the Poet, as an "industrious husbandman" creating a "skilful distribution of sweet sounds" like "cool refreshing water . . . diffused / Through a parched meadow ground," D'Israeli's historian also engages in a kind of georgic discipline:

[Anecdotes] produce . . . those leading thoughts which throw the mind into an agreeable train of thinking. A skilful writer of anecdotes, gratifies by suffering us to make something that looks like a discovery of our own; he gives a certain activity to the mind, and the reflections appear to arise from ourselves. He throws unperceivably seeds, and we see those flowers start up which we believe to be of our own creation.[61]

D'Israeli's "agreeable train of thinking" here, and his thorough dependence on a Lockean aesthetics of association throughout the *Dissertation*, should sound familiar, and not only from Bacon or Locke. It is a precise adaptation of Addison's account of the "By-ways" of reading the *Georgics*, later developed into the influential statement of the "secondary pleasures" of the imagination in *Spectator* 417. To recall Addison's account of the virtues of Virgilian precept from my discussion in chapter 1: "For here the Mind, which is always delighted with its own Discoveries, only takes the hint from the Poetry, and seems to work out the rest by the strength of her own Faculties." The anecdote emerges as the historiographer's version of the georgic precept, as interpreted by Addison's "Essay" thus: "a Truth [suggested] indirectly, and without giving us a full and open view of it: To let us see just so much as will naturally lead the Imagination into all the parts that lie conceal'd."[62] D'Israeli, in other words, seeks to infuse historiography with the "principle of pleasure" located in the illusion of mastery and creativity, an illusion he, like Addison before him, finds in our capacity to discover, or think we are discovering, in every "detached particular" some sort of general truth: in the words of the *Dissertation*, "[W]hen anecdotes are . . . animated by judicious reflections, they recall others of a kindred nature; one suggests another; and the whole series . . . impresses on the mind some interesting conclusion in the affairs of human life."[63] We return again to the question that I have suggested resides at the core of georgic: the regulation of the "sensible paths" of precept and information, now "passages of life."

D'Israeli's account of this apparent transfer of power to the listener or reader helps us understand why the anecdote might offer itself to Wordsworth as the fit historiographical form for addressing the open heart, especially the heart in which vulnerability has turned into its other face, indifference. The anecdotal movement from detached, enumerated particulars to "interesting conclusion," or to what the Wanderer, in his initial request to the Solitary, calls "epitome" ("Epitomize the life . . ."), replicates and effects the gradual and compensatory rhythm of the work of mourning, the "labor against death," which seeks to master loss by appropriating to the present the privilege and the pleasure of recapitulating the past as a form of knowledge – to "find in loss a gain to match," as Tennyson put it. The "little strokes" and "little circumstances" of the historical anecdote pique curiosity, stir the apathetic mind into associative activity, but at the same time prevent bottomless brooding by inviting some interpretive distance, or what *The Excursion* calls, with ultimate precision in the Sympson lines quoted above, "closing words" – words that are not only concluding but effect a temporary epistemological and affective closure.[64] Joel Fineman's account of the historiographical operation of the anecdote, so close to D'Israeli's, offers a fine account of the oscillation of a poem he never intended to describe:

[T]he opening of history that is effected by the anecdote . . . is something that is characteristically and ahistorically plugged up by a teleological narration that, though larger than the anecdote itself, is still constitutively inspired by the seductive opening of anecdotal form – thereby once again opening up the possibility, but, again, *only* the possibility, that this new narration, now complete within itself, and thereby rendered formally small – capable, therefore, of being anecdotalized – will itself be opened up by a further anecdotal operation, thereby calling forth some yet larger circumcising circumscription, and so, so on and so forth.[65]

Thus the Wanderer, who fears that the Pastor's "closing words" may not be sufficiently healing, offers some more – circumscribing and transcendently teleological – conclusions of his own: "Behold a thoughtless Man / From vice and premature decay preserved / By useful habits . . . ," etc. Yet no

closing words are ever permitted to rest as verdicts passed, since the poem
moves metonymically on, to another particularized opening, "Here lies one
who. . . ." And so, so on, and so forth, as Fineman says – so that even the
final lines of the poem have the cadences and deferred syntactical structure
(a series of prepositional phrases, deferred main verb) of an invocation:

> To enfeebled Power,
> From this communion with uninjured Minds,
> What renovation had been brought; and what
> Degree of healing to a wounded spirit,
> Dejected, and habitually disposed
> To seek, in degradation of the Kind,
> Excuse and solace for her own defects;
> How far those erring notions were reformed;
> And whether aught, of tendency as good
> And pure, from further intercourse ensued;
> This – if delightful hopes, as heretofore,
> Inspire the serious song, and gentle Hearts
> Cherish, and lofty Minds approve the past –
> My future labours may not leave untold. (*Exc.*, 9.783–96)

If *The Excursion*'s "passages of life" have a "fructifying" or "renovating
virtue" like *The Prelude*'s spots of time, it is not because of the epistemological content that they yield (e.g., the knowledge that "the mind is lord and
master") so much as because, as self-renewing artifacts – indeed, seeds –
they convert the past into a series of present passings and future repassings;
they attempt to perform mastery. Diffused and defused, the absoluteness
of death is offset by the activity of the passerby in the present, who can pass
through in cycles of investment and detachment. Hence the attempt to pass
some life into the Solitary from the dead is not the oddity it first seemed:
the animation or "certain activity" is not communicated by the example
or "lesson" provided by the dead themselves, but from the possibility of
traversing in the slow time of telling, once more and yet once more, their
place of rest.[66]

But Wordsworth is not D'Israeli. He is both an expert deployer of the
anecdote and a critic of aspects of its D'Israelian – and essentially polite –
incarnation. Like many a Romantically tempered historian after him,
D'Israeli wants to speak familiarly with the dead, to "realise the society of
those who are no more." Anecdotes are, for him, experiments in resurrecting,
not merely reconstructing, the past, and if done badly "anecdotes are but
squalid skeletons, unless they are full of the blood and flesh of reflection."[67]
The desire for intimacy edges toward voyeurism at times, for D'Israeli does

not want merely "to join the crowd to see [great men] pass." Like William
Godwin, whose "Of History and Romance" (1797) expressed the desire
to follow the public figure "into his closet," D'Israeli seeks the vantage of
"concealed spies."[68] Wordsworth's innovation, I think, resides less in his
turn from great men to mute inglorious Miltons – he does do that, but
George Crabbe and Gilbert White have already been there and done it
too – than in his refusal to gratify the desire for the immediacy of the
past, or intimacy with the dead. Indeed, his poem persistently frustrates
both: if D'Israeli wants us to peer into the closet of the dead, *The Excursion* just as resolutely keeps us out of it. Where D'Israeli's anecdotes are
like little novels in their effort to illuminate the "minute springs and little
wheels" of human character, to "become more real cotemporaries with the
great men of another age, than were even their cotemporaries themselves,"
Wordsworth's "passages of life" adamantly forego psychological shading.[69]
Such technique would amount to what "A Poet's Epitaph" derogatorily
calls "botanizing upon" the grave. There is therefore something withheld
in almost every story. The Prodigal of Book 6, for example, is described in
terms of the "sets of manners" he puts on, his dress, his acquired arts, and
"If ye enquire / How such consummate elegance was bred / Amid these
wilds, this answer may suffice; / T'was Nature's will" (6.298–301). We hear
of his cycles of prodigality and return ("Thrice he rose, / Thrice sank as
willingly" [334–35]) without knowing why he leaves or why he returns; his
doings are all "report" until his story comes to an abrupt, curious close:

> —Such the too frequent tenour of his boast
> In ears that relished the report; – but all
> Was from his Parents happily concealed;
> Who saw enough for blame and pitying love.
> They also were permitted to receive
> His last, repentant breath; and closed his eyes,
> No more to open on that irksome world.... (359–65)

As in the story of Luke in "Michael," where something like this technique
occurs (Luke, at least, had a name), there is an ascetic refusal not only to
explore the minute springs and little wheels of character but also to answer
such salient questions as "how did he die?" or "why did he return?" These
questions, like the closing words, are left for the listeners to propose, although not finally to answer: "'Tis strange,' observed the Solitary, '. . . That
in a land where charity provides / For all that can no longer feed themselves, /
A man like this should choose to bring his shame / To the parental door'"
(376–91).

The result is curious: although the Pastor argues that the dead are worthiest of the mind's regard because, in them, "[m]ortality's last exercise and proof / Is undergone; the transit made that shows / The very Soul, revealed as she departs" (*Exc.*, 5.665–67), in fact his accounts are distinctive for the way they hide or glide past that transit without revealing or "baring" the soul. As Alison Hickey comments about the churchyard narratives generally, "The unfolding of the stories of human pangs and sad steps often leads nowhere but to an image of the inaccessibility of these pangs" – that "inward hoard / Of unsunned griefs" remains, as in the Reverend Sympson's case above, largely unsunned.[70] We might rephrase the Pastor's declaration to observe that when the soul's passage from life to death is withheld from direct representation, it becomes all the more subject to the mind's watchful regard. So the Miner, whose story (6.212–254) bears an eponymous relation to the entire project of digging the mine of real life, simply vanishes, but because his passage from the region and (presumably) the world is untold, his story becomes subject to tracing and retracing, a narrative passage among the living which takes as its figure the path from his house to the mine's mouth: "He vanished; but conspicuous to this day / The path remains that linked his cottage-door / To the mine's mouth; a long and slanting track" (6.244–46).

In other words, the Pastor's passages resemble less D'Israeli's planted seed than Walter Benjamin's use of that same metaphor, itself Baconian in origin.[71] "The more . . . the storyteller foregoes psychological shading," Benjamin writes, "the greater becomes the story's claim to a place in the memory of the listener, the more completely it is integrated into his own experience (*Erfahrung*), the greater will be his inclination to repeat it to someone else someday, sooner or later." As an example, Benjamin turns to – nothing other than – an historical anecdote, the account in Herodotus's *Histories* of the Egyptian king, Psammenitus, forced to watch his family members, one by one, led to their execution. When the king's stoic, silent calm cracks only when he sees an ancient servant among the prisoners, Benjamin comments:

From this story it may be seen what the nature of true storytelling is. The value of information does not survive the moment in which it was new. It lives only at that moment; it has to surrender to it completely and explain itself to it without losing any time. A story is different. It does not expend itself. It preserves and concentrates its strength and is capable of releasing it even after a long time. Thus Montaigne referred to this Egyptian king and asked himself why he mourned only when he caught sight of his servant. Montaigne answers: "Since he was already overfull of grief, it took only the smallest increase for it to burst through its dams." Thus

Montaigne. But one could also say: The king is not moved by the fate of those of royal blood, for it is his own fate. Or: We are moved by much on the stage that does not move us in real life; to the king, this servant is only an actor. Or: Great grief is pent up and breaks forth only with relaxation. Seeing this servant was the relaxation. Herodotus offers no explanations. His report is the driest. That is why this story from ancient Egypt is still capable after thousands of years of arousing astonishment and thoughtfulness. *It resembles the seeds of grain which have lain for centuries in the chambers of the pyramids shut up air-tight and have retained their germinative power to this day.*[72]

D'Israeli's seed germinates when it brings us close to the dead; his *Dissertation* is critical of those historians (notably Hume) who would keep us distant from the past – theirs is wasted labor. In Benjamin's account and in Wordsworth's practice, the historical anecdote is saved from being Orphean *labor effusus* – in Benjamin's words, it "does not expend itself" – precisely because it does not permit us to approach too closely. Both it and its teller retain an "incomparable aura," a term that Benjamin, borrowing from early modern science and nineteenth-century mysticism, famously defined as a "unique phenomenon of a distance" or "a peculiar web of time and space," in which an object is invested with the ability to look at us in return.[73] Wordsworth simply calls it "finer distance" (1.17) and anticipates all of Benjamin's formulations quite precisely in the opening tableau of *The Excursion*, Book 1, whose "landscape indistinctly glared / Through a pale steam" to the dreaming gazer's eye.[74]

Wordsworth, then, draws on the sort of anecdotal practice he would have found in D'Israeli's *Dissertation* or numerous other collections, but reshapes it. Mindful of the etymology of anecdote as something unpublished, we might say that the problem with D'Israeli, from the point of view of Wordsworth's practice, is that he publishes too much and, in this sense, is not "anecdotal" enough. In this respect unlike the "microscopic eye" in Thomson or the newspaper's "loophole" in Cowper, the "passages of life" strive for a mode of inform*ing*, a "time-release" intelligence. Wordsworth's prime target is not, clearly, D'Israeli, but those familiar nemeses listed in the "Preface" to *Lyrical Ballads*: the "rapid communication of intelligence" that accompanies urbanization and war; also the novel, whose bulkiest representative, "Clarissa Harlowe" – however unlikely as a rapid form of communicating intelligence – is nonetheless criticized similarly for its "outrageous stimulation," untempered by meter.[75] (While D'Israeli emphasized the "slow accession" of knowledge, his emphasis on "detached particulars," as well as his and other anecdotalists' mock complaints about the "evanescence" and "volatility" of the anecdote and the difficulty of ordering such material, might have reminded Wordsworth too much of the "dissociating articles" of newsprint.) When Benjamin defines story-telling against both news, with its preference for close-range information, and the novel, emblem of the isolated modern individual, he is gazing back retrospectively at the period whose inaugural tremors – which occurred earlier in Britain than on the continent or in Russia – Wordsworth is registering.

"The Storyteller" occupies a notoriously ambiguous position in Benjamin's body of work, particularly when juxtaposed with "The Work of Art in the Age of Mechanical Reproduction," "The Author as Producer," or the essay on Baudelaire that I considered in the last chapter's treatment of William Cowper's georgic of the news. To Miriam Hansen, for instance, the tension between "The Storyteller" and the other essays – indeed even within the other essays – has seemed a "problematic slippage" between two tendencies in the writing.[76] In the one direction, Benjamin's work moved toward nostalgia, toward regret over the historical decline of "communicable experience" (*Erfahrung*) largely dependent on auratic modes of transmission; at other times, he took a different direction, engaging in guarded celebration of the decay both of auratic power and the decline of *Erfahrung*, and hoping that the resulting alienated perception could be mobilized, in some utopian future, for the purpose of a revolutionary politics. To these two impulses correspond two different insights about how a literary work can be a historical medium. Leskov in "The Storyteller" and Baudelaire in "Some Motifs" (or film, with its ambiguous shock effect in the "Mechanical Reproduction" essay) represent not only two modes of experience, *Erfahrung* and *Erlebnis* respectively, but they also adumbrate two kinds of historiography: the first mode preserves and releases the force of its content over time; the second registers the blank, unassimilated shock of the present.[77] At least at first glance, this is also the difference between *The Excursion*'s "prolongation of a still response" and *The Task*'s "poring eye" and strangely anxious "indolent vacuity of thought," in which, as we saw, the magic of distance is pierced and the stranger is apprehended in "near approach."

Such formulations are useful, I think, yet matters are *not* so simple for Wordsworth or for Benjamin, who, as theorists of georgic modernity, are far more dialectical thinkers than these categories suggest. In Wordsworth's case, to leave it at that risks merely reestablishing the conservatism of Wordsworth's project as a protest against an Enlightenment "ethos of letters,"[78] without quite capturing all of its interest as an experiment in historiography. To begin with, we would lose the crucial relation in his poetry (as in Benjamin's work) between "passage" and peril, traversing and danger, a link that both Phillipe Lacoue-Labarthe and Roger Munier remind us resides even in the etymologies of "experience" (the same Latin root enters both *periri*, to cross, and *periculum*, danger) and *Erfahrung* (whose older radical *fara* went into *gefährden*, to endanger, and *Gefahr*, danger). As Munier writes: "The boundaries between one meaning and another are imprecise. . . . The idea of experience as a crossing is etymologically and semantically difficult to separate from that of risk. From the beginning and no doubt in a fundamental sense, *experience* means to endanger."[79] Yet Wordsworth never forgets this association between a passage and peril: an "efficacious spirit chiefly lurks / Among those passages of life," as *The Prelude* put it, but the carefully chosen and distinctively ominous "lurks," retained during the forty-five years of revision, seems to suggest that counter-spirits less benignly "renovating" ("fructifying" [*1799*], or "repairing" [*1850*]) may lurk there too. Only by retaining this link can we understand the momentary peculiarity in the relaying of the life story of the Sympsons to the listeners. Notwithstanding the Pastor's gentle skirting of the facts of death and disappointment – his own "lenient terms" (7.288), as in Ciceronian rhetoric, where an *oratio lenis* (sometimes *lenitas verborum*) is a smooth style – the Wanderer fears "[l]est in those passages of life were some / That might have touched the sick heart of his Friend / Too nearly." There is a tension here between the intentional, renovating discipline of *The Excursion*'s "passages of life" from one character to another and their means, that other, more worrisome "passage" which *The Excursion* elsewhere calls "the passages / Through which the ear converses with the heart" (4.1154–55). As Wordsworth's "Ode on the Power of Sound" acknowledges, a danger lurks in the "intricate labyrinth" of the ear: in the unpredictable movement of words as they enter there and pass to the heart.

The Excursion, in other words, is intent not just on orality and what Milton nicely called "due process of speech," but on aurality or – risking the solecism to avoid confusion with Benjamin's "aura" – auricularity, and these two emphases sometimes work against each other. (Indeed, remembering Coleridge's famous complaint, since reiterated in various forms – "Is there one word for instance, attributed to the pedlar in the Excursion, characteristic of a pedlar?"[80] – one might wonder if the poem's celebration of "oral record" is something of an occasion for the more intent focus on the auricular career of words adjacent but not identical to it; for Wordsworth seems either less competent or, as I suspect, less interested than usual in rendering the "language really used by men" in low and rustic situations.) In *The Excursion*'s anti-apocalyptic revision of *The Prelude*'s dream of the Arab, the Wanderer serenely seeks to maintain that to the "ear of Faith," the conch-shell of the Universe imparts the "central peace, subsisting at the heart / Of endless agitation" (4.1146–47), but the poem's recurrent and persistent images of sound are not so easily able to separate such aggressive drives toward purification from their counterplots of danger. The Pastor's histories, for instance, are said to be "strains of power" that overpower as well, in order "to seize and occupy the sense" (7.22–23). There is even something strangely terrifying in the Wanderer's own example of nature's ceaseless utterance, the "iron knell" of a wandering raven whose cry "fades upon the ear, / Diminishing by distance till it seemed / To expire; yet from the abyss is caught again. / And yet again recovered" (4.1184–87). After all, only one half of the poet's famous proposition in "Expostulation and Reply" ("The eye it cannot chuse but see, / We cannot bid the ear be still") is true. The eye can close its lid, or just avert the gaze; the ear has no such protection and, as in these lines, will not be still. Hence Geoffrey Hartman, in a different context, notes the peculiar vulnerability of the ear: "The ear must deal with sounds that not only cannot be refused entry, but penetrate and evoke something too powerful for any defense."[81] Insofar as the echo therein cannot be economized, the ear may lead "beyond" the pleasure principle. Any attempt, like the Pastor's and the Wanderer's, to instill it with life may also court the infusion of death, more like the "leperous distilment" poured "in the porches" of King Hamlet's ears (cf. *Hamlet*, 1.5.63–64).

The Excursion's auricularity or "otopathy," then, must be sharply distinguished from the Benjaminian aura, which is a phenomenon of distance, a web of time and space, achieved in vision at a distance or by the unfolding of oral discourse.[82] Sound, Susan Stewart has demonstrated, "will not readily 'fit' an epistemology of spatiality, horizon, or location."[83] Indeed, as we have seen in chapter 2, where the noise of "nameless nations" thrusts forth from the visual field established by the microscope and "bursts on" the senses, the trope of sound and auricular perception, that pathway that leads into the ears, renders uncomfortable proximity.[84] It can "*touch*," as the lines on the Sympsons' lives and deaths puts it, "too *nearly*," and such cognitive "noise" signals an excess that eludes the Lockean idea. At the same time, Wordsworth's difficult, antithetical suggestion seems to be that distance and proximity are themselves often inseparably correlative, like origin and tendency, or like the raven's cry which returns by receding in the Wanderer's description. So, for example, when, in the transition that initially marked the interstices between Parts I and II of "The Ruined Cottage," the Wanderer pauses at the climax of Margaret's tale and blandly diverts attention to the "calm of nature," the narrator responds, after the pause, by thinking "in my own despite . . . of that poor Woman as of one / Whom I had known and loved" and returns to "be[g] of the old Man that, *for my sake,* / He would resume his story" (see *Exc.*, 1.590–624, my emphasis). The Sympson sequence is one of many in the later books that establish a *link* between euphemizing speech – in this case the Pastor's exceedingly lenient rendering of death as an "unexpected sleep," as a "shadow thrown / Softly and lightly from a passing cloud," as repose on the "warm lap of his mother earth" – and a perilous echoic effect. It is as if the words touch too nearly precisely *because*, not in spite of, the degree of their tensely "fair-speaking" (*eu-phemos*) interposition.

Only by keeping this dialectic in mind, and thereby preserving the equally dialectical recognition of Kenneth Burke that "implicit in the idea of protection there is the idea of something to be *protected against*" and "that the *threat* is the basis of beauty," can we see *The Excursion's* sometimes aggressively fair-speaking strand as something other than regrettable complacency on the part of an author past his prime.[85] (It is doubtless that, at times, too.) Whether in the form of a display of the flowers of consolatory rhetoric, the flowers of English literary history (the Pastor's account of Sympson's death recalls the "gentle sleep" that seems to pass Adam into his "former state / Insensible" in *Paradise Lost* [8.286–95]), or just a more subtle obliquity, euphemism is also, I think, a deliberate attempt to introduce within the written poem an *acoustical unconscious*, a reverberation that tends in the opposite direction, toward dysphemistic knowledge.[86] Euphemistic language, like effective irony, does not fail to make quite clear the muted content for which it is a substitute; if it does, then it misses its mark as euphemism and becomes enigma. (To read such lines as "she sleeps in the calm earth, and peace is here" [*Exc.*, 1.941] is also to sustain, at least as an internal mutter, the knowledge of death.) Such fair-speaking may seem to resemble closely an instance of denial, negation, repression, suppression, or erasure of unpleasurable content, but I would want to maintain that it is finely different. Although euphemism has been and may certainly still be enlisted in the service of ideology – George Orwell's damning derision of "some comfortable English professor" defending totalitarianism by dropping "a mass of Latin words ... upon the facts like soft snow, blurring the outlines and covering up the details" should remain a corrective occupational mantra[87] – I would also hold the door open for a more vexed or compulsive kind of fair-speaking that is neither snow-job nor silence, but rather more like static or stutter: a disturbance of speech that acknowledges a history beyond the pleasure principle but not beyond representation. Viewers and readers of *Hamlet* know, an Ophelia gathering and scattering her flowers is an Ophelia publishing, not hiding, her wounds.

CODA: FLORAL HISTORIES AND REGISTERS OF MUTENESS

Nec sum animi dubius, verbis ea vincere magnum
Quam sit et angustis hunc addere rebus honorem . . .
. . . magno nunc ore sonandum.
Georgics, 3: 289–90, 294

The "negative allegory" that Marjorie Levinson and others have found to be the unconscious strategy – that is, unknown to the poem but identifiable by the belated critic – at work in the famous longer lyrics and *The Prelude* becomes, thus, the object of a pained self-reflection in *The Excursion*.[88] I take it to be a remarkable piece of methodological self-consciousness on Wordsworth's part to place as the very first of the Pastor's "passages" a narrative about what can, and what cannot, be achieved by the "flowers of speech" – this is, of course, the older, conventional rhetorical conception of euphemistic fair-speaking and a version of the Virgilian *magno ore* (lofty words). Recent readers of *The Excursion* have not failed to recognize in the second story, about the Miner (*Exc.*, 6.212–61), an eponymous passage among "passages" for the Wanderer's project of extracting didactic ore from the mine of real life.[89] But it is the *leading* story, the tale of a love-sick Botanist (6.95–211), that may illuminate more about the poem's historiographical experiment, never reducible to the Wanderer's prescriptions. This flower-gatherer presents another figure of unfulfilled desire, here represented as amorous rather than social (e.g., the Prodigal) or political (the Jacobite and the Hanoverian): in a rather nasty twist on the Eurydice plot, his beloved "had vanished from his prospects and desires; / *Not* by translation to the heavenly choir" but to another suitor (6.137–38). The beginning of his story offers an instance of the failure of the language of chivalric or courtly love: he "[l]oved fondly, truly, fervently; and dared / At length to tell his love, but sued in vain" (6.119–20). Showing the physical symptoms of his inward wound, he is directed by his friends away from the flowers of language to their literal substitute, the language of flowers, an increasingly popular cultural practice imported from the continent as early as Lady Mary Wortley Montagu's letters of mid-century and developed more extensively after the Revolution: "'Do you, for your own benefit, construct / A calendar of flowers, plucked as they blow / Where health abides'"(6.173–74).[90] The cure intended here is not, as the Wanderer has apparently told the Solitary, directly from the herbal remedy ("some virtuous herb of power / To cure his malady") but a function of the act of gathering, the excursive "passage" to and fro. Yet even in this instance, the

Wanderer's typically impatient therapeutic interruption – "'Impute it not to impatience if,' exclaimed / The Wanderer, 'I infer that he was healed / By perseverance in the course described'" – is, as Celeste Langan points out, heavily ironized by the previous information and subsequent reminder that the Botanist has suddenly died.[91] *Despondency* may not be corrected in this poem, but prolepsis, the Wanderer's signature mode of defense, almost always is.

Yet its failure or transience as cure is not the last we learn of this calendar. At his death, the botanist turns it, or some version of it, into a material medium of communication, with one final request to the woman he loves:

> That, from his dying hand, she would accept
> Of his possessions that which most he prized;
> A book, upon whose leaves some chosen plants
> By his own hand disposed with nicest care
> In undecaying beauty were preserved;
> Mute register, to him, of time and place,
> And various fluctuations in the breast;
> To her, a monument of faithful love
> Conquered, and in tranquility retained! (*Exc.*, 6.203–11)

What had been intended as part of the cure becomes instead ("to him") a curious document, the "mute register" that attempts to preserve both outward "time and place" and the "various fluctuations in the breast." What sort of record is this? The imbalance between the ungiving modesty of the function described in lines 208–09 – which is neither reparation nor excavation but simply auscultation of time, place, and breast – and the cloying conclusion that she is said in the two succeeding lines to draw from it ("To her, a monument of faithful love / Conquered, and in tranquility retained!") calls into question the validity of consolation and the possibility of consensus, even as, like D'Israeli's anecdote, it aspires to both.[92] To the extent that it is a register that *is* mute – an artifact that is unreadable and therefore easily misread – the floral calendar rehearses all the dangers of unrepresentability, aporia, and so on, that I noted in my discussion of the farmer's *mirabitur* at the start of this chapter. But the episode suggests that it might also be something rather different: a register *of muteness*, the correlative of the botanist's inability all along to use language to his desired end. It offers a kind of calendric structure of feeling, one that asks for a hearing, although not by any single character within the poem.

With its georgic affiliations, including the "works and days" tradition that influenced Virgil's *Georgics*, *The Excursion* is a calendar of sorts. It is one that can (and has) been understood as an arrogant, prosing attempt to strew flowers on the grave, naturalizing and covering up the diseases of urban industrialization and rural indigence, which are in fact diagnosed by the Wanderer and the Solitary respectively at some length in Book 8 (83–433). At first glance Wordsworth's "mute register" may resemble the pathos drummed up by the original "mute inglorious Miltons" of Thomas Gray's "Elegy, Written in a Country Churchyard," and brilliantly diagnosed by William Empson, who was irritated "by the complacence in the massive calm of the poem": "By comparing the social arrangement to Nature [Gray] makes it seem inevitable, which it was not, and gives it a dignity which was undeserved."[93] However, *The Excursion*'s dramatic structure repeatedly displays the resounding, ironic inadequation between such visible objects as the floral calendar and the meanings attached to them by the various characters, as between the frustrated lives and the fair-speaking, closing words offered as epitomes. It thus presents us with a more contradictory, less naturalizing entity: a register *of* muteness, a stethoscope that tries to make audible the thwarted or aborted histories which call forth either defensive recoil or defensive complacencies to begin with. The poem once chastised by Geoffrey Hartman for offering us "not a vision, but a voice" – even worse, a "flight from vision that causes a warp of obliquity" – for that very same reason also provokes and stages a disturbance in the ear, the poetic obliquity's acoustical unconscious.[94]

I hope it is clear that this is not the same thing as the staging of a failure of signification, a deconstruction of meaning, since something *is* "registered," namely muteness – which far more actively than "silent" (the plausible synonym we might have expected to modify "register" here) suggests a forceful hindrance, external or physical, or else something too difficult to be uttered. Mindful of the horror of the Solitary with whose lines this chapter began, we might say that there is a sense in which the "mute earth" is made to speak in the poem after all. And while Wordsworth's effort to make muteness audible without prompting "recoil" has understandably enough won him the charge of "drowsy, frowsy" complacence from its first readers on, *The Excursion* seems to me to be a difficult poem to convict securely on such a charge. Certainly it would have been more acceptable to readers of our own time if it had been a noisier, less muted poem. It also would be more easily dismissable if it were just a tedious proto-Victorian piece of unchallenged consolation. I hope to have suggested that it is a work that has learned the difficult georgic lesson that history lies neither in the recovered *res* nor in the covering *verba* (a familiar Hobson's choice), but in the interferences and discrepancies between them. In this version of georgic, as a result, there are plenty of "closing words," but no final ones. The very "prolongation of some still response" that is part of the poem's compensatory project also – simultaneously – provides the interval within which all commonplaces, positively recommended for epitaphic writing by the *Essays upon Epitaphs*, instead ring hollowly.

Notes

INTRODUCTION. GEORGIC MODERNITY: SENSORY MEDIA AND THE AFFECT OF HISTORY

1. I follow the Loeb Classical Library edition of Virgil's *Georgics: Eclogues, Georgics, Aeneid 1–6*, trans. H. Rushton Fairclough, rev. edn. (Cambridge, MA: Harvard University Press, Loeb Classical Library, 1986), and, except where otherwise noted, I adopt Fairclough's translation.
2. The term belongs to Paul Alpers, *What is Pastoral?* (Chicago: University of Chicago Press, 1996). For Alpers, drawing in large part on Kenneth Burke, the representative anecdote is a " 'summation' which has generative powers" (14) and permits both modal continuity and historical change.
3. John Philips, *Cyder* 1.238–41, in *The Poems of John Philips*, ed. M. G. Lloyd Thomas (Oxford: Basil Blackwell, 1927); Charlotte Smith, *Beachy Head*, in *The Poems of Charlotte Smith*, ed. Stuart Curran (New York: Oxford University Press, 1993), lines 417–19.
4. Alan Liu, *Wordsworth: the Sense of History* (Stanford: Stanford University Press, 1989), 18–19.
5. James Turner, *The Politics of Landscape: Rural Scenery and Society in English Poetry 1630–1660* (Cambridge, MA: Harvard University Press, 1979), 7; Raymond Williams, *The Country and the City* (New York: Oxford University Press, 1973), 32; John Barrell, *The Dark Side of the Landscape: the Rural Poor in English Painting, 1730–1840* (Cambridge: Cambridge University Press, 1980), 38.
6. The first two quotations come from Kurt Heinzelman, "Millenarial Poetics: Wordsworth's 'Nutting,'" *Raritan* 19 (2000): 149–50; the second comes from an earlier, more detailed article, "Roman Georgic in a Georgian Age: a Theory of Romantic Genre," *Texas Studies in Literature and Language* 33 (1991): 182. Since 1991, Heinzelman has authored at least seven articles on some aspect of Romantic (largely Wordsworthian) or later eighteenth-century georgic. I discuss a number of them in chapter 1, and see also note 32 below.
7. George Crabbe, "The Village," 1.47–48. In *George Crabbe: the Complete Poetical Works*, ed. Norma Dalrymple-Champneys, 3 vols. (Oxford: Clarendon Press, 1988), 1:158.

8. *The German Ideology*, in *The Marx–Engels Reader*, ed. Robert C. Tucker (New York: W. W. Norton and Co., 1978), 154. Quoted in part by Turner, *Politics of Landscape*, 190.

9. See Barrell's *Dark Side* for the origin of his title: a 1783 review of Crabbe's *The Village*, in which the reviewer notes that Crabbe "represents 'only the dark side of the landscape, the poverty and misery attendant on the peasant'" (166 n. 40).

10. Quotations from Raymond Williams, *Marxism and Literature* (New York: Oxford University Press, 1977), 128–29, 133–34. The chemical trope of "precipitate" and "solution" appears broadly in Williams's writing and in his interviews with the *New Left Review*, almost whenever he attempts to articulate the meanings and uses of the term "structure of feeling."

11. In conversation with the interviewers, who point out that Williams's earlier suggestion (in *The Long Revolution* [1961]) that the structure of the present is less available to us for past periods than the present in which we are immersed is misleading, since "the fluidity and indeterminacy of the present surely render it at least as, if not more, difficult to interpret than the past," Williams admits the earlier confusion and adds: "What I would now wish to say is that while a structure of feeling always exists in the present tense, so to speak grammatically, I do not now think it more recoverable or more accessible in the temporal present than in the past." See Raymond Williams, *Politics and Letters: Interviews with the New Left Review* (London: Verso, 1981), 162–63.

12. This admittedly fine line – between a discomfort that cannot be easily named and public displays of identifiable emotions (such as pity, pride, or other performances in the repertoire of sensibility) – distinguishes my focus from those of two studies from which I have learned a great amount: Julie Ellison, *Cato's Tears and the Making of Anglo-American Emotion* (Chicago: University of Chicago Press, 1999) and Adela Pinch, *Strange Fits of Passion: Epistemologies of Emotion, Hume to Austen* (Stanford: Stanford University Press, 1996). What I have in common with both Ellison and Pinch is the understanding that talking about feeling, affect, or emotion does not mean talking about an individual or unified "subject." In Pinch's words, "the history of feeling and the history of the individual are not the same thing"; feelings are, she argues, circulating, "transpersonal" entities (13). Ellison summarizes: "An emerging interdisciplinary conversation in the humanities and social sciences is advancing the view that emotion, including personal emotion felt to be inward or private, is a social phenomenon, though one not separable from bodily response" (5). The "affect" and "feeling" I analyze in the chapters that follow are, similarly, not the mark of a centered subject, a Cartesian sun, but denote a corona of forces and effects extending inward and outward from the body.

As to terminology: Pinch and Ellison use "passion," "emotion," "feeling," and "affect" almost interchangeably in order to emphasize what the terms have in common and because, in Pinch's words, during the eighteenth-century and Romantic periods, "the many names for emotion travel as freely as the emotions themselves" (16). It might not make sense for a historical study of eighteenth-century feeling, then, to distinguish between these terms as finely as does Rei Terada, in her work on poststructuralist philosophy and theory (see *Feeling in Theory: Emotion after the "Death of the Subject"* [Cambridge MA: Harvard University Press, 2001], 4). Nonetheless, I am mindful that the many names can travel a little too freely; in what follows I refer to affect and to feeling (rather than emotion), both of which I take to include (both) physiological sensations and psychological states, although the latter may not be clearly articulated.

13. Pierre Bourdieu, *Outline of a Theory of Practice*, trans. Richard Nice (Cambridge: Cambridge University Press, 1977), 72, 78.

14. Fredric Jameson, *The Political Unconscious: Narrative as a Socially Symbolic Act* (Ithaca: Cornell University Press, 1981), 102.

15. Liu, *Wordsworth*, 47–48, emphasis added.

16. The phrasing is Liu's, as he discusses and adopts Althusser's understanding of historical structure as an "absent cause": see *Wordsworth*, 39 and Louis Althusser and Etienne Balibar, *Reading Capital*, trans. Ben Brewster (London: Verso, 1997), 188–89.

17. Raymond Williams, *Marxism and Literature*, 128, 132, 133–34.

18. Williams, *Politics and Letters*, 167; Joan W. Scott, "The Evidence of Experience," *Critical Inquiry* 17 (1991): 781–84. As valuable as Scott's essay is for its qualification of certain naive constructions of "experience," particularly as such accounts disable the force of histories of difference, the limitation or partiality of her treatment of Williams becomes apparent at the point that she counters what she takes to be Williams's emphasis on individuals with a citation from Teresa de Lauretis: "[In the process by which subjectivity is constructed] one perceives and comprehends as subjective . . . those relations – material, economic, and interpersonal – which are in fact social and, in larger perspective, historical" (from *Alice Doesn't*, cited in "The Evidence of Experience," 782). Yet this position, if I am reading him correctly, is precisely Williams's own. Compare the observation from *Marxism and Literature* cited in my text above: because of the limitations of the analyst, Williams writes, "all that escapes from the fixed and the explicit and the known *is grasped and defined* as the personal[,] this, here, now, alive, active 'subjective,'" rather than recognized as social experience "in solution." This grasping and defining is, for Williams, a misprision, if an inevitable one.

19. The critique of Williams for his failure to account for imperialism's influence in shaping British culture is a frequent one. Of particular note, because of its generosity and its ability to frame the problem in terms of the limitations of British Marxism more generally, is the analysis offered by Gauri Viswanathan, "Raymond Williams and British Colonialism," *Yale Journal of Criticism* 4 (1991): 47–66. Viswanathan locates Williams's "methodological difficulties in his conflicting models of interpretation that approach culture in terms of process . . . while, in reverse fashion, presenting imperialism as a full-blown enactment of economic motives that are encompassed by a larger system of economic determination" (49). So, on the one hand, Williams sensitively

questions the simpler versions of base-superstructure in his analysis of British culture, but because he is unwilling to dispense altogether with the more useful insights of related Marxian categories, economic determinism returns in his analysis of Britain's relation to global power: "the peculiar paradox of Williams's critical position [is that] at the very moment he sought to disengage culture from deterministic explanations, he was locked into a reading of imperialism as the end point of European market forces" (59). Viswanathan locates the origin of this paradox in the conflict between Romanticism and Marx's legacy. Incorporating empire into Williams's "country and city" model is also one of the chief motivations behind the essays collected in Gerald MacLean, Donna Landry, and Joseph P. Ward, eds., *The Country and the City Revisited: England and the Politics of Culture, 1550–1850* (Cambridge: Cambridge University Press, 1999), in particular the contribution of Karen O'Brien, "Imperial Georgic, 1660–1789" in that volume.

20. Fredric Jameson, "Cognitive Mapping," in *Marxism and the Interpretation of Culture*, eds. Cary Nelson and Lawrence Grossberg (Urbana: University of Illinois Press, 1988), 349–50.

21. Williams, *Politics and Letters*, 167–68. Catherine Gallagher observes that "'comparison' isn't exactly the right word here, for Williams denies that 'the articulated' and 'the lived' are a pair of equal and opposite entities. . . . This 'lived' material cannot have an explicit content; it not only appears at the level of consciousness and language as inchoate disturbance, but also *feels* like pure 'trouble'" ("Counterhistory and the Anecdote," in Catherine Gallagher and Stephen Greenblatt, *Practicing New Historicism* [Chicago: University of Chicago Press, 2000], 63).

22. Raymond Williams, "Means of Communication as Means of Production," in *Problems in Materialism and Culture: Selected Essays* (London: New Left Books, 1980), 50–63; see especially 59–63.

23. "Experience becomes a forbidden word, whereas what we ought to say about it is that it is a limited word" (*Politics and Letters*, 172). For an account of the sterility of the choice between naively reducing all experience to the mediations that produce it or naively upholding the possibility of experiential immediacy, as well as a discussion of those poststructuralist thinkers who may have gone beyond it, see Martin Jay, "The Limits of Limit-Experience: Bataille and Foucault," in *Cultural Semantics: Keywords of Our Time* (Amherst: University of Massachusetts Press, 1998), 62–78.

24. Williams, *Politics and Letters*, 164.

25. Jean-François Lyotard, *The Differend: Phrases in Dispute*, trans. Georges Van Den Abbeele (Minneapolis: University of Minnesota Press, 1988), 13.

26. Williams offers a pointed critique of McLuhan in "Means of Communication as Means of Production," *Problems in Materialism and Culture*, 51–53.

27. David Simpson, "Raymond Williams: Feeling for Structures, Voicing 'History,'" *Social Text* 10 (1992): 15.

28. I think, for example, of Simpson's introduction to *Wordsworth's Historical Imagination: the Poetry of Displacement* (New York: Methuen, 1987): "I have

found it most productive to regard the Wordsworthian subjectivity as a particular medium (and entity) that was, by virtue of its openness to the energies of language and experience, extraordinarily articulate about the pressures and tensions that we may with hindsight regard as central to the culture at large" (4). Why *does* Simpson (instinctively? deliberately?) use the word "medium" here? My hope is that this book will do something to answer just that question.

29. Probably following the *Oxford English Dictionary*, Raymond Williams states that the plural "media" became available as a general plural only in the mid-nineteenth century (*Keywords: a Vocabulary of Culture and Society*, rev. edn. [New York: Oxford University Press, 1983], 203). However, the *OED* and Williams are wrong: the plural "media" is in use at least as early as the mid-eighteenth century. See, for example, "Music, Painting, and Poetry," the second of James Harris's *Three Treatises* (1744): "To prevent confusion, it must be observed, that in all these arts there is a difference between the sensible media, through which they imitate, and the subjects imitated. The sensible media, through which they imitate, must always be relative to that sense, by which the particular art applies to the mind; but the subject imitated may be foreign to that sense, and beyond the power of its perception" (*The Works of James Harris, Esq. with an Account of His Life and Character By His Son The Earl of Malmesbury* [Oxford: Printed by J. Vincent, 1841], 28 n). Harris's use of "media" is consistent throughout.

    More may be at stake than a grammatical quibble. As I discuss below, current usage risks turning "media" into a singular noun and homogenous category: "The Media." For an excellent and suggestive account of the dangers inherent in such a singularization, see Jean-Luc Nancy, "Why are there Several Arts and not just one," in *The Muses*, trans. Peggy Kamuf (Stanford: Stanford University Press, 1996).

30. Francis Bacon, *The Advancement of Learning*, ed. Michael Kiernan (Oxford: Clarendon Press, 2000), 111, 135. Hereafter *Advancement* and cited in my main text. Bacon's famous celebration of "these Georgickes of the Mind" occurs in the immediate context of his treatment of ethics, but as many have noted, *The Advancement* is full of quotations and appeals to this particular work by Virgil, which provides the governing trope of Bacon's whole text. For a discussion of the politics and implicit coding of Bacon's choice of quotations from Virgil, see Annabel Patterson, *Pastoral and Ideology: Virgil to Valéry* (Berkeley and Los Angeles: University of California Press, 1987), 133–63. For a discussion of the tropes of agriculture and gardening in *The Advancement*, see Brian Vickers, *Francis Bacon and Renaissance Prose* (Cambridge: Cambridge University Press, 1968), 187–98.

31. Discussing the rivalry among various postmodern spatial media, Fredric Jameson describes "a process whereby the traditional fine arts are *mediatized*: that is, they now come to consciousness of themselves as various media within a mediatic system in which their own internal production also constitutes a symbolic message and the taking of a position on the status of the medium

in question." Jameson notes that while the significance of media and, more generally, the underlying materiality of all things "has finally risen dripping and convulsive into the light of day" during the phase of late capitalism, nonetheless we are now in the position to wonder whether, at some less salient level, such movements and rivalries "were always the case" (*Postmodernism or, the Cultural Logic of Late Capital* [Durham: Duke University Press, 1991], 162, 67–68). I will be suggesting that something like this, if in a local and more limited way, is occurring in some versions of georgic from the seventeenth century on.

32. I have benefited from all of the following accounts, some on genre and mode, others turning to the georgic for the various issues of labor, culture, politics, ideology, and empire that instances of the genre and the mode have raised. Many will be treated in the pages and chapters that follow.

For the late sixteenth and seventeenth centuries: Ralph Cohen, "Innovation and Variation: Literary Change and Georgic Poetry," in *Literature and History: Papers Read at a Clark Library Seminar, March 3, 1973*, eds. Ralph Cohen and Murray Krieger (Los Angeles: William Andrews Clark Memorial Library, 1974), 3–42; Alastair Fowler, "The Beginnings of English Georgic," in *Renaissance Genres: Essays on Theory, History, and Interpretation*, ed. Barbara Kiefer Lewalski (Cambridge, MA: Harvard University Press, 1986), 105–25 and also Fowler's "Georgic and Pastoral: Laws of Genre in the Seventeenth Century," in *Culture and Cultivation in Early Modern England: Writing and the Land*, eds. Michael Leslie and Timothy Raylor (Leicester: Leicester University Press, 1992), 81–87; Anthony Low, *The Georgic Revolution* (Princeton: Princeton University Press, 1985); Annabel Patterson, *Pastoral and Ideology*; William Sessions, "Spenser's Georgics," *English Literary Renaissance* 10 (1980): 202–38; and Jane Tylus, "Spenser, Virgil, and the Politics of Poetic Labor," *ELH* 55 (1988): 53–77. James Turner's *Politics of Landscape* (cited earlier), while more concerned with pastoral, bears significantly on the study of seventeenth-century georgic.

For the eighteenth century, one would have to start with the several studies by John Barrell, which I engage throughout this study, particularly in chapter 2. These include, in addition to *The Dark Side of the Landscape* already cited: *The Idea of the Landscape and the Sense of Place, 1730–1840: an Approach to the Poetry of John Clare* (Cambridge: Cambridge University Press, 1972); *English Literature in History, 1730–1780: an Equal, Wide Survey* (London: Hutchinson, 1983); and several essays in *The Birth of Pandora and the Division of Knowledge* (London: Macmillan, 1992). Next, I have found very useful the different perspectives of: Rachel Crawford, *Poetry, Enclosure, and the Vernacular Landcape* (Cambridge: Cambridge University Press, 2002); Frans de Bruyn, "From Virgilian Georgic to Agricultural Science: an Instance of the Transvaluation of Literature in Eighteenth-Century Britain," in *Augustan Subjects: Essays in Honor of Martin C. Battestin*, ed. Albert J. Rivero (Newark: University of Delaware Press, 1997), 47–67; Richard Feingold, *Nature and Society: Later Eighteenth-Century Uses of Pastoral and Georgic* (New Brunswick: Rutgers

University Press, 1978); Dustin Griffin, "The Bard of Cyder-Land: John Philips and Miltonic Imitation," *Studies in English Literature 1500–1900* 24 (1984): 441–60 and Griffin's "Redefining Georgic: Cowper's *Task*," *ELH* 57 (1990): 865–79; Donna Landry, "The Resignation of Mary Collier: some Problems in Feminist Literary History," in *The New Eighteenth Century: Theory, Politics, English Literature*, eds. Felicity Nussbaum and Laura Brown (New York: Methuen, 1987); Kate Lilley, "Homosocial Women, Martha Sansom, Constantia Grierson, Mary Leapor, and Georgic Verse Epistle," in *Women's Poetry in the Enlightenment: the Making of a Canon, 1730–1820*, eds. Isobel Armstrong and Virginia Blain (New York: Macmillan, 1999); Alfred Lutz, "'The Deserted Village' and the Politics of Genre," *Modern Language Quarterly* 55 (1994); Douglas Lane Patey, "Anne Finch, John Dyer, and the Georgic Syntax of Nature," in *Augustan Subjects: Essays in Honor of Martin C. Battestin*, ed. Albert J. Rivero (Newark: University of Delaware Press, 1997), 29–46; and Ronald Paulson, "The Aesthetics of Georgic Renewal: Pope," in *Breaking and Remaking: Aesthetic Practice in England, 1700–1820* (New Brunswick: Rutgers University Press, 1989). Lastly, many of the essays revisiting Williams's legacy in *The Country and the City Revisited* (cited in earlier note) will be of special interest; in addition to O'Brien, "Imperial Georgic," already mentioned, I would single out also Elizabeth Heckendorn Cook, "Frances Burney and the Reconstruction of Britishness," and John Barrell's "Afterword: Moving Stories, Still Lives."

For Romanticism (for Wordsworth studies in particular there have been quite a large number of studies), Kurt Heinzelman's work on georgic has been especially prolific and sophisticated. In addition to the articles cited earlier, "Roman Georgic in a Georgian Age" and "Millenarial Poetics," see also "The Last Georgic: *Wealth of Nations* and the Scene of Writing," in *Adam Smith's* Wealth of Nations: *New Interdisciplinary Essays*, eds. Stephen Copley and Kathryn Sutherland (Manchester: Manchester University Press, 1995), 172–94; "Economics, Rhetoric, and the Scene of Instruction," *Stanford French Review: International Journal of Interdisciplinary Research* 15 (1991): 349–71; "The Uneducated Imagination: Romantic Representations of Labor," in *At the Limits of Romanticism: Essays in Cultural, Feminist, and Materialist Criticism*, eds. Mary Favret and Nicola Watson (Bloomington: Indiana University Press, 1994); "The Cult of Domesticity: Dorothy and William Wordsworth at Grasmere," in *Romanticism and Feminism*, ed. Anne K. Mellor (Bloomington: Indiana University Press, 1988); and "Poetry and Real Estate: Wordsworth as Developer," *Southwest Review* 84 (1994): 573–88. Yet even Heinzelman has not quite cornered the market so far. In the chapters that follow, particularly chapter 4, I will also have occasion to discuss Bruce Graver, "Honorable Toil: the Georgic Ethic of *Prelude* I," *Studies in Philology* 92 (1995): 346–60 and "Wordsworth's Georgic Beginnings," *Texas Studies in Literature and Language* 33 (1991): 137–59; John Murdoch, "The Landscape of Labor: Transformations of the Georgic," in *Romantic Revolutions: Criticism and Theory*, eds. Kenneth R. Johnston, Gilbert Chaitin, Karen Hanson and Herbert Marks

(Bloomington: Indiana University Press, 1990); and Clifford Siskin, *The Work of Writing: Literature and Social Change in Britain, 1700–1830* (Baltimore: Johns Hopkins University Press, 1998), chapter 4.

Two older surveys remain helpful points of reference: John Chalker, *The English Georgic: a Study in the Development of a Form* (London: Routledge and Kegan Paul, 1969) and Dwight Leonard Durling, *The Georgic Tradition in English Poetry* (New York: Columbia University Press, 1935).

In the "jeu d'esprit" category, I would recommend Norman O. Brown, "My Georgics," in *Apocalyse and/or Metamorphosis* (Berkeley and Los Angeles: University of California Press, 1991) and Paul H. Fry, "Georgic Comedy: the fictive Territory of Jane Austen's *Emma*," *Studies in the Novel* 11 (1979): 129–46.

No list would be sufficient without some mention of classicists' studies of the *Georgics* themselves. I have found particularly useful Gary Miles, *Virgil's Georgics* (Berkeley and Los Angeles: University of California Press, 1980); Christine Perkell, *The Poet's Truth: a Study of the Poet in Virgil's* Georgics (Berkeley and Los Angeles: University of California Press, 1989); Michael C. J. Putnam, *Virgil's Poem of the Earth: Studies in* The Georgics (Princeton: Princeton University Press, 1979); David O. Ross, Jr., *Virgil's Elements: Physics and Poetry in the* Georgics (Princeton: Princeton University Press, 1987); and Richard F. Thomas, *Reading Virgil and his Texts: Studies in Intertextuality* (Ann Arbor: University of Michigan Press, 1999).

33. John Philips, *Cyder* (1708), John Gay, *Rural Sports* (1713; revised 1720), William Somervile, *The Chace* (1735), Christopher Smart, *The Hop-Garden* (1752), John Dyer, *The Fleece* (1757), James Grainger, *The Sugar-Cane* (1764), Richard Jago's *Edge Hill* (1767). Thomson's *The Seasons*, first collected edition in 1730, revised continuously until 1746, is sometimes included in this category, although one sees more mixing with affiliated philosophical and topographical genres. The phrase "true Georgics" is from Turner, *Politics of Landscape*, 185. The phrase may be ironic, since even the Virgilian progenitor is notably impure: a motley mix of myth, agriculture, viniculture, animal culture, historiography, and rhetoric received from numerous, heterogeneous sources.

34. Heinzelman, "Roman Georgic," 201. Heinzelman is here contesting Fredric Jameson's narrower construction of genre in *Political Unconscious*, noting that in the baggy, messy, flexible case of the georgic, this "notion of genre would lead us to see only the institutionalized idea of the 'English Georgic,' which evolved in the century following Dryden's translation (1697) and which implied a kind of mold or even divers kinds of form, not the invisible way in which georgic supplied *both* the very 'materials of Poetry' and the productive powers to use them."

35. Ibid., 185.

36. Viswanathan, "Raymond Williams and British Colonialism," especially 52–53, 57.

37. I take the term from Jay David Bolter and Richard Grusin's *Remediation: Understanding New Media* (Cambridge, MA: MIT Press, 2000). Bolter and Grusin's

discussion of the representation of one medium in another is a development of Marshall McLuhan's "the 'content' of any medium is always another medium"; they argue that remediation is the defining characteristic of new digital media, although not unique to it. I find the term "remediation" useful for its acknowledgment that remediation is not only "re-mediation" but also remedy, or remedial. (See *Remediation*, 45, 53–62; for McLuhan, see *Understanding Media: the Extensions of Man*, intro. Lewis H. Lapham [Cambridge, MA: MIT Press, 1994], 8–9).

38. Jameson, *Political Unconscious*, 17.

39. Friedrich A. Kittler, *Gramophone, Film, Typewriter*, trans. Geoffrey Winthrop-Young and Michael Wutz (Stanford: Stanford University Press, 1999), 5–6. Notwithstanding the important work by Eric Havelock and others in the 1960s on the specific issue of orality, Kittler's periodizing assumptions are widely shared, or assumed, in much media and communications theory written today; as a result, there has been relatively little of the sort of retrospective reading I am trying to accomplish. Happy exceptions to this generalization certainly exist, although the identification of media with technology remains widespread even in them. Jay David Bolter and Richard Grusin's *Remediation* makes clear that few of the qualities they find intensified by "new" (digital) media are specific to global culture circa 2000. Their occasional but interesting backward forays into Renaissance perspective art, or the medieval illuminated manuscript, give glimpses of this prehistory. Gillen D'Arcy Wood's *The Shock of the Real: Romanticism and Visual Culture, 1760–1860* (New York: Palgrave, 2001) offers a series of startling juxtapositions in order to argue "that the social and technological foundations for twentieth-century visual culture were set in the century preceding photography's emergence as a mass medium circa 1860" (14), and John Durham Peters proposes Augustine as the "inventor of the concept of 'medium'" somewhat in passing (see his *Speaking into the Air: a History of the Idea of Communication* [Chicago: University of Chicago Press, 1999], 69). Also important to mention here is an article I will treat again in notes to chapters 1 and 3, Celeste Langan, "Understanding Media in 1805: Audiovisual Hallucination in *The Lay of the Last Minstrel*," *Studies in Romanticism* 20 (2001): 49–70, as well as Peter J. Manning's response to Langan in the same issue: "'The Birthday of Typography': a Response to Celeste Langan," *Studies in Romanticism* 40 (2001): 71–83.

For a far-reaching semantic history of the intersecting trajectories of "medium," "media," and "mediation," one cannot do better than to start with two discussions by Raymond Williams: *Keywords*, 203–07 and *Marxism and Literature*, 85–100 and 158–64. Williams notes the scientific origins of the word, as well as its movement by the end of the eighteenth century into discussions of print and news culture (pertinent to my chapter 3). He does not include the word's use in memorialization or historiography – or, for that matter, later, nineteenth-century spiritualism, the popularized version of wanting to talk to the dead – but the examples noted in chapter 4 suggest that area as a necessary addition to his exemplary account.

1 THE *GEORGICS* AND THE CULTIVATION OF "MEDIUMS," 1660–1712

1. George Chapman, *The Poems of George Chapman*, ed. Phyllis B. Bartlett (Oxford: Oxford University Press, 1941), D2 margin. Robert Burton, *The Anatomy of Melancholy*, eds. Thomas C. Faulkner, Nicolas K. Kiessling, and Rhonda L. Blair, 6 vols. (Oxford: Clarendon Press, 1989–2000), 1:150.

2. Aristotle, *De Anima* 419a, 16–21; for the combination of passivity and activity that characterizes the medium – again *to metaxu* – see *De Anima* 434b, 28–30. For the Greek I follow *Aristotle: On the Soul, Parva Naturalia, On Breath*, trans. W. S. Hett (Cambridge, MA: Harvard University Press, Loeb Classical Library, 1957). Aristotle also uses *metaxu* as an adverb in the important discussion of the four causes or *aitiai* (material, formal, efficient, and final) in the *Physics*. The instrumental "media" in *Physics* 2.3 (194b) are not one of the causes but the *kinesantos metaxu*, the movers (or agents) in between the efficient and final causes (*Physics*, trans. Philip H. Wicksteed and Francis M. Cornford [London: William Heinemann/Loeb Classical Library, 1929]). For the idea of a "mean" – as in the *Nichomachean Ethics*'s discussion of a "mean state between two vices" (2.6.15–16 [1107a]) – Aristotle uses *mesotes*, which has a rather different sense from the "in-between" agents and substances of *De Anima*. My thanks go to Kimberly Johnson for help with the Greek.

3. When talking about touch, Aristotle uses both *to metaxu* and *to mesou*; the latter also means the space between, if not as assertively spatial as *metaxu*. For treatments of Aristotle's discussion of the media of the senses, see the very helpful work of Louise Vinge, *The Five Senses: Studies in a Literary Tradition* (Lund, Sweden: LiberLäromedel/CWK Gleerup, 1975), 17–20 and Susan Stewart, *Poetry and the Fate of the Senses* (Chicago: University of Chicago Press, 2002), 20–21, 164, 337 n. 38, and 362 n. 49.

4. See Leo Spitzer, "Milieu and Ambiance," in *Essays in Historical Semantics* (New York: S. F. Vanni, 1948), 203–05. For a treatment of Newton's impact on eighteenth-century descriptive poetry, see Marjorie Hope Nicolson, *Newton Demands the Muse: Newton's Opticks and the Eighteenth-Century Poets* (Princeton: Princeton University Press, 1946).

5. Niklas Luhmann, *Art as a Social System*, trans. Eva M. Knodt (Stanford: Stanford University Press, 2000), 111, 104.

6. Samuel Weber, *Mass Mediauras: Form, Technics, Media*, ed. Alan Cholodenko (Stanford: Stanford University Press, 1996), 2–3.

7. Bacon, *Advancement of Learning*, 119–20.

8. Aristotle, *On Interpretation*, 1.1–6 (16a), in *The Categories, On Interpretation, Prior Analytics*, trans. Harold P. Cooke and Hugh Tredennick (Cambridge, MA: Harvard University Press/Loeb Classical Library, 1996).

9. George Snel[l], *The Right Teaching of Useful Knowledge, to fit Scholars for some honest Profession* . . . (London: Printed for W. Dugard, 1649), 208.

10. See Low, *Georgic Revolution*, especially chapter 4; Ralph Cohen, "Innovation and Variation: Literary Change and Georgic Poetry," and the two essays by

Alastair Fowler cited in earlier notes: "The Beginnings of English Georgic," in *Renaissance Genres*, eds. Lewalski, and "Georgic and Pastoral," in *Culture and Cultivation*, eds. Leslie and Raylor. For Cohen, literary change is more gradual than for Low, and the new energy of georgic does not so much displace pastoral and epic as insinuate into both a greater didacticism and unembarrassed celebration of what Virgil ambivalently called *labor improbus*, or unremitting labor. I think that Low is right to say that "in this task [of dispelling anti-georgic prejudices] the New Scientists helped Virgil and Virgil helped the new Scientists," but, as I explain below, my account of this mutually advantageous choreography is quite different from Low's largely thematic, though usefully comprehensive survey.

The *Georgics* had been available in English since 1589, when they were translated by "A. F." (identified by the Huntington Library as A. Fleming): *The Georgicks of Publius Virgilius Maro, Otherwise called his Italian Husbandrie . . . Grammaticallie translated into English meter in so plaine and familiar sort, as a learner may be taught thereby to his profit and contentment* (London, 1589). Seventeenth-century translations before Dryden's included Thomas May, *Virgil's Georgicks, Englished by Tho: May, Esqr.* (London: Printed for Thomas Walkley, 1628) and John Ogilby's *The Works of Publius Vergilius Maro*, issued by a number of printers, with ever more elaborate illustrations or "sculpture," in 1649, 1650, 1654, 1665, 1668, and 1684. Although there are a number of sixteenth-century works on husbandry – notably Thomas Tusser's *A Hundreth Good Pointes of Husbandrie* (1557), later expanded to *Five Hundreth Good Pointes* (1573) – these seem to have been largely indigenous growths in which, as in Tusser, the classical influence is not significant. For sixteenth-century and earlier examples of georgic and, more generally, instructional verse see L. P. Wilkinson, *The Georgics of Virgil: a Critical Survey* (Cambridge: Cambridge University Press, 1969), 270–96 and Durling, *The Georgic Tradition in English Poetry*, especially 3–16.

11. John Dryden, "Defence of Essay of Dramatic Poesy," in *John Dryden: Selected Criticism*, eds. James Kinsley and George Parfitt (Oxford: Clarendon Press, 1970), 87.

12. Crawford, *Poetry, Enclosure, and the Vernacular Landscape*, 97. Since Crawford's treatment of georgic is limited to instances of the genre and sustained formal imitations, she argues for its "loss of authority" after 1767, the date of Richard Jago's *Edge Hill*, so that she can make the case – to my mind rather too schematically – for the emergence of a fascination for enclosed spaces (e.g., the kitchen garden) and confined forms (sonnets and short lyrics) at the end of the century.

13. See Introduction, note 29.

14. Robert Hooke, *Micrographia: or some Physiological Descriptions of Minute Bodies Made by Magnifying Glasses with Observations and Inquiries thereupon* (London: Printed by Jo. Martyn and Ja. Allestry, 1665), "Preface," a3^a–b1^a. Available as a facsimile edition (Lincolnwood, IL: Science Heritage, 1987).

15. Ibid., b4^b–c1^a.

16. Bolter and Grusin, *Remediation*, 53–62.
17. The phrase originates in Hans Blumenberg, *Die Lesbarkeit der Welt*, 2nd edn. (Frankfurt am Main: Suhrkamp, 1983), 68.
18. Hooke, *Micrographia*, "Preface," d3ª-d4ᵇ.
19. Fuller accounts include: R. F. Jones, *Ancients and Moderns: a Study in the Rise of the Scientific Movement in Seventeenth-Century England* (Saint Louis: Washington University Studies, 1961); George Williamson, *The Senecan Amble: a Study in Prose Form from Bacon to Collier* (Chicago: University of Chicago Press, 1951); Ian Hacking, *The Emergence of Probability: a Philosophical Study of Early Ideas About Probability, Induction and Statistical Inference* (Cambridge: Cambridge University Press, 1975); Murray Cohen, *Sensible Words: Linguistic Practice in England, 1640–1785* (Baltimore: Johns Hopkins University Press, 1977); Hans Aarsleff, *From Locke to Saussure: Essays on the Study of Language and Intellectual History* (Minneapolis: University of Minnesota Press, 1982), 3–41 and 225–77; Richard W. F. Kroll, *The Material Word: Literate Culture in the Restoration and Early Eighteenth Century* (Baltimore: Johns Hopkins University Press, 1991); Robert Markley, *Fallen Languages: Crises in Representation in Newtonian England, 1660–1740* (Ithaca: Cornell University Press, 1993); and Mary Poovey, *The History of the Modern Fact: Problems of Knowledge in the Sciences of Wealth and Society* (Chicago: University of Chicago Press, 1998), 97–104. Nancy Armstrong and Leonard Tennenhouse have studied the importance of history-writing that accompanied the new science and did much to endorse a new model of intellectual labor (*The Imaginary Puritan: Literature, Intellectual Labor, and the Origins of Personal Life* [Berkeley and Los Angeles: University of California Press, 1992], especially chapter 4).
20. Thomas Sprat, *History of the Royal Society*, eds. Jackson I. Cope and Harold Whitmore Jones (Saint Louis, MD: Washington University Studies, 1958), 113 and (for Cowley's Ode), B2ª. "Neutrality and transparency" are the adjectives provided by John Bender and David Wellbery, in their introduction to *The Ends of Rhetoric: History, Theory, Practice* (Stanford: Stanford University Press, 1990), 13; see also "Rhetoricality," 3–39. G. A. Starr offers an important warning, arguing that literary scholars too often generalize from Sprat's claims, rather than attending to the prose style used by the virtuosi themselves. See "Defoe's Prose Style: 1. The Language of Interpretation," *Modern Philology* 71 (1974): 277–94.
21. John Webster, *Academiarum Examen, Or the Examination of Academies. . . .* (London, 1654), 27, 24. The restoration of Babel is a frequent trope; see for instance the prefatory poem attributed to Joseph Waite that prefixes Cave Beck's *The Universal Character* (London: Tho. Maxey, 1757).
22. John Wilkins, *An Essay Towards a Real Character and Philosophical Language* (London: Sa. Gellibrand and Jo. Martyn, 1668), "The Epistle Dedicatory," a2ᵇ, b1ª.

In an amusingly earnest section of his *Essay*, Wilkins decides to chart the rooming assignments of Noah's ark in order to prove that (within the cubits prescribed by Genesis) two of each of the forty species might indeed fit on that vessel – with room to spare for the collection of the dung and the health of Noah's family. What becomes quite clear in the course of this excursus on interior design is that anything outside those forty categories of all "notions and things" in Wilkins's philosophy – like anything that might in fact not fit on the ark – are outside of consideration.

23. The John Wilkins of the *Essay* is thus not far from the John Wilkins who in 1641 wrote *Mercury, or the Secret and Swift Messenger*, an exhaustive handbook on the forms and strategies of occluded, or coded, representations (London: Printed by J. Norton, for John Maynard and Timothy Wilkins, 1641). For discussions of *Mercury* in relation to the *Essay* of Wilkins's later life, see Hacking, *Emergence of Probability*, 81 and Kroll, *Material Word*, 187–94 and 205–11.

24. Timothy J. Reiss, *The Discourse of Modernism* (Ithaca: Cornell University Press, 1982), 36. Kroll takes a sharply different view from both Reiss and Bender and Wellbery: "The palpable quality of words – commonly illustrated by metaphors of writing and printing, a consciousness of typography, and an interest in hieroglyphics – approximates something of the palpable quality of the discourse of manners executed in three-dimensional social spaces. Words appear as constituent elements of a mode of verbal behavior and are not imagined as readily disposable utilitarian vehicles of knowledge" (*Material Word*, 4). It will be obvious that behind all of these scholars (Aarsleff, Cohen, Kroll, Markley, Reiss, Bender and Wellbery) looms the large and protean example of Michel Foucault's *The Order of Things: an Archaeology of the Human Sciences*, trans. Alan Sheridan Smith (London: Tavistock Publications, 1970). What makes Foucault both oddly co-optable and refutable by all of these critics is that *The Order of Things* tends to emphasize – and sometimes to conflate – *both* the artificiality *and* the transparency of later seventeenth-century and eighteenth-century language, whereas for Aarsleff et al., "artificiality," or what I would prefer to call a recognition of linguistic *labor*, more or less negates the fiction of "transparency."

25. Bolter and Grusin, *Remediation*, 5–6. Earlier examples for Bolter and Grusin of the double logic of remediation would include the Dutch "art of describing" explored by Svetlana Alpers: the mirrors, windows, paintings within paintings, letters, maps, and so on absorbed and captured within the medium of oil (see Svetlana Alpers, *The Art of Describing: Dutch Art in the Seventeenth Century* [Chicago: University of Chicago Press, 1983]; Bolter and Grusin, *Remediation*, 26–27).

26. Bacon, *Advancement*, 134–35.

27. "Treasury of eloquence" is Bacon's phrase in the "Preparation toward a Natural and Experimental History" of the *Novum Organum* (trans. and eds. Peter Urbach and John Gibson [Chicago: Open Court, 1994], 302). Mary Poovey has recently argued that Bacon's difficulty drawing an absolute distinction between his own notion of experience and experiment (which sought to emphasize the evidence provided by instrumentally produced "singular instances") from the received Aristotelian sense of experience (as a law of nature) led to the strong

emphasis on the difference of his style from the more traditional accounts (*History of the Modern Fact*, 97–104).

28. I am still following the Loeb prose translation here. But early English translations of the *Georgics* tend to draw out this dissonance more than modern ones. One of the earliest of such translations, and one that Bacon may well have seen, is the rendition of A. F[leming]: "For ne doubtfull am in mind / How great a thing it is t'advance or hoist aloft with word, / These matters, and give unto small things this honor due" (*The Georgicks of Publius Virgilius Maro*, n.p.).

29. Cf. Virgil, *Georgics*, ed. Richard F. Thomas, 2 vols. (Cambridge: Cambridge University Press, 1988) 3.294 n.

30. De Bruyn, "From Virgilian Georgic to Agricultural Science," 47–67.

31. Thomas, *Reading Virgil and his Texts*, 142–72. This stylization or, to use the terms of Russian Formalism, foregrounding of device, although well understood by most eighteenth-century commentators at least from Addison on, did not prevent the irony of Adam Smith's indirect use of it to justify a rhetorical practice of "perspicuity": on Smith, and *The Wealth of Nations* in particular, see Kurt Heinzelman, "The Last Georgic," 172–94.

32. The *Georgics* are, in William Empson's terms, literature "'about' but not 'by' or 'for' the people." As such, they would fall under his very capacious category of pastoral in *Some Versions of Pastoral* (New York: New Directions, 1974); quotation from page 6.

33. The first quotation is from Kurt Heinzelman, "Roman Georgic in a Georgian Age," 192; the second is from Heinzelman's "The Last Georgic," 192.

34. For Joseph Farrell's work on the subject, see his *Vergil's* Georgics *and the Traditions of Ancient Epic: the Art of Allusion in Literary History* (New York: Oxford University Press, 1991).

35. Dryden, "The Preface" to *Sylvae: or the Second Part of Poetical Miscellanies* (London: Jacob Tonson, 1685), A5ᵃ.

36. Thomas, *Reading Virgil*, 144–45 n. 12, 159.

37. Robert Wolseley, "Preface" to *Valentinian* (1685), in David Farley-Hills, ed., *Rochester: the Critical Heritage* (New York: Barnes and Noble, 1972), 148. I thank James Turner for calling this fascinating text to my attention.

38. Henry Power, *Experimental Philosophy, in Three Books, Containing New Experiments Microscopical, Mercurial, Magnetical* (London: T. Roycroft, for John Martin and James Allestry, 1664), B2ᵇ–B3ᵃ. For a good account of the attractions offered by the minute to poets during the first three-quarters of the seventeenth century – the intricate wit of attempting *multum in parvo* or "much in little" – see Kitty W. Scoular, *Natural Magic: Studies in the Presentation of Nature in English Poetry from Spenser to Marvell* (Oxford: Clarendon Press, 1965), 81–117. The examples chosen by Scoular emphasize the responses of wonder and celebratory wit; the horror heralded by the microscopic eye, which I discuss below, seems to me to point to a later, second stage of artistic reception.

39. On dating, see William H. Youngren, "Addison and the Birth of Eighteenth-Century Aesthetics," *Modern Philology* 79 (1982): 269.

40. I use the following edition of each of these texts: Addison's essay is included in *The Works of Virgil in English*, eds. William Frost and Vincent A. Dearing, vol. 5 of *Works of John Dryden*, eds. Edward Niles Hooker and H. T. Swedenberg, Jr. (Berkeley and Los Angeles: University of California Press, 1987), 145–53. For Trapp, see the facsimile edition reprinted in Joseph Trapp, *Lectures on Poetry* (Hildesheim: Georg Olms Verlag, 1969), 187–201. Tickell's *De Poesi Didactica* is available in Richard E. Tickell, *Thomas Tickell and the Eighteenth-Century Poets* (London: Constable and Co., 1931), 198–209.

41. On the *Georgics* as an index of the gradual separation, during the eighteenth century, between "literature" and "science," see De Bruyn, "From Virgilian Georgic to Agricultural Science," 47–67. De Bruyn is interested in the other half of this story of division: agricultural and scientific authors appeal to the literary prestige of the *Georgics* in order to give their writing a pedigree. While I, too, see the gradual division, separating the scientific or "technical" from the "poetical" occurring during the eighteenth century, I would observe that De Bruyn's (and others') argument cuts both ways: the *Georgics*, with their appeal to human *tekhnē*, their bookish display of rhetorical technique, by their hybrid nature also resist such separations even as they become the occasion for attempting them.

42. Addison, "Essay," 5:150–51.

43. Tickell, *De Poesi Didactica*, 201.

44. Quoted in Chalker, *English Georgic*, 59.

45. John Armstrong, *The Art of Preserving Health, to which is prefixed a critical essay on the poem by J. Aikin, M.D.* (London: T. Cadell, Jun. and W. Davies, 1795), 3–4.

46. Trapp, "Of Didactic or Preceptive Poetry," in *Lectures on Poetry*, 188. Sir Philip Sidney, *An Apology for Poetry*, ed. Geoffrey Shepherd (London: Thomas Nelson and Sons, 1967), 102.

47. Barbara M. Stafford, *Artful Science: Enlightenment Entertainment and the Eclipse of Visual Education* (Cambridge, MA: MIT Press, 1994), 226. See also Stephen Copley, "The Fine Arts in Eighteenth-Century Polite Culture," in *Painting and Politics of Culture: New Essays on British Art*, ed. John Barrell (New York: Oxford University Press, 1992), 23–24.

48. Trapp, "Of Didactic or Preceptive Poetry," 193.

49. Addison, "Essay," 5:147.

50. See, for example, Heinzelman, "Roman Georgic," 198, 212–13 n. 49 and R. Cohen, "Innovation and Variation," 5, 19.

51. Addison, "Essay," 5:147–48.

52. McLuhan, *Understanding Media*, 23.

53. Addison, "Essay," 5:149.

54. For a well-documented argument establishing the extent to which Addison's role as "Mr. Spectator" was modeled on the practice and tools of Restoration virtuosi like Hooke, see Joanna Picciotto, "Optical Instruments and the Eighteenth-Century Observer," *Studies in Eighteenth-Century Culture* 29 (2000): 123–53. Picciotto offers a more extended view of the same genealogy in

her dissertation, "Literary and Scientific Experimentalism in Seventeenth- and Eighteenth-Century England" (Ph.D. diss., University of California, Berkeley, 2000).

55. Joseph Addison and Sir Richard Steele, *The Spectator*, ed. Donald F. Bond, 5 vols. (Oxford: Clarendon Press, 1965), 3:535–82.

56. Ibid., 3:537.

57. Ibid., 3:559–60.

58. Ibid., 3:562, emphases added.

59. Ibid., 3:569.

60. Ibid., 3:566. Shaun Irlam, *Elations: the Poetics of Enthusiasm in Eighteenth-Century Britain* (Stanford: Stanford University Press, 1999), 88–89.

61. Addison and Steele, *Spectator*, 3:567.

62. In this instance, then, I disagree with Youngren's perceptive essay, which considers Addison's discussion of the by-ways by which precept – or dung – enters the mind an aberration in an essay otherwise "juvenile, superficial, uninstructive" (Johnson's verdict, cited by Youngren) and only interesting as an augury of the more mature author of *The Spectator* ("Birth of Eighteenth-Century Aesthetics," 272–73).

63. On this point, see Neil Saccamano, "The Sublime Force of Words in Addison's 'Pleasures'," *ELH* 58 (1991): 83–106, especially 91.

64. Addison and Steele, *Spectator*, 3:559–60.

65. Ibid., 3:560. Addison, "Essay," 5:149.

66. Ibid., 3:559.

67. Kittler, *Gramophone, Film, Typewriter*, 6. This book is the sequel to Kittler's *Discourse Networks 1800/1900* (Stanford: Stanford University Press, 1990), whose first part explores the steps by which silent reading became the norm, bypassing the vocal organs. In a discussion of Walter Scott's *Lay of the Last Minstrel*, Celeste Langan has contested Kittler's claim in an argument that I have found most helpful; she concludes that "once print has achieved its would-be transparency . . . the storage system of 'oral literature' would seem to be obsolete. But precisely for that reason, it becomes available as the ostensible content of the broadcast medium of print . . . In that poem, the medium of print becomes recognizable *as* a medium (contra Kittler), by its attempt to 'deliver' audiovisual information" ("Understanding Media in 1805," 70). To Langan's analysis of Scott I would want to add, given the context of my argument about earlier georgic, the original definition of "to broadcast": "to scatter (seed) abroad with the hand." Long before the expression was taken over by radio at the beginning of the twentieth century, the action was georgic at root. For "broadcasting," see John Durham Peters, *Speaking into the Air*, 34–35, 207–11.

68. Heinzelman, "Roman Georgic," 198.

69. Addison and Steele, *Spectator*, 3:538.

70. For Heinzelman's work on economics and rhetoric, including an analysis of Adam Smith's *The Wealth of Nations* as a georgic, see "The Last Georgic," 173–75 and "Economics, Rhetoric, and the Scene of Instruction," 349–71.

2 THE MICROSCOPIC EYE AND THE NOISE OF HISTORY IN THOMSON'S *THE SEASONS*

1. John Barrell, *Dark Side of the Landscape*; for his discussion of Thomson, see 37–41. His larger argument is pursued over a series of studies, including *The Idea of Landscape, English Literature in History*, and *The Birth of Pandora*. For the ideological constraints on representation, see also Ann Bermingham's *Landscape and Ideology: the English Rustic Tradition, 1740–1860* (Berkeley and Los Angeles: University of California Press, 1986). For a detailed account of the rhythms of agriculture and Thomson's mixed attentiveness to them (and some helpful comparisons between Thomson and the working class poets, Stephen Duck and Mary Collier), see John Goodridge, *Rural Life in Eighteenth-Century English Poetry* (Cambridge: Cambridge University Press, 1995).

2. James Thomson, *The Seasons*, ed. James Sambrook (Oxford: Clarendon, 1981); further references in text and identified by season (*Sp., Su.*, etc.) and line(s).

3. Tim Fulford, *Landscape, Liberty, and Authority: Poetry, Criticism, and Politics from Thomson to Wordsworth* (Cambridge: Cambridge University Press, 1996), 18–19, and 18–38 for Fulford's argument about Thomson more generally.

4. John Murdoch, "The Landscape of Labor: Transformations of the Georgic," 192.

5. For Wordsworth's comment, which offers something of a digest of much eighteenth-century commentary on Thomson, see "Essay, Supplementary to the Preface," *The Prose Works of William Wordsworth*, eds. W. J. B. Owen and Jane Worthington Smyser, 3 vols. (Oxford: Clarendon Press, 1974), 3:74.

6. Adam Smith, "The History of Astronomy," in *Essays on Philosophical Subjects*, eds. W. P. D. Wightman and J. C. Bryce (Oxford: Clarendon Press, 1980), 45. For a helpful account of Smith's interest in connecting principles, which derives from his interest in stoicism, see Christopher Herbert, *Culture and Anomie: Ethnographic Imagination in the Nineteenth Century* (Chicago: University of Chicago Press, 1991), 79–105.

7. Adam Smith, *An Inquiry into the Nature and Causes of the Wealth of Nations*, eds. R. H. Campbell and A. S. Skinner, 2 vols. (Oxford: Clarendon Press, 1976), 1:21–22. In addition to his *English Literature in History*, this paragraph's discussion of Barrell's argument draws on two further essays by Barrell: "The Public Prospect and the Private View: the Politics of Taste in Eighteenth-Century Britain" and "Visualising the Division of Labour: William Pyne's *Microcosm*." Both appear in *The Birth of Pandora* (41–62 and 89–118).

8. Joseph Warton, *An Essay on the Genius and Writings of Pope*, 2nd edn., 2 vols. (London: R. and J. Dodsley, 1762), 1:47. The comment about Thomson's microscopic vision comes from James Thomson, *The Seasons*, with "A Critical Essay on The Seasons" by Robert Heron (Perth, 1793) and is quoted, along with Warton and others, in Patricia Meyer Spacks's fine account of the patterning of meaning in *The Seasons*. See her *The Poetry of Vision: Five Eighteenth-Century Poets* (Cambridge, MA: Harvard University Press, 1967), 14–15.

9. On the genealogy, see Picciotto, "Optical Instruments and the Eighteenth-Century Observer," 123–53.

10. Bruce Robbins, "The Sweatshop Sublime," *PMLA* 117 (2002): 84–97.

11. On Thomson's Newtonianism, including his time at Watts, and for his poem to Newton, see *Liberty, The Castle of Indolence, and other Poems*, ed. James Sambrook (Oxford: Clarendon Press, 1986), 1–14.

12. Georg Lukács, *History and Class Consciousness: Studies in Marxist Dialectics*, trans. Rodney Livingstone (Cambridge, MA: The MIT Press, 1972), 157, emphasis added.

13. Fredric Jameson, *Political Unconscious*, 287.

14. Some publication history: "Winter," the earliest composed of the *Seasons*, went through five editions in its first year, 1726, and was reissued as a separate poem in 1728, 1730, and 1734. "Summer," "Spring," and "Autumn" went through more than eleven editions in the first years of their publications. The collected *Seasons* first appeared in 1730 and went into three editions that year. It was reprinted over forty-eight times before 1800, not counting the twenty-two editions of Thomson's works that included it in the same period. Four more editions in both 1802 and 1803, then five in 1805, followed by forty-four reprintings between 1800 and 1820, show the poem's renewed appeal during the years most of the Romantic poets wrote their major work. These are minimal figures for England only; foreign translations and publications in English-speaking countries (particularly America) add to the number. See the checklist provided by Ralph Cohen, in *The Art of Discrimination: Thomson's* The Seasons *and the Language of Criticism* (Berkeley and Los Angeles: University of California Press, 1964), 472–507; Cohen's compendious study also discusses the illustration history and record of adaptations of the poem.

15. For Hazlitt's comment, see *The Complete Works of William Hazlitt*, ed. P. P. Howe, 21 vols. (New York: AMS Press, 1967), 5: 87–88. For the 1842 review and helpful synopses of less obvious (as well as better known) texts in Thomson reception history, see Hilbert H. Campbell, *James Thomson (1700–1748): an Annotated Bibliography of Selected Editions and the Important Criticism* (New York: Garland Publishing, 1976), 42. For Altick's conclusions, see Richard Daniel Altick, *The English Common Reader: a Social History of the Mass Reading Public 1800–1900* (Chicago: University of Chicago Press, 1957), 252–57.

16. See John Barrell and Harriet Guest, "On the Use of Contradiction: Economics and Morality in the Eighteenth-Century Long Poem," in *The New Eighteenth Century: Theory, Politics, English Literature*, eds. Felicity Nussbaum and Laura Brown (New York: Methuen, 1987), 123. For a sensitive analysis of style that treats the paradoxes contained by what he calls Thomson's "urbane sublime," see Marshall Brown, *Preromanticism* (Stanford: Stanford University Press, 1991), 29–34.

17. Although the *Opticks* was not published until 1704, the year of Hooke's death, many of Newton's optical theories were known to his students at Cambridge from his lectures in the late 1660s, and to the Royal Society from a 1672 letter. In turn, Newton's "aetherial medium" in the *Opticks* and the *Principia* is itself a

development of Henry Power's 1664 use of the same phrase: the "greatest part of the world" is the "aetherial medium" (*Experimental Philosophy*, "Preface," b4ᵃ). On the reception of Newton's *Opticks* in specialized and more popular circles, see Marjorie Hope Nicolson, *Newton Demands the Muse: Newton's Opticks and the Eighteenth-Century Poets* (Princeton: Princeton University Press, 1946), chapter 1.

18. "Naming power" is Heidegger's well-known phrase in "The Age of the World Picture" (in *The Question Concerning Technology and Other Papers*, trans. William Lovitt [New York: Harper and Row, 1977], 132), but I use it also to designate the voracious appetite for naming all natural objects with maximum efficiency in Wilkins's and others' universal language schemes.

19. Kurt Heinzelman ("The Last Georgic," 171–94) makes the case for the *Georgics* as an unspoken influence on the utilitarian model of communication proposed and disseminated in Adam Smith's *Lectures on Rhetoric and Belles-Lettres*, ed. John M. Lothian (London: Thomas Nelson and Sons, Ltd., 1963), which takes "perspicuity" as its keyword, as well as on Smith's *Wealth of Nations*.

20. Power, *Experimental Philosophy*, B3ᵇ–B4ᵃ.

21. Hooke, "Discourse concerning Telescopes and Microscopes" (written in 1692), published in *Philosophical Experiments and Observations*, ed. William Derham (1726; reprint, London: Cass, 1967), 261. For a good account of the decline of the fortunes of the microscope, see Catherine Wilson, *The Invisible World: Early Modern Philosophy and the Invention of the Microscope* (Princeton: Princeton University Press, 1995), chapters 6 and 7.

22. [Henry] Baker, *The Microscope Made Easy* (London: R. Dodsley, 1742). In addition to Wilson's work, see Marjorie Hope Nicolson, *The Microscope and English Imagination* (Northampton, MA: Smith College, 1935) for a detailed study of the popularization of the microscopic in the later seventeenth and eighteenth centuries. Baker himself discusses the diminishing expense of the microscope, which made it available to the "publick" (i.e., as middle-class entertainment) in *The Microscope Made Easy*, ii–iii.

23. See Margaret Cavendish, Duchess of Newcastle, *Observations upon Experimental Philosophy*, ed. Eileen O'Neill (Cambridge: Cambridge University Press, 2001), 50.

24. Ibid., 51–52.

25. John Locke, *An Essay Concerning Human Understanding*, ed., Peter H. Nidditch (Oxford: Clarendon Press, 1975), 2.23.12.

26. Power, *Experimental Philosophy*, "Preface," B1ᵃ.

27. George Berkeley, "An Essay Toward a New Theory of Vision," in *The Works of George Berkeley, D.D.*, ed. Alexander Campbell Fraser, 4 vols. (Oxford: Clarendon Press, 1871), 1:75.

28. What Berkeley casually alludes to as "a certain observable connection betwixt the divers perceptions of sight and touch" (1:75) has a complex history. Although Descartes's privileging of sight as the "noblest of the senses" goes back to the long tradition of the hierarchy of senses, charted by Louise Vinge, Aristotle, while giving the same priority to sight, also suggests that seeing and

tasting are forms of touch, and then, at the end of *De Anima* widens the importance of touch as the only sense than an animal cannot live without. See Vinge, *The Five Senses*, 17–20. As Susan Stewart and David Summers have discussed, there is also a tradition that valorizes the greater immediacy of touch over the distance of visual perception (see Stewart, *Poetry and the Fate of the Senses*, 171 and chapter 4, more generally; for Summers, see *The Judgment of Sense: Renaissance Naturalism and the Rise of Aesthetics* [Cambridge: Cambridge University Press, 1987], 103–04, 326–27).

29. See *An Essay on Man: Epistle I* (189–206) in *The Poems of Alexander Pope*, ed. John Butt (New Haven: Yale University Press, 1963). The passage is worth citing here:

> Why has not Man a microscopic eye?
> For this plain reason, Man is not a Fly.
> Say what the use, were finer optics giv'n,
> T'inspect a mite, not comprehend the heav'n?
> Or touch, if tremblingly alive all o'er,
> To smart and agonize at ev'ry pore?
> Or quick effluvia darting thro' the brain,
> Die of a rose in aromatic pain?
> If nature thunder'd in his op'ning ears,
> And stunn'd him with the music of the spheres,
> How would he wish that Heav'n had left him still
> The whisp'ring Zephyr, and the purling rill? (1.193–204)

30. Bentley's and other Boyle lectures are collected in Sampson Letsome and John Nicoll, eds., *A Defence of Natural and Revealed Religion: Being a Collection of the Sermons Preached at the Lecture founded by the Honourable Robert Boyle, Esq. (From the Year 1691 to the Year 1732)* (London: D. Midwinter et al., 1739), H1ª.

31. John Milton, *Paradise Lost*, 6.350–51, in *John Milton: Complete Poems and Major Prose*, ed. Merritt Y. Hughes (Indianapolis: Bobbs-Merrill, 1957).

32. Wilson does note that post-Renaissance "military and mathematical mastery of new territory threatened as well as enhanced confidence" (*Invisible World*, 180). For accounts of the specific seventeenth-century senses of experience and the relation of experience (*experientia*) to experiment (*experimenta*), see, for example, Peter Robert Dear, *Discipline and Experience: the Mathematical Way in the Scientific Revolution* (Chicago: University of Chicago Press, 1995); Lorraine Daston, *Classical Probability in the Enlightenment* (Princeton: Princeton University Press, 1988); and Daston, "Baconian Facts, Academic Civility, and the Prehistory of Objectivity," *Annals of Scholarship* 8 (1991): 337–64.

33. Locke, *Essay*, 2.11.17. Jonathan Crary, *Techniques of the Observer: on Vision and Modernity in the Nineteenth Century* (Cambridge, MA: MIT Press, 1990), 58–66. Other accounts of the camera obscura model of the mind that I have found helpful include Sarah Kofman, *Camera Obscura: of Ideology*, trans. Will Straw (Ithaca: Cornell University Press, 1999) and Martin Jay, *Downcast*

Eyes: the Denigration of Vision in Twentieth-Century French Thought (Berkeley and Los Angeles: University of California Press, 1993), particularly chapters 1 and 2.

34. See note 29 above. There are many related examples, including Marvell's destabilizing of the viewer's identity from shifting perspectives, metamorphoses and anamorphoses of the landscape. For a discussion of Marvell's responsiveness to the new optical technology, characteristically combined with older conventions exalting the sight over other senses, see Donald Friedman, "Sight and Insight in Marvell's Poetry," *Approaches to Marvell: the York Tercentenary Lectures*, ed. C. A. Patrides (Boston MA: Routledge and Kegan Paul, 1978), 306–30. For a reading of the tricky optics of "Upon Appleton House," see James Turner, *Politics of Landscape*, 78. On vertigo more generally, see Stewart, *Poetry and the Fate of the Senses*, 178–95.

35. Locke, *Essay*, 2.1.6.

36. Buck-Morss traces the development of ideas about the human sensorium, as well as the detrimental separation between natural science (including physiology of the brain) and philosophy of mind, in "Aesthetics and Anaesthetics: Walter Benjamin's Artwork Essay Reconsidered," *October* 62 (1992): 3–41; see especially 11–13. Jerome McGann is also interested in complicating the subject–object divide of classical philosophy in his treatment of the poetry of sensibility in relation to its Lockean background (see *The Poetics of Sensibility: a Revolution in Literary Style* [Oxford: Clarendon Press, 1996], especially 13–18).

37. This passage from Kepler's *Ad Vitellionem Paralipomena* (1604) is cited – at greater length – by A. C. Crombie, "The Mechanistic Hypothesis and the Scientific Study of Vision: Some Optical Ideas as a Background to the Invention of the Microscope," in *Historical Aspects of Microscopy* (Cambridge: Heffer, for the Royal Microscopical Society, 1967), 55.

38. Locke, *Essay*, 2.9.8.

39. Michel Foucault, *The Birth of the Clinic: an Archaeology of Medical Perception*, trans. A. M. Sheridan (New York: Pantheon, 1973), 65. Discussions of the Molyneux problem that I have found useful include Jay, *Downcast Eyes*, Michael J. Morgan, *Molyneux's Question: Vision, Touch, and the Philosophy of Perception* (Cambridge: Cambridge University Press, 1977), William R. Paulson, *Enlightenment, Romanticism, and the Blind in France* (Princeton: Princeton University Press, 1987), and Martha Brandt Bolton, "The Real Molyneux Question and the Basis of Locke's Answer," in *Locke's Philosophy: Content and Context*, ed. G. A. J. Rogers (Oxford: Clarendon Press, 1994), 75–100. For an account of the modern updates – and "remediation" – of the Molyneux problem in Hollywood film of the 1990s (e.g., *At First Sight*, the film version of an Oliver Sacks story), see Naomi Schor, "Blindness as Metaphor," *differences: A Journal of Feminist Cultural Studies* 11 (1999): 76–105, especially 96–101. Book III of Richard Jago's late formal imitation of Virgil's *Georgics*, the "mining" georgic *Edge Hill* (1767), offers a sentimentalized version of the story as an inset vignette.

40. Alenka Zupančič, "Philosophers' Blind Man's Buff," in *Voice and Gaze as Love Objects*, eds. Renata Salecl and Slavoj Žižek (Durham: Duke University Press, 1996), 40.
41. For an elaboration of the two-step process and the ways in which Locke's influential form of conceptualism arose from linguistic considerations (were we to base our names on every particular idea that arises from each particular thing, then names would be endless), see William H. Youngren, "Conceptualism and Neo-Classic Generality," *ELH* 47 (1980): 705–74.
42. Locke, *Essay*, 3.2.7, 3.2.2; compare 3.9.6.
43. Zupančič, "Philosophers' Blind Man's Buff," 41.
44. Murray Cohen helpfully negotiates some of the continuities and shifts between Locke's late-century and other mid-century linguistics (*Sensible Words*, chapter 1, especially 38–42). For a brief but useful discussion of the way that "communication breakdown looms large in Locke's scenario," see John Durham Peters, *Speaking into the Air*, 84.
45. John Rogers, *The Matter of Revolution: Science, Poetry, and Politics in the Age of Milton* (Ithaca: Cornell University Press, 1996), 2. Rogers is following Otto Mayr's exploration of these analogical structures in *Authority, Liberty, and Automatic Machinery in Early Modern Europe* (Baltimore, MD: Johns Hopkins University Press, 1986).
46. To take on this subject directly would have brought Locke to a more thorough exploration of the controversial suggestion (redolent of atheism to divines like Bentley) that thinking is at root a material process. This suggestion is in fact included in the Fourth Book of the *Essay*, where Locke proposes that it is conceivable that "God can, if he chooses, superadd to matter a faculty of thinking," but then gingerly dropped, and assigned to the domain of revelation rather than experiential knowledge (4.3.6). For an account of the physiology of thought and action in Locke and in the eighteenth century more generally, see John W. Yolton, *Thinking Matter: Materialism in Eighteenth-Century Britain* (Minneapolis: University of Minnesota Press, 1983), chapter 8.
47. Locke, *Essay*, 2.3.1.
48. One finds a version of the presence room, or at least the problem of conveyance between the eye and the "seat of Sense within" in Richard Blackmore's physico-theological poem, *The Creation* (London, 1715):

> Since all Perception in the Brain is made,
> (Tho' where and how was never yet display'd)
> And since so great a distance lies between
> The Eye-ball, and the Seat of Sense within,
> While in the Eye th'arrested Object stays,
> Tell, what th'Idea to the Brain conveys?
> (7.134–39; quoted by Nicolson, *Newton Demands the Muse*, 103)

49. Cf. Zupančič, "Philosophers' Blind Man's Buff," 38–39.
50. Locke's own concern not only about the consistency and consensual basis of naming but also about the importance of thinking and speaking "in train," on

the "Connexion, Restriction, Distinction, Opposition, Emphasis [a man] gives to each respective part of his Discourse" offers an implicit acknowledgment of this shift (*Essay*, 3.7.2). What Murray Cohen has called "the growing interest in the syntactical as opposed to the lexical functions of language" – that is, in the relation of parts of speech rather than in isolated markers – is, if anything, even more apparent in Locke's contemporaries and can be understood as an attempt to restore order in the presence room of collective and individual human understanding (*Sensible Words*, 25). One could cite many examples, as Cohen does, but one, fairly typical, contemporary handbook makes the point quite directly, if comically, by literalizing Locke's metaphor. In Samuel Shaw's *Words Made Visible, or Grammar and Rhetorick Accommodated to the Lives and Manners of Men*, the various parts of speech (Lord Verbum; Ralph Pone and Jeffrey Prae – two prepositions – and so on) present their grievances against the others' usurpations to the Lords Commissioners of the court of King Syntaxis (duly named Dico, Audio, Lego, and Amo – I Say, I Hear, I Read, I Love), who restore the order, or syntax, of speech and writing. See Samuel Shaw, *Words Made Visible, or Grammar and Rhetorick Accommodated to the Lives and Manners of Men* (London: B. G. for Daniel Major, 1679).

51. All quotations from Addison and Steele, *The Spectator*, ed., Donald F. Bond.
52. Blumenberg, *Die Lesbarkeit der Welt*, 68. Also quoted in Wilson, *Invisible World*, 180.
53. Addison, "Essay on the Georgics," in Dryden, *Works*, 5:147–48. See also my discussion in chapter 1 above.
54. Addison and Steele, *Spectator*, 3:538.
55. Ibid., 3:569.
56. Ibid., 3:559.
57. Ibid., 3:575.
58. Ibid., 4:346.
59. Ibid., 3:576.
60. Wilson, *Invisible World*, 191.
61. For some hair-raising examples of the way that the Great Chain of Being could be used as an apology for social and economic inequity, see Arthur O. Lovejoy, *The Great Chain of Being: a Study of the History of an Idea* (Cambridge, MA: Harvard University Press, 1957), 205–07.
62. Barrell, *Idea of the Landscape*, 27.
63. W. J. T. Mitchell, "Imperial Landscape," in *Landscape and Power*, ed. W. J. T. Mitchell (Chicago: University of Chicago Press, 1994), 17. Elizabeth A. Bohls similarly argues that the semiotics of the English landscape were extended to the imperial holdings of the Empire (her example is the Jamaica of Edward Long's *History of Jamaica*) in an effort "to advance the imperial project" (Bohls, "The Gentleman Planter and the Metropole: Long's *History of Jamaica* [1774]," in *The Country and the City Revisited*, Maclean, Landry, and Ward, 180.
64. Laura Brown, *Alexander Pope* (Oxford: Basil Blackwell, 1985), 13–14; see also 44–45, 131–39.

65. Jill Campbell, "Colonial Trade and the Laboring Body in Thomson's *The Seasons*" (paper delivered at the annual meeting of the New England Society for Eighteenth-Century Studies, October 1990). I am grateful to Professor Campbell for sharing her unpublished work.

66. Karen O'Brien discusses the difficulty of maintaining this artifice in colonial georgic, where witnessing slavery is inescapable. In *Sugar-Cane,* James Grainger does his best to uphold the pastoral fiction, stressing the fertility of the Caribbean soil and the spontaneity of the sugar-cane, which grows all year round, but, in O'Brien's apt assessment, ends up courting "ethical and tonal bathos" when he tries to deliver instructions for how to pick a slave. (See her "Imperial Georgic," 160–79, quotation from 174.)

67. Barrell, *Idea of the Landscape,* 30.

68. The arrested empty gaze is itself a recurrent and significant figure, whose history I examine in the next chapter.

69. The study of Thomson's revisions, almost as much as Wordsworth's, is a small industry itself. For a collation of the texts, see Otto Zippel, *Thomson's Seasons: Critical Edition* (Berlin: Mayer and Muller, 1908). For a general discussion of certain of Thomson's principles and problems of revision, one needs to consult Ralph Cohen, *Art of Discrimination,* especially chapter 1.

70. Campbell, "Colonial Trade," 17–18. Campbell's fine paper is notable as well for its resistance to the rhetoric of critical demystification: "One lesson my experience of *The Seasons* has offered me has to do with the danger of our own reification of particular authors in our attempts to locate the ideological force of their works. To separate, absolutely or habitually, the operations of our negative and our positive hermeneutic methods . . . seems to me not to recognize the lived, dynamic, and contradictory labor of their own intellectual struggles – or our own" (19).

71. Virgil's periphrases are also that poet's way of insinuating historical density and particularity: *Quirites,* a proper noun, is the appellation given to the Roman citizens considered in their civic (and explicitly not their military) capacity after the union of the Romans and the Sabines. For a useful tabulation of poetic diction across several languages, see the appendixes in John Arthos, *The Language of Natural Description* (Ann Arbor: University of Michigan Press, 1949). Although he does not discuss this passage (or, very often, James Thomson), I would point to Donald Davie as one of the more sensitive and sympathetic readers of eighteenth-century poetic diction, precisely because he resists the Wordsworthian pressures to condemn a priori all circumlocutions, periphrases, etc. See Davie, *Purity of Diction in English Verse* (London: Routledge and Kegan Paul, 1967), especially chapter 3. Geoffrey Tillotson (*Augustan Poetic Diction* [London: Athlone Press, 1964]) also gives an important account of Virgil's influence on early eighteenth-century poetic diction and the precision such diction could and did afford Thomson and others, but Tillotson has a more strongly Wordsworthian preference for nineteenth-century (by which he means largely Romantic) poetry.

72. Philips, *Cyder*, 1.344–60. For Baker, see *The Universe. A Poem. Intended to Restrain the Pride of Man* (London: Printed for T. Worrall, 1734), D3^a.

73. See O'Brien, "Imperial Georgic," 165. O'Brien also gives a helpful account of how Dryden's decisions (and considerable translator's license) helped to push the georgic further toward imperial concerns (163–66).

74. My first assumption was that eighteenth-century imperial ideology might seek to keep the populations of the "torrid zones" nameless (outside of language and easy reference); in fact what one sees, in cartography and narratives of exploration, is assiduous naming. For a sampling of primary texts, albeit slightly earlier, see V. T. Harlow, ed., *Colonizing Expeditions to the West Indies and Guiana, 1621–1667* (London: Hakluyt Society, 1925). For an overview, see Anthony Pagden, *Lords of All the World: Ideologies of Empire in Spain, Britain, and France, c.1500–c.1800* (New Haven: Yale University Press, 1995).

75. Locke, *Essay*, 3.2.7-8.

76. Ibid., 3.6.13.

77. This "bursting" proximity is one among the factors that should keep us from too quickly amalgamating the "microscopic eye" with the aesthetic category of the sublime. The element of distance that is critical to British eighteenth-century accounts of the sublime is missing in the topos; its horror is not mitigated, as in Edmund Burke's later account of the "delightful horror" and "tranquility tinged with terror" exercised in the movement of the sublime (*A Philosophical Enquiry into the Origin of Our Ideas of the Sublime and Beautiful*, ed. Adam Phillips [Oxford: Oxford University Press, 1990], 123). I would distinguish, then, between the microscopic sublime that one finds in Philip's, Baker's or Addison's wonder (see the *Spectator* passages quoted earlier) – all of which are typically followed by praise or identification with the divine maker – and the microscopic eye. The latter, because it cannot be removed like the actual instrument, permits no self-preserving distance and offers no compensatory movement.

78. On Thomson and the training of the ear, see Lisa Steinman's comments in *Masters of Repetition: Poetry, Culture, and Work in Thomson, Wordsworth, Shelley, and Emerson* (New York: St. Martin's Press, 1998), chapter 1, especially 9–25. On elocutionary practice, and its "cultural capital," see John Guillory, *Cultural Capital: the Problem of Literary Canon Formation* (Chicago: University of Chicago Press, 1993), 99–102.

79. Samuel Johnson, *Lives of the English Poets*, ed. George Birkbeck Hill (Oxford: Clarendon Press, 1905), 3:300; for *The British Journal*, see Alan Dugald McKillop, ed., *James Thomson (1700–1748): Letters and Documents* (Lawrence: University of Kansas Press, 1958), 52. Both passages are cited by Steinman, who gives an interesting but unduly narrow, or at least unduly (Harold) Bloomian, reading of the phrase, "stunned with noise," by arguing that the noise comes from Thomson's poetic precursors, particularly Milton and Spenser.

80. Spacks, *Poetry of Vision*, 29.
81. On the complex ideal of "purity of diction" during the eighteenth century, see Davie, *Purity of Diction* and Marjorie Barstow, *Wordsworth's Theory of Poetic Diction: a Study in the Historical and Personal Background of the Lyrical Ballads* (New Haven: Yale University Press, 1917). The notion of a "pure diction" (the language of a vernacular fine yet natural enough to rival Latin and Greek and to represent the "English character") is never that far from edging toward the ideal of a "pure poetry" – poetry that pretends to be free of doctrines, morals, ideology, and particular topical reference, aspiring to be a kind of music free from the practical order of existence. On this second but related notion, see, for instance, Geoffrey H. Hartman, *Criticism in the Wilderness: the Study of Literature Today* (New Haven: Yale University Press, 1980), 115–60, and Annabel Patterson on Valéry, in *Pastoral and Ideology*, 316–32.
82. Addison, *Spectator*, 3:559.
83. The adjective comes during Johnson's not entirely sympathetic discussion of Milton's stylistic optics: "But he does not confine himself within the limits of rigorous comparison: his excellence is amplitude, and he expands the adventitious image beyond the dimensions which the occasion demanded. Thus, comparing the shield of Satan to the orb of the Moon, he crowds the imagination with the discovery of the telescope and all the wonders which the telescope discovers" (*Lives of the English Poets*, 1:179).
84. See Slavoj Žižek, "I Hear You with My Eyes," in *Gaze and Voice as Love Objects*, eds. Renata Salecl and Slavoj Žižek (Durham: Duke University, 1996), 93.
85. Michel Serres, *Hermes: Literature, Science, Philosophy*, trans. Lawrence R. Schehr, eds. Josué V. Harari and David F. Bell (Baltimore: Johns Hopkins University Press, 1982), 66.
86. Ibid., 76–77. Serres gives no reference, but he clearly has in mind *Monadology's* paragraph 21 and its surrounding paragraphs: "But when there is a great multitude of little perceptions, in which there is nothing distinct, one is stunned; as when one turns continuously round in the same way several times in succession, whence comes a giddiness which may make us swoon, and which keeps us from distinguishing anything. Death can for a time put animals into this condition." See Gottfried Wilhelm Leibniz, *The Monadology*, trans. Robert Latta (New York: Oxford University Press, 1965), 230–31.
87. See Lukács, *History and Class Consciousness*, 156. Lukács's remarks shortly thereafter on the artist's representation of the landscape and its presupposition of spatial distance are pertinent to my discussion as well (157–58).
88. Walter Benjamin, "Theses on the Philosophy of History," in *Illuminations: Essays and Reflections*, trans. Harry Zohn, ed. Hannah Arendt (New York: Schocken Books, 1968), 256.
89. See Charlotte Sussman, *Consuming Anxieties: Consumer Protest, Gender, and British Slavery, 1713–1833* (Stanford: Stanford University Press, 2000), 119, 115. Sussman is quoting from "A Second Address to the People of Great Britain . . ." (Rochester, 1792). Compare also Charlotte Smith's rendition of the microscopic

eye in *Beachy Head*, where the narrator stands, at home, looking at "the ship of commerce" as it is

> Bound to the orient climates, where the sun
> Matures the spice within its odorous shell,
> And, rivalling the gray worm's filmy toil,
> Bursts from its pod the vegetable down;
> Which in long turban'd wreaths, from torrid heat
> Defends the brows of Asia's countless casts.
> There Earth hides within her glowing breast
> The beamy adamant, and the round pearl
> Enchased in rugged covering, which the slave,
> With perilous and breathless toil tears off
> From the rough sea-rock . . .

Then, moments later, Smith's narrator will make explicit something of the protest that Thomson's poem registers as noise: "And they who reason, with abhorrence see / Man, for such gaudes and baubles, violate / The sacred freedom of his fellow man – / Erroneous estimate!" (see Smith, "Beachy Head," 36–60, in *Poems*, 218–219).

90. Lyotard, *The Differend*, 13.

3 COWPER'S GEORGIC OF THE NEWS: THE "LOOPHOLE" IN THE RETREAT

1. All quotations from *The Task* are cited by book and line from *The Poems of William Cowper*, eds. John D. Baird and Charles Ryskamp, vol. 1 (Oxford: Clarendon Press, 1980). Bruce Redford's reading of Cowper's letters emphasizes the poet's habitation and movement within a concentric series of ever-contracting retreats, consisting of Olney, Orchardside, garden, summerhouse, greenhouse, cucumber frame, and so on. See Redford, *The Converse of the Pen: Acts of Intimacy in the Eighteenth-Century Familiar Letter* (Chicago: University of Chicago Press, 1986), 50 and chapter 2 ("William Cowper: Invitations to the Microcosm") more generally.

2. Kenneth MacLean, "William Cowper," in *The Age of Johnson: Essays Presented to Chauncey Brewster Tinker*, ed. Frederick W. Hilles (New Haven: Yale University Press, 1949), 263.

3. Leonore Davidoff and Catherine Hall, *Family Fortunes: Men and Women of the English Middle Class, 1780–1850* (Chicago: University of Chicago Press, 1987), 165.

4. The phrase "the flight from history" originated with John Sitter, in *Literary Loneliness in Mid-Eighteenth-Century England* (Ithaca: Cornell University Press, 1982), chapter 3 ("The Flight from History in Mid-Century Poetry"), although Sitter does not treat Cowper specifically, since his emphasis is on mid-century poets (e.g., Thomas Gray, James Thomson). Richard Feingold's work on later eighteenth-century uses of pastoral and georgic (Feingold uses "bucolic" to indicate their mingling during this period) sees the forfeiture of

a public vision as a gradual process in *The Task*, to which he devotes two chapters of his *Nature and Society*. For Feingold, Cowper initially conceives of an engaged retirement as a "middle ground," consisting of participation-at-a-distance in the *vita activa*, between alternatives of frenetic involvement or cloddish sensibility (135); however, as the poet is "unable to reconcile the fact of an inherently corrupt political corporation with the normative idea of a healthy community, for which his poem imagines no political home," he shifts his focus from political to spiritual freedom, and the ultimate goal of retirement becomes not participation but religious peace (156). Although Feingold does resist a flight from history thesis, then, he does ultimately put Cowper on a trajectory toward lyric in which the public promise of the georgic mode is lost (82).

5. John Barrell, "Afterword: Moving Stories, Still Lives," in *The Country and the City Revisited*, eds. Maclean, Landry, and Ward, 245; Griffin, "Redefining Georgic: Cowper's *Task*," 876. For a richly suggestive discussion of Cowper's peculiar brand of masculine domesticity and closeted, wounded anxiety about masculinity, see Andrew Elfenbein, *Romantic Genius: the Prehistory of a Homosexual Role* (New York: Columbia University Press, 1999), chapter 3.

6. *The Letters and Prose Writings of William Cowper*, eds. James King and Charles Ryskamp, 5 vols. (Oxford: Clarendon Press, 1979–86), 2:219–20 (hereafter cited in the main text as *Letters*, followed by the relevant volume and page). Cowper's addiction to the newspaper has been recently noticed and superbly discussed by Julie Ellison, "News, Blues, and Cowper's Busy World," *Modern Language Quarterly* 62 (2001): 219–37. Below I return to discuss Ellison's article, and the ways in which our approaches to Cowper are complementary and different.

7. Although they are both important elements of contemporary journalism, and share certain topics, it is helpful to distinguish between the periodical publications, including miscellanies like *The Gentleman's Magazine*, and the newspapers, such as the daily *Morning Chronicle* and *The General Evening Post*. Even where they do not present an organizing point of view or "voice," as did *The Spectator*, *The Tatler*, *The Rambler*, and others, periodicals display a certain continuity, regularity, and predictable organization (including, in the case of *The Gentleman's Magazine* as well as *The London Magazine*, quite elaborate tables of contents and volume indexes). By contrast, the habits of news journalists, as J. Paul Hunter has observed, "were calculated to keep the public off balance" (*Before Novels: the Cultural Contexts of Eighteenth-Century English Fiction* [New York: W. W. Norton and Co., 1990], 176). The first London daily was published in 1702.

8. This "hot chronology," to borrow Levi-Strauss's phrase, is noted by Baird and Ryskamp, the modern editors of Cowper's poems: see *The Poems of William Cowper*, 2:379 n. For an account of the constitutional crisis of 1783–84, see Paul Langford, *A Polite and Commercial People: England 1727–1783* (Oxford: Clarendon Press, 1989), 559–63.

9. "Preface," *The Gentleman's Magazine* 32 (1782).

10. See Jürgen Habermas, *The Structural Transformation of the Public Sphere*, trans. Thomas Burger (Cambridge, MA: MIT Press, 1994), 61–62; also Langford, *Polite and Commercial People*, 526, 705–6.

11. Under "loophole," n. 1, the *Oxford English Dictionary* lists "opening," with specialized senses in fortification (for the passage of missiles), in nautical terminology (a port-hole), and more general usage as any "similar opening to look through, or for the admission of light and air." Cowper almost certainly had in mind Milton's influential use of the term in *Paradise Lost*: Adam and Eve, moments after the fall, turn for garments to the figtree (or banyan): "such as to this day to Indians known / In Malabar or Deccan spreads her arms" (9.1102–03). Milton then opens up the counterplot of the epic simile: "There oft the Indian herdsman shunning heat / Shelters in cool, and tends his pasturing herds / At loopholes cut through thickest shade . . . " (1108–10). For reasons that will become apparent below, I think that Cowper turns to Milton's image for an aperture between worlds in part because of its evocation of a geographically remote land.

12. Cowper was well-known during the 1770s as coauthor, with John Newton, of the *Olney Hymns*. For a general discussion of the tension between personal and collective, or "exemplary," expression in Cowper and in the eighteenth-century hymn more generally, see Madeleine Forell Marshall and Janet Todd, *English Congregational Hymns in the Eighteenth Century* (Lexington: University Press of Kentucky, 1982), particularly chapters 1 and 5, and Donald Davie, *The Eighteenth-Century Hymn in England* (Cambridge: Cambridge University Press, 1993), especially 16–19 for the transformation of classical into congregational hymn.

13. Benedict Anderson, *Imagined Communities: Reflections on the Origin and Spread of Nationalism*, rev. edn. (London: Verso, 1991), 35. Habermas's "audience-oriented [*publikumbezogem*] subjectivity" similarly complicates the usual public/private binarism he is sometimes thought to encourage; he argues that even "included in the private realm was the authentic 'public sphere' – i.e., the public sphere constituted by private people coming together for the discussion of politics and letters" (See *Structural Transformation*, 29–30).

In thinking about the various ways in which the lair of the skull can be a public place, I have been greatly helped by Steven Goldsmith's discussion of Blake in "Blake's Agitation," *South Atlantic Quarterly* 95 (1996), 753–96. Goldsmith asks – and proceeds to answer, via a subtle treatment of Anderson, Habermas, early print culture (including the important work of Jay Fliegelman), Kant, Lyotard, and others – the questions: "What understanding of social formation allowed Blake to think of the general and the particular not as antithetical but somehow as nearly one and the same thing . . . ? Within what understanding of society could one experience private agitation, independent acts of resistant critical judgment, as something essential to the health of one's nation? And what if such resistance, concentrated in the individual experience of the aesthetic, were the very act that *constituted* social order?" (764–65). As the last question indicates, Goldsmith is ultimately skeptical about, if interested by, Blake's (and Kant's) elision of the difference between mental fight and public agitation, such that a private experience might be experienced as a form of public action. Much of what Goldsmith has to say about Blake is relevant to Cowper's peculiar private publicity, or sense of collective subjectivity – but with a crucial exception. Unlike Blake, Cowper was not shy about publication, micro-managing the process with the help of his London agents, Unwin and, later, John Johnson and William Hayley. Cowper, that is, invented a voice meant to be heard in public, even as it talked all about privacy. His privacy is thus remarkably public, and publicized.

14. Homi K. Bhabha, *The Location of Culture* (New York: Routledge, 1994); Adela Pinch, *Strange Fits of Passion*, Julie Ellison, *Cato's Tears*.
15. Donald M. Lowe, *History of Bourgeois Perception* (Chicago: University of Chicago Press, 1982), 38.
16. As Lowe comments: "Newspapers contracted time to the instantaneous and the sensational. . . . The present became much more diverse and complex, no longer containable within a single chronological framework" (Ibid., 38). For an account of what he nicely calls "the culture of now" as it took shape in the early British news culture of the Restoration and early eighteenth century, see Hunter, *Before Novels*, chapter 7.
17. Anderson, *Imagined Communities*, 24.
18. Raymond Williams, *Marxism and Literature*, 133, 128; see also my introduction to this book.
19. Joanna Picciotto, "Optical Instruments and the Eighteenth-Century Observer," 124, 142. For Addison's ambitions (quoted by Picciotto on 134), see *Spectator*, 4:370. Picciotto concludes her discussion of Addison by arguing that in Mr. Spectator we might find the "ancestral traces" of our own practice of ideological analysis. If so, I want to add, then we have to be far more critical than Addison (perhaps than Picciotto herself) of the contemporary intellectual's claims to "proper" vision. At least we must pose the question: " 'Proper' to whom?"
20. Most of the details in the newspaper sequence of *Task* 4 have been traced by Baird and Ryskamp to issues from the fall and early winter of 1783 – the beginning of the winter that gives the titles to Books 4–6: "The Winter Evening," "The Winter's Morning Walk," "The Winter Walk at Noon," respectively (see *Poems of William Cowper*, 2:379–84).
21. Entry dated April 11, 1757, printed in *The London Magazine* 26 (April 1757): 160.
22. Preface to "The Newspaper: a Poem," in *George Crabbe: the Complete Poetical Works*, 1:179.
23. Jeremy Black, *The English Press in the Eighteenth Century* (London: Crook Helm, 1987), 201, and see chapter 7 more generally for the "major role" of foreign news in relation to the "small quantity of local news." For a helpful account of the daily press in the later decades of the century, see also Lucyle Werkmeister, *The London Daily Press, 1772–1792* (Lincoln: University of Nebraska Press, 1963).

24. See Benjamin's "On Some Motifs in Baudelaire," in *Illuminations*, 155–200. I return to discuss the greater relevance of this essay and Cowper's relation to Benjamin's categories of *Erfahrung, Erlebnis,* and lyric later in this chapter.

25. Printed in *London Magazine* 35 (December 1766): 638.

26. *London Magazine* 49 (August 1780): 354.

27. Crabbe, "The Newspaper," 245–46.

28. *London Magazine* 35 (December 1766): 639–40.

29. Eagleton, *The Function of Criticism: from "The Spectator" to Post-Structuralism* (London: Verso, 1984), 10; also quoted by Jon Klancher in *The Making of English Reading Audiences, 1790–1832* (Madison: University of Wisconsin Press, 1987), 23.

30. Very early on in the century, the avidity of the writers of "daily histories," as the news writers were called, led to a complaint that the smallest trifle could become news; hence a contributor to the *Universal Spectator* for March 8, 1735, writing with the name "A. Trifle," complained that news writers are speedier than undertakers, and they "carefully instruct us in the Life and Circumstances of the Deceased, who perhaps never made the least Noise till he was dead" (printed under "Weekly Essays," *The Gentleman's Magazine* 5 [March 1735]).

31. On selection and "objectivity," see Black, *English Press*, 24–49.

32. Richard Terdiman, *Discourse/Counter-Discourse: the Theory and Practice of Symbolic Resistance in Nineteenth-Century France* (Ithaca: Cornell University Press, 1985), 122. Terdiman is finely ambivalent about this "representation of dissonance about which it appears that nothing can or will be done.... The form of the newspaper projects no thought or expectation of [its elements'] harmonization or resolution, . . . instructs us in the apparently irreducible fragmentation of daily experience and prepares us to live it" (135). Yet the very resistance to (false) harmonization is potentially, if not always in practice, subversive for Terdiman, who is particularly interested in satirical impulses within the news medium that "sap its own protocols of domination" (121).

33. Relevant to the relationship that I am describing here is Bolter and Grusin's observation about the logic of immediacy and hypermediacy in digital media: "Transparent digital applications seek to get to the real by bravely denying the fact of mediation; digital hypermedia seek the real by multiplying mediation so as to create a *feeling of fullness, a satiety of experience, which can be taken as reality*" (*Remediation*, 53; emphasis added). On the dialectic or "double logic" of immediacy and hypermediacy, more generally, see 3–50, and my discussion in chapter 1. As they make clear throughout their work, the phenomena Bolter and Grusin are investigating have a long prehistory, and their citation of Jacques Derrida's account of Kant's third *Critique* is apposite, both for their purposes and mine. Derrida defines "true mimesis" in Kant as follows: it "is not the representation of one thing by another . . . the reproduction of a product of nature by a product of art. It is not the relation of two products but of two productions . . . The artist does not imitate things in nature or, if you will, in *natura naturata*, but the acts of *natura naturans*, the operations of the *physis*" ("Economimesis," *Diacritics* 11 [1981]: 9). The newspaper's "as if," in

other words, mimes that aspect of presentness which resists known historical categories and structures because the terms which will describe it are not yet fully formed or known.

34. Fredric Jameson, "Cognitive Mapping," 347–57. Also pertinent to my discussion is Gillen D'Arcy Wood's study of simulated reality effects in the Romantic period: focusing canonical authors' resistance to the proliferation of popular entertainments, Wood pursues the connection between "the pictorial representation of [apparently] unmediated reality with an experience of shock in the viewer" (*Shock of the Real*, 5 and Wood's introduction more generally).

35. Ellison, "News," 230–31. Ellison's article, which also has a very fine discussion of the gendering of parlor newspaper reading, came out after I had drafted this chapter; I admire it greatly, and see that we coincide on certain points. The differences between our work fall into two categories: [1] Where her emphasis falls on Cowper's therapeutic and pleasurable management of variety, I am less interested in the therapy, whose success seems tenuous to me, than in the aberrant sound ("noise" and the tense silence) that does not get managed (or, as I phrase it below, cannot be made "conversable") and therefore resists the Addisonian "principle of pleasure." [2] Where Ellison focuses mostly on the poet as consumer, I treat Cowper as at once consumer and producer of sound.

36. Ibid., 228–29.

37. Ibid., 232–33.

38. Davidoff and Hall, *Family Fortunes*, 157.

39. "I am induced by your readiness in publishing some hints which I sent you a few days ago on this subject to trouble you with the following extracts from an ingenious author . . ." (*Morning Chronicle*, September 30, 1783).

40. For Davie's discussion of Arnold's "tone of the centre," see *Purity of Diction*. On the difference between early and later eighteenth-century prose and the trend, in the latter, toward "gentrification" and "writtenness," see Carey McIntosh, *The Evolution of English Prose, 1700–1800: Style, Politeness, and Print Culture* (Cambridge: Cambridge University Press, 1998), 22–38.

41. I have summarized Guillory's long and subtle chapter, "Mute Inglorious Miltons: Gray, Wordsworth, and the Vernacular Canon," in *Cultural Capital*, 85–133. Since Guillory, Maureen McLane has offered a different, although complementary, account of poetry's (or rather an idealized "Poetry's") struggle to maintain a distinction from "literature" by defining itself as the opposite not of prose but of particular (prose) *discourses*, namely moral philosophy and science. McLane's interest, then, is in the move by which poetry frees itself from mere technique (metrical composition) or even technology (print) and defines itself as a discourse of "genius" with special humanizing powers (see her *Romanticism and the Human Sciences: Poetry, Population, and the Discourse of the Species* [Cambridge: Cambridge University Press, 2000], 10–42). As McLane notes, the process of distinction is a long and gradual one, since one can find examples as early as Sir Philip Sidney's declaration that verse is "but an

ornament and no cause to Poetry, since there have been many most excellent poets that never versified, and now swarm many versifiers that need never answer to the name of poets" (*Apology for Poetry*, 103), but she, like Guillory, finds an intensified pressure to distinguish in the Romantic period. As I suggested in chapter 1's treatment of eighteenth-century commentary on the *Georgics* beginning with Addison's "Essay," I find the acceleration of attempts to create a hierarchy within print beginning earlier, waged within the reception and adaption of Virgil's poem.

42. Like "poetic," "prosaic" undergoes a gradual extension from the more limited, older sense – "of or pertaining to prose"; "writing in prose" (i.e., without meter) – to the extended sense, now common: "plain, matter of fact, lacking in feeling or imagination"; this process we can identify as the counterpart to the more frequently described abstraction and idealization of Poetry from versification (see preceding note).

43. Walter J. Ong, *Orality and Literacy: the Technologizing of the Word* (New York: Methuen, 1982), 136.

44. George Puttenham, *The Arte of English Poesie* (London, 1589) 3:2, available as facsimile reproduction, intro. Baxter Hathaway (Kent, OH: Kent State University Press, 1970), 151. See also Louis Milic's pointed demystification of the conversational style: "Observations on Conversational Style," in *English Writers of the Eighteenth Century*, ed. John H. Middendorf (New York: Columbia University Press, 1971), 274.

45. I quote from Wlad Godzich and Jeffrey Kittay, *The Emergence of Prose: an Essay in Prosaics* (Minneapolis; University of Minnesota Press, 1987), 204. While this study is focused on thirteenth-century French prose, its theoretical sophistication and wide range of reference makes it most helpful for considering the interdependency and rivalry between poetry and prose – particularly the way that modern (written) verse is conditioned by the existence of prose (always written, a later development than oral verse) – in later periods as well; their conclusion, entitled "The Prosaic World," considers the wider historical sweep that follows and extends the emergence of prose in France. As Godzich and Kittay point out, "Poetics has not provided us with adequate terminology for the designation of verse and prose because these terms exceed the scope of the broadest category of poetics: genre. In fact, we commonly recognize the existence of genres *within* prose and verse" (xii). They speak of both prose and verse as "signifying practices," a term that includes the context of the signifying act (presence of a speaker, numbers and situation of addressees, the role of ritual, etc.) as well as its content. Although less dependent on technology other than writing because of the earlier historical focus, Godzich and Kittay's "signifying practice" is in certain respects related to McLuhan's "medium," although the distinction between signifying practices is more fine and gradual than between media. Compare their statement – "a new signifying practice may – perhaps *must* – initially pretend to 'hold' the old, to contain it" (7) with McLuhan's inescapable formulation: "the 'content' of any medium is always another medium" (*Understanding Media*, 8).

46. Writing about Sir Walter Scott's *The Lay of the Last Minstrel*, Celeste Langan contrasts Scott's practice of rhyme, as well as his play upon Northern dialect, with the blank verse of Wordsworth, Coleridge, and Cowper (as poetry that, as Coleridge put it, "affects not to be poetry"). For Langan, the establishment of blank verse as a poetic norm marks the redefinition of English poetry by the silent, invisible, or naturalized medium of print, and Langan reads Wordsworth's rejection of rhyme in his 1802 revision of the "Preface" as a recognition of the "fully residual status of sound" in the poetry of a print culture ("Understanding Media in 1805," 53). Yet Cowper's desire to make "verse *speak* the language of prose" differs, I think, from Wordsworth's claim for a "strict affinity of metrical language with that of prose" because, while both Wordsworth and Cowper are affirming the shared diction of poetry and prose, *Cowper* is simultaneously differentiating speech (better rendered by poetry) from silent reading (prose). *The Task*'s representation of the (largely prose) newsprint thus offers us – notwithstanding Cowper's choice of blank verse – an example of the internal differentiation between sight and sound *within* print that Langan finds in Scott's *Lay*, however different these two long poems otherwise are.

47. Coleridge's phrase, which finds equivalents in Wordsworth and many later readers of Cowper, originates in a letter to John Thelwall of December, 1796; see *Samuel Taylor Coleridge: a Critical Edition of the Major Works*, ed. H. J. Jackson (New York: Oxford University Press, 1992), 491.

48. For the text of "Conversation," see *The Poems of William Cowper*, 1:354–77. I quote from line 82.

49. Ong, *Orality and Literacy*, 136.

50. Matthew Prior, "Preface" to *Solomon on the Vanity of the World*, in *The Literary Works of Matthew Prior*, eds. H. Bunker Wright and Monroe K. Spears, 2 vols. (Oxford: Clarendon Press, 1959), 1:309.

51. Both Martin Priestman and Tim Fulford offer different analyses of Cowper's celebration of Prior, neither of which is incompatible with the one I offer here (or with each other), but which do not take up what might be at stake in Cowper's translation of prose into verse or the question of the different sound offered by the two signifying practices. Priestman argues, on thematic grounds, that the significant Prior poem for Cowper is Prior's *Alma, or the Progress of the Mind*, since this poem, like *The Task*, is a conversation about the meandering progress, or digressiveness, of the mind (see Priestman, *Cowper's Task: Structure and Influence* [Cambridge: Cambridge University Press, 1983], 22–23). Fulford argues that Prior provides Cowper with a model for a political, patriotic poetry that adapts the familiar style for public expression (see *Landscape, Liberty, and Authority*, 66–69).

52. Reading the cucumber mock-georgic of *Task* 3, Priestman comments aptly on "the way in which working for the open market alienates the poet as worker from the benefits of his own labour": "Cowper is producing this history of a soul out of his own manure but not necessarily for his own consumption" (*Cowper's Task*, 103 and chapter 3 more generally).

53. For the origin of the phrase "the conversable world," see David Hume, "Of Essay Writing," in *Essays, Moral, Political, and Literary*, ed. Eugene F. Miller (Indianapolis: Liberty Fund, 1985), 533–34.

54. Henry Fielding, "An Essay on Conversation," in *Miscellanies*, ed. Henry Knight Miller, 3 vols. (Oxford: Clarendon Press, 1972–97), 1:120. Alison Hurley offers an excellent discussion of Fielding's essay in relation to the polite culture of conversation as it emerged in the English resort town (Bath, Tunbridge Wells, etc.): "The Culture of Conversation: a Social and Literary History of the Eighteenth-Century Watering Place" (Ph.D. diss., University of California, Berkeley, 2002). My understanding of conversation and the larger discourse of politeness has also been much aided by the work of Lawrence E. Klein: "Courtly Politesse and Civic Politeness in France and England," *Halcyon* 14 (1992): 171–81; "Berkeley, Shaftesbury, and the Meaning of Politeness," *Studies in Eighteenth-Century Culture* 16 (1986): 57–68; "Gender, Conversation and the Public Sphere in Early Eighteenth-Century England," in *Textuality and Sexuality: Reading Theories and Practices*, eds. Judith Still and Michael Worton (Manchester: Manchester University Press, 1993); *Shaftesbury and the Culture of Politeness: Moral Discourse and Cultural Politics in Early Eighteenth-Century England* (Cambridge: Cambridge University Press, 1994); "Politeness for Plebes: Consumption and Social Identity in Early Eighteenth-Century England," in *The Consumption of Culture 1600–1800: Image, Object, Text*, ed. J. A. Brewer (New York: Routledge, 1995). As those titles indicate, Klein focuses on the first part of the century; for the continuing development of the culture of conversation, see Adam Potkay, *The Fate of Eloquence in the Age of Hume* (Ithaca: Cornell University Press, 1994), and the work of David Simpson and Geoffrey Hartman, cited in the subsequent notes below.

55. David Hume, "Of Essay Writing," 533. For a discussion of Hume's term, see, *inter alia*, Nancy S. Streuver, "The Conversable World: Eighteenth-Century Transformations of the Relation of Rhetoric and Truth," in *Rhetorical Traditions and British Romantic Literature*, eds. Don H. Bialostosky and Lawrence D. Needham (Bloomington: Indiana University Press, 1995), 233–49.

56. As David Simpson remarks, "No conversation can ever subsist unless it excludes from the table those voices that must seem unmannerly, impatient, unwilling to listen, pressed by needs too urgent to be put on hold, or simply shy and unable to join in" ("The Cult of 'Conversation,'" *Raritan* 16 [1997], 77). For Simpson's more extended demystification of the tea- and table-talk ideal, which traces our own postmodern fetish for "getting into the conversation" (a slogan that begs the question of who gets into the dialogue and how), see *The Academic Postmodern and the Rule of Literature: a Report on Half-Knowledge* (Chicago: University of Chicago Press, 1995), chapter 2. Earlier, Geoffrey H. Hartman offered his own skeptical account of what he wittily called the "teatotaling" style in familiar or essayistic prose: it is pre-professional, attempts to cancel class, and advances an "unconsciousness [that] tends to quiet the real unconscious" (political, psychic, and otherwise). See Hartman's "Tea and Totality" and "From Common to Uncommon Reader," in *Minor*

Prophecies: the Literary Essay in the Culture Wars (Cambridge, MA: Harvard University Press, 1991); quotation from "Tea and Totality," 63.

57. I cite here from Serres, *Hermes*, 67. However, the phenomenon of "noise" is writ large, or loud, across Serres's works, perhaps most extensively in *The Parasite*, trans. Lawrence R. Schehr (Baltimore: Johns Hopkins University Press, 1982).

58. Jameson, "Cognitive Mapping," 349.

59. "Cowper and his fire at twilight" also makes it into Jane Austen's *Emma* in a paragraph describing Knightley's suspicious meditations about Frank Churchill (see volume 3, chapter 5: Jane Austen, *Emma*, ed. Lionel Trilling [Boston: Houghton Mifflin, 1957], 269).

60. Locke, *Essay*, 2.1.1; 2.27.9.

61. Ibid., 2.1.11–12, 2.1.10.

62. Reid's protest (from *Essays on the Intellectual Powers of Man* [1785]), as well as the many precursors throughout the eighteenth century, is cited by Fox, *Locke and the Scriblerians: Identity and Consciousness in Early Eighteenth-Century Britain* (Berkeley and Los Angeles: University of California Press, 1988), 10. The project of Fox's book is to insist that it is with Locke, and not later (e.g., with Hume, to whom the image of the mind-as-theater and discussion of identity are usually credited), that the fixity of personal identity is undermined; Locke's positing of identity in consciousness led, from its first reception by the Scriblerians and others, to the opposite conclusion, the recognition of the self as transient. Jean Hagstrum's genealogy ("Toward a Profile of the Word *Conscious* in Eighteenth-Century Literature," in *Psychology and Literature in the Eighteenth Century*, ed. Christopher Fox [New York: AMS Press, 1987], 23–50) also touches on the identity-in-consciousness debate, in order to argue that the eighteenth-century trajectory of the word and concept "conscious," in its precariousness, opens up the possibility for the nascent idea of an unconscious.

63. Brown, *Preromanticism*, 69.

64. Coleridge, "Frost at Midnight," line 26. Coleridge, of course, would offer the famous gloss in early editions of his poem: "In all parts of the kingdom, these films are called *strangers*, and are supposed to portend the arrival of some absent friend" (*Samuel Taylor Coleridge: a Critical Edition*, 701).

Where Cowper is Coleridge's source text, one of Cowper's probable influences is Edward Young's *Conjectures on Original Composition* (1759), but the difference is interesting, for where Young's "stranger within thee" is "the depth, extent, bias, and full fort of thy mind," a deep or "true" self, Cowper's stranger-on-the-outside is a composite of other selves altogether. Cowper has Young in his mind more generally in the brown study sequence: line 290 ("myself creating what I saw") derives from Young's *Night Thoughts*, 6.424 ("half create the wondrous world they see").

65. In the *Elements of Criticism* (Edinburgh: Printed for A. Miller, London, and for A. Kincaid and J. Bell, Edinburgh, 1762), I.ii.1.7, Kames defines ideal presence as a "waking dream" (Cowper's phrase as well in the brown study [4.287]) in which the "idea of a thing I never saw" is so vivid that "I am insensibly transformed into a spectator and have an impression that every

incident is passing in my presence." He distinguishes ideal presence from both "real presence" (direct eyesight or contact that can be verified by sense perception) and remembrance, where an event may be vivid but it is recognized as something that has occurred in the past.

A comprehensive survey of the shifting senses of "fancy," frequently personified, during the eighteenth century is beyond the scope of this book let alone this note, but a helpful account, particularly of the relationship between fancy and the imagination, is available in James Engell, *The Creative Imagination: Enlightenment to Romanticism* (Cambridge, MA: Harvard University Press, 1981), especially chapter 13. Julie Ellison's work is especially pertinent for any discussion of the role of Fancy in imperial and/or topographical verse of the eighteenth century. In addition to "News, Blues, and Cowper's Busy World," see *Cato's Tears*, chapter 4. Where Ellison understands Fancy primarily as a mode of subjective "mastery and escape" (*Cato's Tears*, 100), I place more stress than she does – although her account is a finely dialectical one – on Fancy's involuntary and intersubjective engagement and movements.

66. See Hans Blumenberg, *Shipwreck with Spectator: Paradigm of a Metaphor for Existence*, trans. Steven Rendall (Cambridge, MA: The MIT Press, 1997), 73. Blumenberg's study locates at one pole the stances adopted by Lucretius and Montaigne, whose spectators enjoy the safe consideration of the "*alterius . . . laborem*" (the travails of others); at the other pole, he places, among others, Pascal and Nietzsche, whose spectators have lost their safety and are themselves already embarked on rough seas – for whom, that is, the Epicurean or skeptical abstention is no longer an option. The paradigm, as Blumenberg suggests, takes on different specificities at different moments; whereas in Lucretius's scientific imagination it functioned as a metaphor for man's relation to the natural world, it later becomes increasingly central as a figure for reckoning with the immediate prospect of history. Blumenberg's examples are almost exclusively continental; I would locate a part of its trajectory in Britain. Martin Jay, whose work first alerted me to the significance of Blumenberg, has extended *Shipwreck with Spectator* in a tempered critique of the postmodern fin-de-siècle suspicion of Lucretian spectatorship and cult of the Nietzschean–Pascalian alternative ("Diving into the Wreck" [lecture delivered at the University of California, Berkeley, October 1999]).

67. With its famous last lines ("No light divine the storm allay'd, / No light propitious shone, / When, snatch'd from all effectual aid, / We perish'd, each, alone; / But I, beneath a rougher sea, / And whelm'd in deeper gulphs than he"), "The Castaway" is based on the fate of one of the seamen in the Royal Navy squadron commanded by George Anson off Tierra del Fuego and related in Richard Walter's *A Voyage Around the World by George Anson* (1748). See Cowper, *Poems*, 3:357.

68. Claude Levi-Strauss, *Introduction to the Work of Marcel Mauss*, trans. F. Baker (London: Routledge, 1987); quoted by Bhabha in *The Location of Culture*, 150.

My comparison of the English view (and construction from the outside) of Omai with Smith's "impartial spectator" – that imagined or projected being which *The Theory of Moral Sentiments* locates simultaneously inside and outside the body, the "great inmate of the breast" who judges us as we imagine others to view our actions – is intended to indicate the extent to which "Omai" was useful as a kind of mild national conscience, a noble savage able to diagnose the corruptions of British plenty even as his imagined castigation freed the national conscience to enjoy the plenty itself. Cf. Cowper's lines, "Thou art sad / At thought of [England's] forlorn and abject state" (*Task*, 1.558–59) with Smith's account of the disciplinary role of the impartial spectator: "It is from him only that we learn the real littleness of ourselves, and of whatever relates to ourselves, and the natural misrepresentations of self-love can be corrected only by the eye of this impartial spectator" (*The Theory of Moral Sentiments*, eds. D. D. Raphael and A. L. Macfie [Oxford: Clarendon Press, 1976], 137). For an interesting discussion of Omai-as-national-conscience outside of *The Task* in popular culture (epistles, theater, and other forms of social satire), see Bernard Smith, *European Vision and the South Pacific* (New Haven: Yale University Press, 1985), 82–84.

69. See, for example, the following issues of *The General Evening Post* and *Morning Chronicle*: *General Evening Post*, July 14–16, 1774, July 19–21, 1774, July 21–23, 1774, July 26–28, 1774, August 6–9, 1774, August 9–11, 1774; *Morning Chronicle*, July 16, 1774, July 26, 1774, July 29, 1774, August 5, 1774, August 8, 1774, November 9, 1774, etc. Articles or accounts are also frequent in *The London Magazine* for 1774–76. Omai's visit was watched by interested on-lookers like the Burney family (Fanny's brother James served on Furneaux's ship and befriended Omai), Dr. Johnson, Boswell, and others; Burney's diaries are accordingly a good source for following polite English society's interest in the visitor (especially *The Early Diary of Frances Burney*, ed. Annie Raine Ellis [London: G. Bell, 1907]). A very thorough documentation of Omai's visit as well as its considerable aftermath – journalistic and literary – during the rest of the eighteenth century is offered by E. H. McCormick, *Omai, Pacific Envoy* (Auckland, New Zealand: Auckland University Press, 1977).

70. *Morning Chronicle*, August 5, 1774 and *The General Evening Post*, August 6–9, 1774.

71. McCormick, *Omai*, 114.

72. Joseph Roach, *Cities of the Dead: Circum-Atlantic Performance* (New York: Columbia University Press, 1996), 6, although Roach's entire first chapter (1–31) is pertinent to my discussion of Omai's visit.

73. On the opening of the South Pacific, see Bernard Smith, *European Vision*, especially chapters 1–4; see also Jonathan Lamb, Robert P. Maccubbin, and David F. Morrill, eds., "The South Pacific in the Eighteenth-Century: Narratives and Myths," Papers from the Ninth Annual David Nichol Smith Memorial Seminar, *Eighteenth-Century Life* 18 (1994): 1–242; and Jonathan Lamb, Vanessa Smith, and Nicholas Thomas, eds., *Exploration and Exchange: a South Seas Anthology, 1680–1900* (Chicago: University of Chicago Press, 2000).

74. For a fine and wide-ranging account of the way the eighteenth-century "literature of sensibility exposes a complicated awareness of the human costs of

national and imperial economies," see Julie Ellison, *Cato's Tears* (the quotation is from page 7). Homi Bhabha treats these issues in a post-colonial context, citing, as a statement of the conundrum of understanding a history that has in part happened, or is in part happening, elsewhere, the inebriated wisdom of Salman Rushdie's S. S. ("Whiskey") Sisodia in *The Satanic Verses*: "The trouble with the Engenglish is that their hiss hiss history happened overseas, so they do do don't know what it means" (Bhabha, *Location of Culture*, 166–67).

75. *London Magazine*, 44, 20–22 April, 1775, 382. The older sense of conversation, quite pertinent here, is of course sexual intercourse.

76. See McCormick's chapter on "The End of Omai," in *Omai*, 261–94.

77. *General Evening Post*, September 23–25, 1784; see also September 25–28, 1784.

78. These transitions are quite startling for any modern reader trying to follow a single story. The *Morning Chronicle* of August 5, 1774, for example, moves straight from the observation that "His Majesty will defray all the expences [Omai] shall incur during his stay here" to the observation, in the next paragraph, that "[t]he pigmy first fiddle at Vauxhall ought not to be indulged by the Manager to play only what he approves."

79. Jameson, "Cognitive Mapping," 350.

80. Charlotte Smith's *The Emigrants*, dedicated to William Cowper, is replete with such abjected starers placed in the Revolutionary context: there is the exiled French mother by the seashore, "wearied by the task / Of having here, with swol'n and aching eyes / Fix'd on the grey horizon, since the dawn / Solicitously watch'd the weekly sail / From her dear native land" (*Emigrants* 1.215–19 in *Poems of Charlotte Smith*). Earlier in the poem, a group of emigrants is said to "hang / Upon the barrier of the rock, and seem / To murmur [their] despondence, waiting long / Some fortunate reverse that never comes" (1.108-11). See also the opening lines of *Beachy Head*, in the same edition.

81. Suvir Kaul, *Poems of Nation, Anthems of Empire: English Verse in the Long Eighteenth Century* (Charlottesville: University Press of Virginia, 2000), 5. Kaul treats the Omai incident briefly, suggesting that Cowper emphasizes Omai's sense of loss, in leaving Britain behind, in order to balance his poem's critique of the nation's mercantile policy, so that the reproof of the principle of trade that concludes the Omai sequence works as a small but necessary check to the poem's ideological affirmation of the "genuine superiority of English culture and morality" (235). As a whole, Kaul's thorough and significant study emphasizes the overt and programmatic statements of the numerous poems he studies, but he does have a fine sense that the poems are trying to resolve a perceived contradiction in the experience of empire.

82. Adam Phillips, "On Being Bored," in *On Kissing, Tickling, and Being Bored: Psychoanalytic Essays on the Unexamined Life* (Cambridge, MA: Harvard University Press, 1993), 77 and 68–78 more generally. Patricia Meyer Spacks gives Phillips's psychoanalytic insights historical specificity by arguing that while something like boredom may have existed earlier by a different name, boredom was in the eighteenth century "a new concept, if not necessarily a new event" (*Boredom: the Literary History of a State of Mind* [Chicago: University

of Chicago Press, 1995], 28). Among the historical determinants of boredom, Spacks identifies the emergence of leisure as a condition and a problem that defined certain times as empty times; the decline of religious faith; and a newly elaborated notion of individual rights (including the right to be interested and occupied). She offers, as an exemplar of privileged, but unhappy and anxious, boredom, Johnson's *Rasselas*, who puts the condition this way: "That I want nothing, *or that I know not what I want*, is the cause of my complaint" (quoted in *Boredom*, 47, my emphasis). I look at Johnson's own unhappy relation to boredom below. For more general studies of boredom, ennui, and their relatives, see Sean Desmond Healy, *Boredom, Self, and Culture* (Rutherford, NJ: Fairleigh Dickinson University Press, 1984) and Reinhard Kuhn, *The Demon of Noontide: Ennui in Western Literature* (Princeton: Princeton University Press, 1976). For a consideration of the relation of boredom to the twentieth-century culture of information, which I believe offers a difference in degree more than in kind, see Orrin E. Klapp, *Overload and Boredom: Essays on the Quality of Life in the Information Society* (New York: Greenwood Press, 1986).

83. W. Benjamin, "A Berlin Chronicle," *Reflections: Essays, Aphorisms, Autobiographical Writings*, trans. Edmund Jephcott, ed. Peter Demetz (New York: Schocken Books, 1986), 14. For good discussions, in rather different contexts, of Benjamin's conception of consciousness as a social medium or in relation to ongoing history, see Sarah M. Zimmerman, *Romanticism, Lyricism, and History* (Albany: SUNY Press, 1999), 24–28 and Pinch, *Strange Fits of Passion*, 150–54. Gillen D'Arcy Wood's *Shock of the Real* is similarly interested in the historical pertinence of Benjamin's observations (based on Second Empire Paris) to late-eighteenth and early nineteenth-century British culture, pointing out that Benjamin's "historical timeline may be misleadingly shortened."

84. Benjamin, "Some Motifs in Baudelaire," *Illuminations*, 158–59, 162. Elsewhere, Benjamin assigns to the newspaper an as yet unrealized but nonetheless revolutionary potential: see "The Author as Producer," *Reflections*, 220–38.

85. Benjamin, "Some Motifs," *Illuminations*, 162.

86. Benjamin, "Theses," *Illuminations*, 261; Martin Jay, "Experience without a Subject," in *Cultural Semantics*, 49–50.

87. Quoted from Benjamin, *Gesammelte Schriften* by Cynthia Chase, "Translating the Transference: Psychoanalysis and the Construction of History," in *Telling Facts: History and Narration in Psychoanalysis*, eds. Joseph H. Smith and Humphrey Morris (Baltimore, MD: Johns Hopkins University Press, 1992) 120.

88. See Siskin, *Work of Writing*, 126. For Wordsworth's quotation from "Frost at Midnight," see *1799 Prelude* 1.6–8: "For this didst thou, / O Derwent, travelling over the green plains / Near my 'sweet birthplace' . . ." (in *The Prelude, 1799, 1805, 1850*, eds. Jonathan Wordsworth, M. H. Abrams, and Stephen Gill [New York: W. W. Norton and Co., 1979]).

89. Kant writes: "Beautiful objects are to be distinguished from beautiful views of objects. . . . In the latter case taste appears, not so much in what the imagination apprehends in this field, as in the impulse it thus gets to fiction, i.e. in the

peculiar fancies with which the mind entertains itself, while it is continually being aroused by the variety which strikes the eye. An illustration is afforded, e.g. by the sight of the changing shape of a fire on the hearth or of a rippling brook; neither of these has beauty, but they bring with them a charm for the imagination because they entertain it in free play" (*Critique of Judgment*, trans. J. H. Bernard [New York: Hafner Press, 1951], 81).

90. Addison and Steele, *Spectator*, 1:44.
91. On print culture and character formation more generally, see the masterful study of Deidre S. Lynch, *The Economy of Character: Novels, Market Culture, and the Business of Inner Meaning* (Chicago: University of Chicago Press, 1998).
92. Addison and Steele, *Spectator*, 1:395.
93. Samuel Johnson, *The Rambler*, eds. W. J. Bate and Albrect Strauss, vols. 3–5 of *The Yale Edition of the Works of Samuel Johnson*, ed. Allen T. Hazen, 16 vols. (New Haven: Yale University Press, 1958–90); quotation from 4:212.
94. Addison and Steele, *Spectator*, 2:386.
95. Ibid., 1:18, 1:46.
96. Samuel Johnson, *The Idler*, eds. W. J. Bate, J. M. Bullitt, and L. F. Powell, *The Yale Edition of the Works of Samuel Johnson*, 2:23.
97. Ibid., 2:94.
98. Ibid., 2:23–24.
99. Michael Warner, *Letters of the Republic: Publication and the Public Sphere in Eighteenth-Century America* (Cambridge, MA: Harvard University Press, 1990), 5–7 and chapter 1 more generally.
100. Johnson, *Idler*, 2:22.
101. In addition to Priestman's comments on poetic alienation, noted above (n. 52), and for a slightly later period, Guinn Batten's work on Blake, Wordsworth, Byron, and Shelley offers a thoughtful discussion of the melancholy of the poet as a producer for a growing commodity culture (*The Orphaned Imagination: Melancholy and Commodity Culture in English Romanticism* [Durham: Duke University Press, 1998]).
102. Dustin Griffin also observes the transformation ("Redefining Georgic," 871–72). Virgil's *ignobilis oti* offers a subtext to many 1780s and 1790s poets, troubled by a common anxiety of indolence. Coleridge ends his 1795 "Reflections on Leaving a Place of Retirement" by opposing the bliss of his "happy cot" with a vaguely conceived public life of "honorable toil"; Wordsworth ends the first part of the Two Part *Prelude* with the hope that, having "fetch[ed] / Reproaches from my former years," he might now move on to "honorable toil"; Cowper himself, earlier in *The Task*, had lashed out with anxious acrimony at the gypsies who "prefer / Such squalid sloth to honorable toil" (*Task* 1.578).
103. Willard Spiegelman, *Majestic Indolence: English Romantic Poetry and the Work of Art* (New York: Oxford University Press, 1995). For some further interesting comments on the "blank void" in William Cowper and Charlotte Smith, and the "vacancy" of disappointment in Wordsworth, see Laura Quinney, *The*

Poetics of Disappointment: Wordsworth to Ashbery (Charlottesville: University Press of Virginia, 1999), chapter 1.

104. Spiegelman, *Majestic Indolence*, 4.
105. Kenneth Burke, *The Philosophy of Literary Form: Studies in Symbolic Action*, 2nd edn. (Baton Rouge: Louisiana State University Press, 1967), 61 and 293–304.

4 "PASSAGES OF LIFE": AURAL HISTORIES IN *THE EXCURSION*

1. All quotations from *The Excursion* in this chapter are from vol. 5 of *The Poetical Works of William Wordsworth*, eds. Ernest de Selincourt and Helen Darbishire, 5 vols. (Oxford: Clarendon, 1940–49; reprint, 1966). Quotations from other poems will also be from this edition (hereafter *PW*), with the volume and page designated.
2. William Godwin, *The Political and Philosophical Writings of William Godwin*, ed. Mark Philp, 7 vols. (London: William Pickering, 1993), 6:20–21.
3. For a twentieth-century amplification of Godwin's position, see Frank Ankersmit, "Can We Experience the Past?," in *History-Making: the Intellectual and Social Formation of a Discipline: Proceedings of an International Symposium, Uppsala, September 1994*, eds. Rolf Torstendahl and Irmline Veit-Brause, Vitterhets Historie och Antikvitets Akademien, *Konferenser*, no. 37 (Stockholm: Kungl, 1996), 47–76. Ankersmit questions those historical methodologies (primarily constructivism) which rule out the possibility of "experiencing" or sensing the past and celebrate context and probable narrative over "experiential content." His concern about the denigration of "experience" in twentieth-century historiography leads him to draw into the historian's repertoire of "evidence" certain complex aesthetic experiences prompted by artifacts from the past – just as, conversely, the Solitary would draw away from the "volume" of the earth.

   On Godwin specifically and the rising emotional register in late eighteenth-century and early nineteenth-century historiography more generally, see Mark Salber Phillips, *Society and Sentiment: Genres of Historical Writing in Britain, 1740–1820* (Princeton: Princeton University Press, 2000), especially chapter 12. On the "desire for history" during the Romantic period, see Stephen Bann, *Romanticism and the Rise of History* (New York: Twayne Publishers, 1995).
4. For a learned discussion of the Aristotelian and Renaissance interest in "particular," preconceptual, and "confused" knowledge in relation to the later discourse of aesthetics formulated during the eighteenth century by Alexander Baumgarten and others, see Summers, *Judgement of Sense*, 23–31, 182–97.
5. About this concern for transmission, Susan Stewart nicely remarks in a parenthetical note that "although georgic is often written in the past and present tenses, its entire orientation is toward the future; what it records is meant to be taken up by future generations" (*Poetry and the Fate of the Senses*, 367 n. 32).

6. Simpson's skepticism is directed at the *unacknowledged* persistence of old literary paradigms (anecdote, localism, storytelling) in postmodern theories aspiring to radical innovation. He is worried about the "tendency for the tellers of little tales to smuggle back, behind the rhetoric of modesty or of radical alternative, precisely the most uncritical and traditional formations of self and subject, along with the unacknowledged grand narratives that surreptitiously maintain them" (*Academic Postmodern*, 30). His call, then, is for the acknowledgment of the history that we inhabit, sometimes blithely unaware of the shadows at our backs. In a similar vein of self-critique ("Local Transcendence: Cultural Criticism, Posmodernism, and the Romanticism of Detail," *Representations* 32 [1990]: 75–113), Alan Liu anatomizes the rhetoric of detail as an instrument of anti-foundationalism in late twentieth-century cultural criticisms, which he describes as "methodologies as much *against* as of knowledge" (81). However, since "the *etc.* of cultural-critical detail is at base emphatically sublime," "only the reactive phase of the romantic sublime . . . can intervene: insignificance becomes the trope of transcendental meaning. By this trope, the least detail points to a total understanding" (92–93). If unacknowledged, Liu argues, this reactive phase amounts to the "hidden agenda of Western individualism" (cf. Simpson's reappearing "formations of self and subject"). These exemplary self-critiques – both Liu and Simpson acknowledge their own earlier celebrations of the particular over the general – are protests, then, against the hidden compensations of professional academic narratives, above all those that disclaim the compensation of master-narratives; these thinkers offer remarkable, honest accounts of the difficulty steering between the reductiveness of grand claims and the reductiveness of disclaiming them. I hope this chapter on Wordsworth as historiographer participates in the histories that Simpson and Liu call for; going back to Wordsworth again and again, I have come to feel that the compensatory and anti-compensatory drives in his work are more interwined than we have entirely measured. Whether this is truly dialectic or a bad postmodern case of half-claims, I will not presume to answer. I do think that my earlier article on the new historicism, insofar as it emphasized the healing and sealing powers of the "aesthetic medium" (a word I then used without any particular thought or research) was telling only half the story. If "medium" was then seriously underthought, then "aesthetic" was also a tiger held neatly behind bars ("Making Time for History: Wordsworth, the New Historicism, and the Apocalyptic Fallacy," *Studies in Romanticism* 35 [1996], 563–77).

7. Jameson, *The Political Unconscious*, 82; Jean-Luc Nancy, "Finite History," in *The Birth to Presence*, trans. Brian Holmes and others (Stanford: Stanford University Press, 1993), 148.

8. Michel de Certeau, *The Writing of History*, trans. Tom Conley (New York: Columbia University Press, 1988), 5; Conley's fine introduction (vii–xxiii) notes the same ambivalence.

9. For a valuable discussion of the difference between consolatory and anti-consolatory elegy (which he also calls anti-elegy), see the first chapter of Jahan Ramazani's *Poetry of Mourning: the Modern Elegy from Hardy to Heaney*

(Chicago: University of Chicago Press, 1994), 1–30. Ramazani's literary history tends to be more schematic than my own, for he identifies consolatory conventions with elegies written before the twentieth century, and the anti-consolatory rebuff to convention with the poetry of the last century, but he does acknowledge that the categories are not absolute and do not map neatly onto chronology. On the ethics of anti-consolatory mourning, I have learned a great amount from R. Clifton Spargo's *The Ethics of Mourning* (Baltimore: Johns Hopkins University Press, 2004).

10. Thus the Holocaust scholar Saul Friedlander criticizes an earlier generation of historians for remaining "caught between hasty ideological closure (such as the 'catastrophe and redemption theme' [which assimilates the Shoah to a comfortingly familiar Old Testament pattern]) and a paralysis of attempts at global interpretation." See Friedlander's "Trauma, Transference, and Working Through in Writing the History of the Shoah," *History and Memory: Studies in the Representation of the Past* 4 (1992): 51. Lurking behind Friedlander's contradictory constraints, as indeed behind much of this chapter, is Theodor Adorno's famous statement, whose "Yet" clause is often forgotten: "[T]o write lyric poetry after Auschwitz is barbaric. . . . Yet this suffering . . . also demands the continued existence of art while it prohibits it."

11. Saree Makdisi, *Romantic Imperialism: Universal Empire and the Culture of Modernity* (Cambridge: Cambridge University Press, 1998), 36.

12. Michel Foucault, "The Lives of Infamous Men" (1977); the English translation of this essay by Meaghan Morris and Paul Foss is available in *Michel Foucault: Power, Truth, Strategy*, eds. Meaghan Morris and Paul Patton (Sidney: Feral Publications, 1979), 76–91.

13. Nichols, *Anecdotes, Biographical and Literary; Comprizing Biographical Memoirs of William Bowyer, Printer . . .*, 9 vols. (London: Nichols, son, and Bentley, 1812–16), 1:A3[b]. Nichols is largely quoting from, and acknowledging, Johnson's *Rambler*, No. 60.

14. As discussed in chapter 1, Samuel Weber similarly distinguishes between "aesthetically-oriented notions of art and reality, form and work" and the notion of "media," which (he argues) move us away from the usual oppositions between self and object, or between objects, to "places and positioning" (*Mass Mediauras*, 2–4).

15. Stephen Greenblatt, *Shakespearean Negotiations: the Circulation of Social Energy in Renaissance England* (Berkeley and Los Angeles: University of California Press, 1988), 1.

16. Alan Liu, "The New Historicism and the Work of Mourning," *Studies in Romanticism* 35 (1996): 560. Liu's earlier work describes the work of the new historicism as a desire to "pry apart the sides of the raw gap of history to prevent any too-easy credence in an interstitial 'subject' able to heal the wound" (*Sense of History*, 456–57). In his subsequent critique of an array of postmodern historicism, including the new historicism of his own earlier work, Liu suggests that there is an unaddressed longing for epistemological compensation, for a reanimation of the past, in the cultural criticism's romanticization of detail: "A

phrase such as *some fragment of lost life* [Greenblatt's] thus implies, by its genitive construction, that 'lost life' is not really lost, that 'some fragment' despite its discontinuity with the lost life-world can be discovered to be part 'of' the lost world and thus to be big with wholeness" ("Local Transcendence," 86). David Simpson similarly finds "a desire to forestall death" in the postmodern academic culture of storytelling, anecdotes, and conversation (*Academic Postmodern*, 68).

17. This is the argument of one of the best of the many readings of the epyllion: Jane Tylus's "Spenser, Virgil, and the Politics of Poetic Labor," *ELH* 55 (1988). Tylus, whose interest is in Spenser's use of the episode to protest the economy of the patronage system in early modern England, makes the case that Orpheus's elegiac voice disrupts the *Georgics'* celebration of fertility and organic process. Similarly, an important classicist reading of the *Georgics* depends on a binary opposition between husbandman and poet, so that the husbandman "stands for 'productivity' and for control of nature . . . while Orpheus [and the poet narrator] stand for 'creativity' and 'sympathy' with nature" (Christine Perkell, *The Poet's Truth*, 69–70). Perkell represents a majority view among classicists, with the notable exception of the moving study by Michael C. J. Putnam, *Virgil's Poem of the Earth*. I extended a version of this argument about Virgil into an article on Milton ("'Wasted Labor'? Milton's Eve, the Poet's Work, and the Challenge of Sympathy," *ELH* 64 [1997]: 415–46).

18. For further discussion of Virgil's *labor* and its various synonyms, including its difference from *opus*, see *Thesaurus Linguae Latinae*, 10 vols. (Leipzig: B. G. Teubner, 1977), and Susan Scheinberg Kristol, *Labor and Fortuna in Virgil's* Aeneid (New York: Garland Publishing, 1990), especially 22–26.

19. See William Sessions's discussion of time and labor in Virgil and Spenser in "Spenser's Georgics," 203–4.

20. Harry Berger, Jr., "Archaism, Vision, and Revision: Studies in Virgil, Plato, and Milton," *The Centennial Review of Arts and Sciences* 11 (1967): 32.

21. Those who emphasize the imaginative failure include Esther Schor, who writes of the Solitary's inability "to cross the gap between the mind's visionary powers and the spirit's powerlessness to embrace them for consolation. . . . [to find] 'conceptions equal to the soul's desires,'" and Alison Hickey, who writes of his "unwillingness to accept such elusive evidence [the sense of immortality] as adequate to 'counteract' the sensory impressions of death that assault us daily." See Schor's *Bearing the Dead: the British Culture of Mourning from the Enlightenment to Victoria* (Princeton: Princeton University Press, 1994), 168, and Hickey's *Impure Conceits: Rhetoric and Ideology in Wordsworth's 'Excursion'* (Stanford: Stanford University Press, 1997), 81. The thesis of a political malaise in need of a cure that it does not entirely find, suggested by Coleridge's commission to Wordsworth to "write a poem . . . addressed to those who, in consequence of the complete failure of the French Revolution, have thrown up all hopes for the amelioration of mankind," is pursued rigorously by Celeste Langan, who argues: "'Despondency' . . . occurs in the aftermath of the shift, much lamented by Burke, from a discourse of obligations to one of rights. The *negative* character of liberty within the regime and discourse of liberalism

effectively eliminates the deontological or ethical aspect of the political; the subject no longer knows himself by virtue of what he owes to past, present, and future generations. But the discourse of rights in fact deepens the debt; 'man' and 'citizen' owe their being to each other." See Langan, *Romantic Vagrancy: Wordsworth and the Simulation of Freedom* (Cambridge: Cambridge University Press, 1995), 226.

22. Wordsworth's translations of the Orpheus and Eurydice sequence as well as a portion of *Georgics* 3 are collected in *PW* I: 283–85. Bruce Graver, who has edited the Cornell Wordsworth edition of the poet's *Aeneid* translations (William Wordsworth, *Translations of Chaucer and Virgil* [Ithaca: Cornell University Press, 1998]), has also provided further archival and linguistic work on the *Georgics* translations ("Wordsworth's Georgic Beginnings"). Frances Ferguson points out Wordsworth's role as translator of the Orpheus sequence in the context of her analysis of echo and epitaph in *Wordsworth: Language as Counter-Spirit* (New Haven: Yale University Press, 1977), 163–65. To my knowledge, no one has identified these lines from *The Excursion* as allusions to Orpheus – and with him the larger georgic problematic of the simultaneous husbandry of the past by means of the husbandry of the present passions. Wordsworth may also have in mind, as an intermediary, Milton's description of Orpheus (a recurrent and haunting figure for Milton, as is well known) in Sonnet 23: "But O, as to embrace me she inclin'd, / I wak'd, she fled, and day brought back my night" (*Complete Poems and Major Prose*, ed. Hughes, 171).

23. Hickey, *Impure Conceits*, 96; her discussion from 94–96 on the labor of story-telling is excellent. The georgic presence in *The Excursion* is by now widely accepted: for earlier notings of the paradigm, see Annabel Patterson, "Wordsworth's Georgic: Genre and Structure in *The Excursion*," *The Wordsworth Circle* 9 (1978): 145–54, as well as Patterson's *Pastoral and Ideology*, 283–84. Before Patterson, Geoffrey Hartman's *Wordsworth's Poetry, 1787–1814* (New Haven: Yale University Press, 1964) noted the influence (see 296–98). For all three versions of *The Prelude*, I quote from *The Prelude, 1799, 1805, 1850*, eds. Jonathan Wordsworth, M. H. Abrams, and Stephen Gill.

24. On graves as furrows in *The Excursion*, see Paul H. Fry, "The Absent Dead: Wordsworth, Byron, and the Epitaph," in *A Defense of Poetry: Reflections on the Occasion of Writing* (Stanford: Stanford University Press, 1995), 160–67.

25. William Wordsworth, *The Prose Works of William Wordsworth*, eds. W. J. B. Owen and Jane Worthington Smyser, 2:51. (Hereafter *PrW*.)

26. Schor, *Bearing the Dead*, 3; G. W. Pigman III, *Grief and English Renaissance Elegy* (Cambridge: Cambridge University Press, 1985). For a trenchant critique of the way the semi-religious elevation of "memory" in recent historical discourse overleaps the question of how, and whether, psychoanalytic categories are applicable to the writing of history, see Kerwin Lee Klein, "On the Emergence of *Memory* in Historical Discourse," *Representations* 69 (2000), 127–50. Klein's criticisms are well founded and well taken, but nonetheless the persistence and indeed vehement recurrence of implicitly psychological rhetoric – emotion, pain, melancholia – in recent historicizing studies that otherwise

abjure the psychological as dangerously "individual" suggests that the premise that historians should strive for intellectual mastery without worrying about psychic mastery and related concerns remains, at the least, open to question.

27. Freud may be there anyway in the presence of Michel de Certeau, whom Schor discusses wonderfully in the opening pages of *Bearing the Dead*, although without mentioning de Certeau's debt to Freud. To integrate de Certeau's use of Freud in *The Writing of History* more fully than she does might be to recognize the ways that the crucial insight of Schor's work – that in an Enlightenment or Romantic culture of mourning the living provide the site for negotiating relations with the dead – coincides precisely with one of Freud's more Enlightenment faiths: the power of the transference as a kind of compensatory community. Schor may attribute to community precisely the power that Freud attributes to the transference, the present ground of relationship established, in dialogue, with the therapist (although hardly contained by that figure).

28. Schor, *Bearing the Dead*, 3.

29. Geoffrey H. Hartman, "'Was it for this . . . ?' Wordsworth and the Birth of the Gods," in *Romantic Revolutions: Criticism and Theory*, eds. Kenneth R. Johnston et al. (Bloomington: Indiana University Press, 1990), 22; Clifford Siskin, *Work of Writing*, 112. A number of other studies have treated the significance to his poetry of Wordsworth's vocational doubts: these notably include Simpson's *Wordsworth's Historical Imagination*, Thomas Pfau, *Wordsworth's Profession: Form, Class, and the Logic of Early Romantic Cultural Production* (Stanford: Stanford University Press, 1997); and Mark Schoenfield, *The Professional Wordsworth: Law, Labor, and the Poet's Contract* (Athens: University of Georgia Press, 1996).

30. See Bruce Graver, "'Honorable Toil': The Georgic Ethic of *Prelude* I," 352–54.

31. *PrW*, 3:82.

32. Among critics, one of the most skeptical of Wordsworth's attempted identification of work with the ability to feel and create feeling is probably Clifford Siskin. Writing in a self-consciously unsympathetic (i.e., un-Romantic, defamiliarizing) way, Siskin has argued that this prescription is "less salubrious and more coercive: for roughly two centuries we have no choice *but* to feel . . ." (*The Historicity of Romantic Discourse* [New York: Oxford University Press, 1988], 67). Compare as well *Work of Writing*, chapter 4. More generally, the economic arrangements underwriting what Alan Liu calls Wordsworth's "vocational imagination" have been well discussed by Liu (*Sense of History*, 325–41), as by both Pfau and Schoenfield.

33. On the tradition, which develops jointly from the "*fortunatus ille*" sequence in Virgil's second *Georgic* and Horace's *beatus vir* in the second *Epode*, see Maren-Sophie Røstvig, *The Happy Man: Studies in the Metamorphosis of a Classical Ideal*, 2 vols. (Oslo: Akademisk Forlag, 1954). On the contest within "The Ruined Cottage" between a natural education associated with Rousseau and a moral discipline associated with Burke, see James Chandler, *Wordsworth's*

Second Nature: a Study of the Poetry and Politics (Chicago: University of Chicago Press, 1984), 120–43.

34. I follow the text of *The Riverside Shakespeare*, ed. G. Blakemore Evans (Boston: Houghton Mifflin, 1974). On the importance of this allusion during the eighteenth century, and its relationship to the rival Lucretian paradigm of the spectator with shipwreck discussed in chapter 3 above, see David Marshall, *The Surprising Effects of Sympathy* (Chicago: University of Chicago Press, 1988), 21, 23, and *The Figure of the Theater: Shaftesbury, Defoe, Adam Smith, and George Eliot* (New York: Columbia University Press, 1986), 208–09.

35. Adam Smith, *The Theory of Moral Sentiments*, 47. For Smith's parsimonious psychic economy in relation to more extravagant displays of emotion, see Marshall Brown, *Preromanticism*, 82–112, especially 101–02. For Christopher Herbert's discussion of the continuity of Smith's thoughts across his diverse works, see *Culture and Anomie*, 79–105. Wordsworth's edgy and excessive vilification of Adam Smith as "the worst critic, David Hume not excepted, that Scotland, a soil to which this sort of weed seems natural, has produced" (*PrW*, 3:71), does not make their shared assumptions any less striking: this is the anxiety of similarity.

36. Sigmund Freud, *Beyond the Pleasure Principle*, in *The Standard Edition of the Complete Psychological Works of Sigmund Freud*, trans. and ed. James Strachey, 24 vols. (London: Hogarth Press, 1953–74), 18:27–29 (hereafter *SE*).

37. John Keats to Richard Woodhouse, October 27, 1818, *The Selected Letters of John Keats*, ed. Lionel Trilling (New York: Farrar, Straus and Young, 1951), 152.

38. Keats, *The Fall of Hyperion*, 1.392, in *Complete Poems*, ed. Jack Stillinger (Cambridge, MA: Belknap Press, 1982).

39. See Wordsworth, Abrams, and Gill, eds., *The Prelude*, 492 for the early MS draft of the Boy of Winander sequence, which became *1805 Prelude*, 5.389–413.

40. For "A Poet's Epitaph," see *PW*, 4:65–67; I quote lines 51–52, 58–61.

41. See de Selincourt's note to *Excursion* 1.368 (*PW*, 5:20).

42. The poem's ongoing debate over the justifiability of Stoic ethics is motivated, I suspect, less by the philosophical or didactic entailments of georgic than by the occasion the discussion provides for questioning the sympathetic "openness" possible in an "unoccupied" existence. With his unusual ability to quote from Seneca and Samuel Daniel, the Wanderer is a mark of Wordsworth's growing interest – and growing library – in Stoic philosophy. On this subject, see Jane Worthington Smyser, *Wordsworth's Reading of Roman Prose* (New Haven: Yale University Press, 1946), especially 43–73. One of the first readers to discuss the extent of "the Wordsworthian quality that is very close to the Stoic *apatheia*, to not-feeling" was Lionel Trilling, in "Wordsworth and the Rabbis," *The Opposing Self: Nine Essays in Criticism* (New York: Viking Press, 1955), 136. For further comments on how Wordsworth's stoic inclinations both enabled and disabled his poetry, see Michael Cooke, *The Romantic Will* (New Haven: Yale University Press, 1976), 201–16 and 250–51 n. 55.

43. Their affinity recalls the doubling of opposites or isomorphic imitation described by Angus Fletcher, yet unlike the more blatant, old-style confrontations

of Virtue and Vice (or enemy knights in Spenser), the meeting of characters may serve as much to illuminate the ambiguities of the Wanderer's calm as to overcome the resistance of the Solitary. See Fletcher's *Allegory: the Theory of a Symbolic Mode* (Ithaca: Cornell University Press, 1964), 190, as well as William Empson on the identity of opposites, in *Seven Types of Ambiguity* (New York: New Directions, 1966), 192–98.

44. Freud, *SE*, 18:29.
45. Cathy Caruth, *Unclaimed Experience: Trauma, Narrative, and History* (Baltimore: Johns Hopkins University Press, 1996), 61.
46. For a use of Freud largely consonant with my own, see Pinch, *Strange Fits of Passion*, 15–16.
47. Freud, "New Introductory Lectures," *SE*, 22:80.
48. For the use of this term, see Eric Santner, "History Beyond the Pleasure Principle," in *Probing the Limits of Representation: Nazism and the "Final Solution,"* ed. Saul Friedlander (Cambridge, MA: Harvard University Press, 1992), 146.
49. *PrW*, 2:58. See also Wordsworth's aggressively consolatory late poem of 1833, "Monument of Mrs Howard (by Nollekens, In Wetheral Church, near Corby, on the banks of the Eden)":

> But Sculpture here, with the divinest scope
> Of luminous faith, heavenward hath raised the head
> So patiently; and through one hand has spread
> A touch so tender for the insensate Child—
> . . .
> That we, who contemplate the turns of life
> Through this still medium, are consoled and cheered . . .

50. These would have to include, in addition to Schor, *Bearing the Dead*, Hickey, *Impure Conceits*, Fry, "Wordsworth, Byron, and the Epitaph," and Ferguson, *Language as Counter-Spirit*, also the following: Sharon Setzer, "Wordsworth's Wanderer, the Epitaph, and the Uncanny," *Genre* 24 (1991): 361–79; Lorna Clymer, "Graved in Tropes: the Figural Logic of Epitaphs and Elegies in Blair, Gray, Cowper, and Wordsworth," *ELH* 62 (1995): 347–86; and Michelle Turner Sharp, "The Churchyard among the Wordsworthian Mountains: Mapping the Common Ground of Death and the Reconfiguration of Romantic Community," *ELH* 62 (1995): 387–407. For a wide-ranging discussion of the epitaph that includes Wordsworth, see Joshua Scodel, *The English Epitaph: Commemoration and Conflict from Jonson to Wordsworth* (Ithaca: Cornell University Press, 1991).
51. See, for example, *PrW*, 2:50. For Chandler's argument, see *Wordsworth's Second Nature*, 140–44 and 206–15; Schor distinguishes between oral epitaphs, with their criterion of "authenticity," in *The Excursion*, and the scriptural epitaphs, which uphold "sincerity," in the *Essays* (*Bearing the Dead*, 177–83).
52. In her "Notes on Distressed Genres," as well as in "Scandals of the Ballad," Stewart argues that the appropriation of folklore results in a residue of lost context and lost presence, which literary (i.e., print) culture at once distances

and imbues with nostalgia; the bid for authenticity, by a trick of irony, instead suffers from an "inauthenticity of presentation." Both essays are in Stewart's *Crimes of Writing: Problems in the Containment of Representation* (Durham: Duke University Press, 1994), 66–101, 102–31.

53. Kenneth R. Johnston, *Wordsworth and the Recluse* (New Haven: Yale University Press, 1984), 306.

54. Chandler also notes the repetition, and he compares the two poems' "spots" as parallel attempts – both Burkean and conservative – to evoke within post-Revolutionary print culture the traditionary tale, with its resistance to written record and emphasis on common usage (*Wordsworth's Second Nature*, 206–15). My treatment of aura and auricular perception, below, qualifies this assessment.

55. Thomas Weiskel, *The Romantic Sublime: Studies in the Structure and Psychology of Transcendence* (Baltimore: Johns Hopkins University Press, 1976; reprint, 1986), 169.

56. For a discussion of Procopius's *Anecdota* and the genre's deployment, *avant la lettre* (and before the translation of Procopius into English), in Tudor historiography, notably Holinshed, see Annabel Patterson, "Foul, his Wife, the Mayor, and Foul's Mare: the Power of Anecdote in Tudor Historiography," in *The Historical Imagination in Early Modern Britain: History, Rhetoric, and Fiction, 1500–1800*, eds. Donald R. Kelley and David Harris Sacks (Cambridge: Cambridge University Press, 1997), 159–78. Joel Fineman (see next note) emphasizes the anecdote's descent from Thucydides and Hippocratic medicine.

57. For treatments of the anecdote in twentieth-century cultural criticism see, in addition to the important work by Liu ("Local Transcendence") and Simpson (*Academic Postmodern*, chapter 2) discussed above, also Joel Fineman, "The History of the Anecdote," in *The New Historicism*, ed. H. Aram Veeser (New York: Routledge, 1989), 49–76 and Catherine Gallagher, "Counterhistory and the Anecdote," in Gallagher and Greenblatt, *Practicing New Historicism*, 49–74. There is a parting of ways between Gallagher and Greenblatt, on the one hand, and Simpson and Liu, on the other, while Fineman is interestingly enlisted for both sides. Where Gallagher and Greenblatt emphasize the anecdotal "opening" and its capacity for brushing history against the grain, Simpson and Liu are considerably more skeptical of the anecdote's subversive power, arguing that it reinstates the grain and an agenda of individualism (see my discussion in note 6 above). In the terms of this chapter: Gallagher and Greenblatt emphasize the opening, and Simpson and Liu the "closing words"; Fineman the dialectical movement between them. I, too, am describing the ways in which the oscillation is crucial to *The Excursion*'s historiographical project.

58. Isaac D'Israeli, *A Dissertation on Anecdotes*, is available in modern reprint (New York: Garland Publishing, 1972), v–vi. For a discussion of D'Israeli's *Dissertation* in relation to Wordsworth's own "Anecdote for Fathers," see David Simpson, "Public Virtues, Private Vices: Reading Between the Lines of Wordsworth's 'Anecdote for Fathers,'" in *Subject to History: Ideology, Class,*

Gender, ed. David Simpson (Ithaca: Cornell University Press, 1991), 188–90. On D'Israeli more generally, see Simpson's *The Academic Postmodern*, 55–58.

59. Nichols, *Anecdotes, Biographical and Literary*, 9:1ᵃ.

60. On experiment and experience in Baconian science and moral philosophy and its difference from Aristotelian "experience" (received wisdom or common-place), see Poovey, *History of the Modern Fact*, chapters 3 and 4. Poovey is in turn drawing on and extending the work of Peter Dear's *Discipline and Experience*, with a particular interest in developing what she calls the paradox of the modern fact which "could be represented either as mere data, gathered at random, or as data gathered in the light of a social or theoretical context that made them seem worth gathering," in which case they carry with them theoretical presuppositions (96).

61. D'Israeli, *Dissertation*, 30.

62. Addison, "Essay on the Georgics," in Dryden, *Works*, 5:147–48.

63. D'Israeli, *Dissertation*, 3.

64. For D'Israeli's "strokes" and "circumstances," see *Dissertation*, 6, 14. Geoffrey H. Hartman, in an essay I return to below, makes explicit the connection between the closure of form and the compensatory work of mourning: "Closure is sealing with a healing effect" ("Words and Wounds," in *Saving the Text: Literature/Derrida/Philosophy* [Baltimore: Johns Hopkins University Press, 1981], 150).

65. Fineman, "History of the Anecdote," 61.

66. Thomas Weiskel's account of the "unpredictable concomitance" of Wordsworth's quest for an efficacious spirit in the "spots of time" sequence is thus quite appropriate for *The Excursion* provided that one places "historical knowledge" in the place that "self-knowledge" occupies in his discussion. Noting that *The Prelude*'s wording makes it clear that, while the passages of life give the knowledge or feeling that "the mind is lord and master," the efficacious spirit does not consist of that knowledge, but rather "lurks" in concealment where such knowledge is openly "given," Weiskel argued that Wordsworth's discovery is a mode of conversation that is emphatically "not a 'communication' (the cant word of our social world); its aim is not the transmission of knowledge or a message but the springing loose of an efficacious spirit which haunts the passages of self-knowledge" (*The Romantic Sublime*, 169). One hardly needs to note the irony whereby "communication" has become, since 1976, even more of a "cant word of our social world."

67. D'Israeli, *Dissertation*, 50, 81.

68. Ibid., 14. Godwin's essay, unpublished in his lifetime, is reprinted in William Godwin, *Things as They Are or The Adventures of Caleb Williams*, ed. Maurice Hindle (New York: Penguin Books, 1988), 359–73; quotation from 364.

69. D'Israeli, *Dissertation*, 50. Schor, by contrast, argues that *The Excursion*'s mini-plots are proto-novelistic: "The Pastor's closest literary affinities are neither with the expansive national epic nor with the contracted epitaph but rather with a nineteenth-century fictional form that modulates between biography and

history, between the personal and the communal; in this respect, *The Excursion* brings to mind such Victorian fictions as George Eliot's *Middlemarch*, Elizabeth Gaskell's *Cranford*, and Margaret Oliphant's *Chronicles of Carlingford*" (*Bearing the Dead*, 186). While I am intrigued by and sympathetic to the large claim suggested in this brief comment – *Middlemarch*, as I have suggested, does seem to be a permutation of georgic – it seems to me that in this instance the difference between Wordsworth's rural anecdotes and D'Israeli's and other familiar anecdotes are important to emphasize.

70. Hickey, *Impure Conceits*, 63.

71. See Bacon's defense of the aphorism over the scholastic method in the second book of *The Advancement of Learning*:

> For it is in Knowledges, as it is in Plantes: if you meane to vse the Plant, it is no matter for the Rootes: But if you meane to remooue it to growe, then it is more assured to rest vppon rootes, than Slippes: So the deliuerie of Knowledges (as it is nowe vsed [e.g. by methods, which compel assent]) is as of faire bodies of Trees without the Rootes: good for the Carpenter, but not for the Planter: But if you will haue Sciences growe; it is lesse matter for the shafte, or bodie of the Tree, so you looke well to the takinge vp of the Rootes.

Slightly later Bacon adds: "*Aphorismes*, representing a knowledge broken, doe inuite men to enquire farther; whereas *Methodes*, carrying the shewe of a Totall, doe secure men; as if they were at furthest." Quoted from *The Advancement of Learning*, ed. Kiernan, 123–24.

Writing about Luke's equally hasty and under-described exit in "Michael," Susan Eilenberg detects the return of "precisely the kind of narrative Wordsworth rejects in the 'Preface' to *Lyrical Ballads:* sensational, unsubtle, characterless," and others, protesting what they take to be the strained foreclosure of that prodigal's narrative, have agreed. I suspect, however, that what has seemed sudden, unsubtle, and undermotivated to some readers results instead from a strategic policy of reticence, understatement, and quite often, irony. For Eilenberg's reading of "Michael" against "Christabel," see *Strange Power of Speech: Wordsworth, Coleridge, and Literary Possession* (New York: Oxford University Press 1992), 94.

72. Walter Benjamin, "The Storyteller," in *Illuminations*, 90–91, emphasis added. Much as Benjamin would not like the comparison, although it is relevant for Wordsworth, we might note that we have seen this "chaste" aesthetic underlying Adam Smith's advice for the evocation of sympathy. For Smith, the man who seeks to represent his suffering to others must "flatten" and "lower" his passion "to that pitch, in which the spectators are capable of going along with him" (*Theory of Moral Sentiments*, 24).

73. Benjamin, "The Storyteller," in *Illuminations*, 109; "On Some Motifs in Baudelaire," in *Illuminations*, 188.

74. Compare Benjamin – "If, while resting on a summer afternoon, you follow with your eyes a mountain range on the horizon or a branch which casts its shadow

over you, you experience the aura of this mountain, of that branch" ("Work of Art in the Age of Mechanical Reproduction," *Illuminations*, 222–23) – with the opening of *The Excursion*:

> 'Twas summer, and the sun had mounted high:
> Southward the landscape indistinctly glared
> Through a pale steam; but all the northern downs,
> In clearest air ascending, showed far off
> A surface dappled o'er with shadows flung
> From brooding clouds; shadows that lay in spots
> Determined and unmoved, with steady beams
> Of bright and pleasant sunshine interposed;
> To him most pleasant who on soft cool moss
> Extends his careless limbs along the front
> Of some huge cave . . .
>   . . .
> With side-long eye looks out upon the scene
> By power of that impending covert thrown
> To finer distance.   (*Exc.*, 1.1–11, 15–17)

75. *PrW*, 1:128, 130.
76. See Miriam Hansen, in "Benjamin, Cinema, Experience: the Blue Flower in the Land of Technology," *New German Critique* 40 (1987): 179–224. Also helpful is the lucid exposition offered by Martin Jay, "Experience without a Subject: Walter Benjamin and the Novel," in *Cultural Semantics*, 48–52.
77. Fredric Jameson, one of the relatively few Marxist theorists fully to appreciate "The Storyteller" as something other than a backward-looking or embarrassing lapse of political correctness, writes (in the context of a comparison between Benjamin and Sartre): "Benjamin is as aware as Sartre of the way in which the tale, with its appearance of destiny, does violence to our lived experience of the present; but for him it does justice to our experience of the past" (*Marxism and Form* [Princeton: Princeton University Press, 1971], 79).
78. I take the phrase "ethos of letters" from James Chandler's argument about Wordsworth's Burkean traditionalism (*Wordsworth's Second Nature*, 140–55). Chandler is one of the few critics to engage the recurrence of the phrase "passages of life" in key moments of *The Prelude* and *The Excursion* at any length; his helpful analysis argues that Wordsworth's attempt to make his writing simulate oral narrative is a protest against this more progressive ethos (as captured in the anti-Burkean spirit of Hazlitt's thesis that the French Revolution was an indirect but inevitable result of the invention of the art of printing).
79. Munier is quoted in Philippe Lacoue-Labarthe, *Poetry as Experience*, trans. Andrea Tarnowski (Stanford: Stanford University Press, 1999), 128 n. 15. Lacoue-Labarthe himself, privileging one of Benjamin's two categories over the other, warns us to "avoid associating [experience, 'crossing through danger'] with what is 'lived,' the stuff of anecdotes. *Erfahrung*, then, rather than *Erlebnis*" (18). Lacoue-Labarthe's association of "the stuff of anecdotes" with *Erlebnis*,

the charged and lived moment, is, of course, quite interesting in the context of my own discussion. One way to put my point about Wordsworth's alteration of anecdotal practice is that he rids it of any association with what Benjamin would later call *Erlebnis*, which finds its form in the isolated and "detached particular," and turns it into a kind of *Erfahrung*. But I have tried for the most part to describe the revision in its own terms for the sake of simplicity and accuracy.

80. See chapter 22 of the *Biographia Literaria*, here quoted from *Samuel Taylor Coleridge: a Critical Edition*, 396.

81. Hartman, "Words and Wounds," *Saving the Text*, 123. Jacques Derrida's *The Ear of the Other: Otobiography, Transference, Translation*, trans. Peggy Kamuf and Avitall Ronell, ed. Christie MacDonald (Lincoln: University of Nebraska Press, 1988) also finds an ethical dimension and a disruption of the author's or speaker's authority in the figure of the ear, so long as it is understood as the "ear of the other." John Hollander comments that "one can shut, or avert, the eyes but not the ears; . . . hearing outlasts vision as one falls through layers of sleep; . . . sound can pierce the dark globe of sleeping consciousness, the planetarium in which are projected our dreams, . . . while light cannot," and he offers a reading of Wordsworth's "Ode on the Power of Sound" in this context (*Vision and Resonance: Two Senses of Poetic Form* [New York: Oxford University Press, 1975], 22–25).

82. Benjamin's aura comes from the Greek word for breeze or breath (i.e., an emanation); auricular from the Latin for ear. I take the apt term "otopathy" from Marshall Brown's description of the essays by Derrida and Hartman cited in the preceding note: "Jacques Derrida has recently given us the otobiography, or life history of the ear, and Geoffrey Hartman's troubling studies of words and wounds have established the study of otopathy. But the track that leads from the voice to the ear, from the soul's voice to the heart's ear, remains, I am convinced, as intact and mysterious as ever" (*Preromanticism*, 21). I have been interested in an even more mysterious track – that which leads from the page to the ear; a question which reinstates the problem of heterogeneous media within Brown's problematic. Although the study of otopathy is far from established, there are, besides Brown's work, some notable contributions, among which I would mention Robert Kaufman, "Aura Still," *October* 99 (2002): 45–80.

83. Stewart, *Poetry and the Fate of the Senses*, 100. Stewart's analysis of the affecting qualities of sound (ibid., 59–105) reminds us that in the case of printed poetry, "we are always *recalling sound*" from an originating auditory experience (68). For this reason I have preferred to talk about the trope or figure *of* sound, or "cognitive noise," but this figure, or moment of recall, is similarly resistant to the epistemology of spatial articulation and "ideas."

84. Discussing *The Excursion*'s shell passage, Hickey writes that "*The Excursion* does not leave room for any such obscure conflations in the hierarchy of transmission, or for garbled or waylaid messages. . . . *The Excursion* expresses more urgency about keeping unobstructed 'the passages / Through which the ear converses with the heart'" (*Impure Conceits*, 151). I am arguing just the

opposite. It is certainly true that the *Wanderer*, whose lines these are, expresses urgency about unobstructed communications, both internal and external, but it would contradict Hickey's own finely argued position elsewhere in *Impure Conceits* – namely, that we cannot identify the author of *The Excursion* with the Wanderer or any other character – to make that substitution here.

85. Kenneth Burke, *Philosophy of Literary Form*, 61.
86. I am adapting here Benjamin's "unconscious optics" ("Work of Art," *Illuminations*, 237).
87. Orwell, "Politics and the English Language," in *A Collection of Essays* (New York: Harcourt, Brace, Jovanovich, 1946), 167.
88. "Negative allegory," or "allegory by absence," are Marjorie Levinson's terms, set forth in the introduction to her *Wordsworth's Great Period Poems: Four Essays* (Cambridge: Cambridge University Press, 1986), see especially 8–13. Levinson's procedure is close to Alan Liu's emphasis on absence and denial in *The Sense of History*; Liu offers an excellent discussion of the difference among terms of negativity (including the difference between his denial and David Simpson's emphasis on "displacement" and Jerome McGann's "occlusion") in a long discussion note on 528–30.
89. See, for instance, Hickey's *Impure Conceits*, 89–93 and Schor's *Bearing the Dead*, 157–58.
90. On the "language of flowers," see (for France, with some mention of Lady Mary Wortley Montague) Jack Goody, *The Culture of Flowers* (Cambridge: Cambridge University Press, 1993), chapter 8, and Ann B. Shteir, *Cultivating Women, Cultivating Science* (Baltimore: Johns Hopkins University Press, 1996), 158, 163, 199.
91. Langan, *Romantic Vagrancy*, 268.
92. Wordsworth seems to be parodying the language of flowers particularly in France, where it aspired to be a universal language or "code," a floral version of the objects waved about in Swift's Academy of Lagado (see Goody, cited above). David Simpson similarly remarks the failure of "consensus" and ironization of dialogue in *The Excursion* more generally (*Wordsworth's Historical Imagination*, 209–10).
93. See Empson, *Some Versions of Pastoral*, 4–5.
94. Quotations are from Geoffrey H. Hartman's *Wordsworth's Poetry*, 292, 295. Hartman's dismissal of *The Excursion* would seem to move oddly against the very insights that are offered in the later essay, "Words and Wounds" (1981, in *Saving the Text*), quoted earlier in my discussion.

Works cited

Aarsleff, Hans. *From Locke to Saussure: Essays on the Study of Language and Intellectual History*. Minneapolis: University of Minnesota Press, 1982.

Addison, Joseph. "An Essay on the Georgics." In *The Works of Virgil in English*, eds. William Frost and Vincent A. Dearing. Vol. 5 of *Works of John Dryden*, eds. Edward Niles Hooker and H. T. Swedenberg, Jr. Berkeley and Los Angeles: University of California Press, 1987.

Addison, Joseph and Sir Richard Steele. *The Spectator*. Ed. Donald F. Bond. 5 vols. Oxford: Clarendon Press, 1965.

Alpers, Paul. *What is Pastoral?* Chicago: University of Chicago Press, 1996.

Alpers, Svetlana. *The Art of Describing: Dutch Art in the Seventeenth Century*. Chicago: University of Chicago Press, 1983.

Althusser, Louis and Etienne Balibar. *Reading Capital*. Trans. Ben Brewster. London: Verso, 1997.

Altick, Richard Daniel. *The English Common Reader: a Social History of the Mass Reading Public 1800–1900*. Chicago: University of Chicago Press, 1957.

Anderson, Benedict. *Imagined Communities: Reflections on the Origin and Spread of Nationalism*. Rev. edn. London: Verso, 1991.

Ankersmit, Frank. "Can We Experience the Past?" In *History-Making: the Intellectual and Social Formation of a Discipline: Proceedings of an International Symposium, Uppsala, September 1994*, eds. Rolf Torstendahl and Irmline Veit-Brause. Vitterhets Historie och Antikvitets Akademien, *Konferenser*, no. 37. Stockholm: Kungl, 1996.

Aristotle. *Physics*. Trans. Philip H. Wicksteed and Francis M. Cornford. London: William Heinemann/Loeb Classical Library, 1929.

——. *Aristotle: On the Soul, Parva Naturalia, On Breath*. Trans. W. S. Hett. Cambridge, MA: Harvard University Press/Loeb Classical Library, 1957.

——. *The Categories, On Interpretation, Prior Analytics*. Trans. Harold P. Cooke and Hugh Tredennick. Cambridge, MA: Harvard University Press/Loeb Classical Library, 1996.

Armstrong, John. *The Art of Preserving Health, to which is prefixed a critical essay on the poem by J. Aikin, M.D.* London: T. Cadell, Jun. and W. Davies, 1795.

Armstrong, Nancy and Leonard Tennenhouse. *The Imaginary Puritan: Literature, Intellectual Labor, and the Origins of Personal Life*. Berkeley and Los Angeles: University of California Press, 1992.

Arthos, John. *The Language of Natural Description in Eighteenth-Century Poetry.* Ann Arbor: University of Michigan Press, 1949.

Austen, Jane. *Emma.* Ed. Lionel Trilling. Boston: Houghton Mifflin, 1957.

Bacon, Francis. *Novum Organum.* Trans. and eds. Peter Urbach and John Gibson. Chicago: Open Court, 1994.

———. *The Advancement of Learning.* Ed. Michael Kiernan. Oxford: Clarendon Press, 2000.

Baker, [Henry]. *The Universe. A Poem. Intended to Restrain the Pride of Man.* London: Printed for T. Worrall, 1734.

———. *The Microscope Made Easy.* London: R. Dodsley, 1742.

Bann, Stephen. *Romanticism and the Rise of History.* New York: Twayne Publishers, 1995.

Barrell, John. *The Idea of the Landscape and the Sense of Place, 1730–1840: an Approach to the Poetry of John Clare.* Cambridge: Cambridge University Press, 1972.

———. *The Dark Side of the Landscape: the Rural Poor in English Painting, 1730–1840.* Cambridge: Cambridge University Press, 1980.

———. *English Literature in History, 1730–1780: an Equal, Wide Survey.* London: Hutchinson, 1983.

———. *The Birth of Pandora and the Division of Knowledge.* London: Macmillan, 1992.

———. "Afterword: Moving Stories, Still Lives." In *The Country and the City Revisited,* eds. MacLean, Landry, and Ward, 1999.

Barrell, John and Harriet Guest. "On the Use of Contradiction: Economics and Morality in the Eighteenth-Century Long Poem." In *The New Eighteenth Century: Theory, Politics, English Literature,* eds. Felicity Nussbaum and Laura Brown. New York: Methuen, 1987.

Barstow, Marjorie. *Wordsworth's Theory of Poetic Diction: a Study in the Historical and Personal Background of the Lyrical Ballads.* New Haven: Yale University Press, 1917.

Batten, Guinn. *The Orphaned Imagination: Melancholy and Commodity Culture in English Romanticism.* Durham: Duke University Press, 1998.

Beck, Cave. *The Universal Character.* London: Tho. Maxey, 1757.

Bender, John and David Wellbery, eds. *The Ends of Rhetoric: History, Theory, Practice.* Stanford: Stanford University Press, 1990.

Benjamin, Walter. *Illuminations: Essays and Reflections.* Trans. Harry Zohn. Ed. Hannah Arendt. New York: Schocken Books, 1968.

———. *Reflections: Essays, Aphorisms, Autobiographical Writings.* Trans. Edmund Jephcott. Ed. Peter Demetz. New York: Schocken Books, 1986.

Berger, Harry, Jr. "Archaism, Vision, and Revision: Studies in Virgil, Plato, and Milton." *The Centennial Review of Arts and Sciences* 11 (1967): 24–52.

Berkeley, George. *The Works of George Berkeley, D.D.* Ed. Alexander Campbell Fraser. 4 vols. Oxford: Clarendon Press, 1871.

Bermingham, Ann. *Landscape and Ideology: the English Rustic Tradition, 1740–1860.* Berkeley and Los Angeles: University of California Press, 1986.

Bhabha, Homi K. *The Location of Culture.* New York: Routledge, 1994.

Black, Jeremy. *The English Press in the Eighteenth Century*. London: Crook Helm, 1987.

Blumenberg, Hans. *Die Lesbarkeit der Welt*. 2nd edn. Frankfurt am Main: Suhrkamp, 1983.

———. *Shipwreck with Spectator: Paradigm of a Metaphor for Existence*. Trans. Steven Rendall. Cambridge, MA: The MIT Press, 1997.

Bohls, Elizabeth. "The Gentleman Planter and the Metropole: Long's *History of Jamaica* [1774]." In *The Country and the City Revisited*, eds MacLean, Landry, and Ward.

Bolter, Jay David and Richard Grusin. *Remediation: Understanding New Media*. Cambridge, MA: The MIT Press, 2000.

Bolton, Martha Brandt. "The Real Molyneux Question and the Basis of Locke's Answer." In *Locke's Philosophy: Content and Context*, ed. G. A. J. Rogers. Oxford: Clarendon Press, 1994.

Bourdieu, Pierre. *Outline of a Theory of Practice*. Trans. Richard Nice. Cambridge: Cambridge University Press, 1977.

Brown, Laura. *Alexander Pope*. Oxford: Basil Blackwell, 1985.

Brown, Marshall. *Preromanticism*. Stanford: Stanford University Press, 1991.

Brown, Norman O. *Apocalypse and/or Metamorphosis*. Berkeley and Los Angeles: University of California Press, 1991.

Buck-Morss, Susan. "Aesthetics and Anaesthetics: Walter Benjamin's Artwork Essay Reconsidered." *October* 62 (1992): 3–41.

Burke, Edmund. *A Philosophical Enquiry into the Origin of Our Ideas of the Sublime and Beautiful*. Ed. Adam Phillips. Oxford: Oxford University Press, 1990.

Burke, Kenneth. *The Philosophy of Literary Form: Studies in Symbolic Action*. 2nd edn. Baton Rouge: Louisiana State University Press, 1967.

Burney, Frances. *The Early Diary of Frances Burney*. Ed. Annie Raine Ellis. London: G. Bell, 1907.

Burton, Robert. *The Anatomy of Melancholy*. Eds. Thomas C. Faulkner, Nicolas K. Kiessling, and Rhonda L. Blair. 6 vols. Oxford: Clarendon Press, 1989–2000.

Campbell, Hilbert H. *James Thomson (1700–1748): an Annotated Bibliography of Selected Editions and the Important Criticism*. New York: Garland Publishing, 1976.

Campbell, Jill. "Colonial Trade and the Laboring Body in Thomson's *The Seasons*." Paper delivered at the annual meeting of the New England Society for Eighteenth-Century Studies, October 1990.

Caruth, Cathy. *Unclaimed Experience: Trauma, Narrative, and History*. Baltimore, MD: Johns Hopkins University Press, 1996.

Cavendish, Margaret, Duchess of Newcastle. *Observations upon Experimental Philosophy*. Ed. Eileen O'Neill. Cambridge: Cambridge University Press, 2001.

Chalker, John. *The English Georgic: a Study in the Develoment of a Form*. London: Routledge and Kegan Paul, 1969.

Chandler, James. *Wordsworth's Second Nature: a Study of the Poetry and Politics*. Chicago: University of Chicago Press, 1984.

Chapman, George. *The Poems of George Chapman*. Ed. Phyllis B. Bartlett. Oxford: Oxford University Press, 1941.

Chase, Cynthia. "Translating the Transference: Psychoanalysis and the Construction of History." In *Telling Facts: History and Narration in Psychoanalysis*, eds. Joseph H. Smith and Humphrey Morris. Baltimore, MD: Johns Hopkins University Press, 1992.

Clymer, Lorna. "Graved in Tropes: the Figural Logic of Epitaphs and Elegies in Blair, Gray, Cowper, and Wordsworth." *ELH* 62 (1995): 347–86.

Cohen, Murray. *Sensible Words: Linguistic Practice in England, 1640–1785*. Baltimore, MD: Johns Hopkins University Press, 1977.

Cohen, Ralph. *The Art of Discrimination: Thomson's* The Seasons *and the Language of Criticism*. Berkeley and Los Angeles: University of California Press, 1964.

———. "Innovation and Variation: Literary Change and Georgic Poetry." In *Literature and History: Papers Read at a Clark Library Seminar, March 3, 1973*, eds. Ralph Cohen and Murray Krieger. Los Angeles: William Andrews Clark Memorial Library, 1974.

Coleridge, Samuel Taylor. *Samuel Taylor Coleridge: a Critical Edition of the Major Works*. Ed. H. J. Jackson. New York: Oxford University Press, 1992.

Cook, Elizabeth Heckendorn. "Frances Burney and the Reconstruction of Britishness." In *The Country and the City Revisited* eds. MacLean, Landry, and Ward.

Cooke, Michael. *The Romantic Will*. New Haven: Yale University Press, 1976.

Copley, Stephen. "The Fine Arts in Eighteenth-Century Polite Culture." In *Painting and the Politics of Culture: New Essays on British Art*, ed. John Barrell. New York: Oxford University Press, 1992.

Cowper, William. *The Letters and Prose Writings of William Cowper*. Eds. James King and Charles Ryskamp. 5 vols. Oxford: Clarendon Press, 1979–86.

———. *The Poems of William Cowper*. Eds. John D. Baird and Charles Ryskamp. 3 vols. Oxford: Clarendon Press, 1980.

Crabbe, George. *George Crabbe: the Complete Poetical Works*. Ed. Norma Dalrymple-Champneys. 3 vols. Oxford: Clarendon Press, 1988.

Crary, Jonathan. *Techniques of the Observer: on Vision and Modernity in the Nineteenth Century*. Cambridge, MA: The MIT Press, 1990.

Crawford, Rachel. *Poetry, Enclosure, and the Vernacular Landscape*. Cambridge: Cambridge University Press, 2002.

Crombie, A. C. "The Mechanistic Hypothesis and the Scientific Study of Vision: some Optical Ideas as a Background to the Invention of the Microscope." In *Historical Aspects of Microscopy*. Cambridge: Heffer, for the Royal Microscopical Society, 1967.

Daston, Lorraine. *Classical Probability in the Enlightenment*. Princeton: Princeton University Press, 1988.

———. "Baconian Facts, Academic Civility, and the Prehistory of Objectivity." *Annals of Scholarship* 8 (1991): 337–64.

Davidoff, Leonore and Catherine Hall. *Family Fortunes: Men and Women of the English Middle Class, 1780–1850*. Chicago: University of Chicago Press, 1987.

Davie, Donald. *Purity of Diction in English Verse*. London: Routledge and Kegan Paul, 1967.

——. *The Eighteenth-Century Hymn in England*. Cambridge: Cambridge University Press, 1993.

De Bruyn, Frans. "From Virgilian Georgic to Agricultural Science: an Instance of the Transvaluation of Literature in Eighteenth-Century Britain." In *Augustan Subjects: Essays in Honor of Martin C. Battestin*, ed. Albert J. Rivero. Newark: University of Delaware Press, 1997.

De Certeau, Michel. *The Writing of History*. Trans. Tom Conley. New York: Columbia University Press, 1988.

Dear, Peter Robert. *Discipline and Experience: the Mathematical Way in the Scientific Revolution*. Chicago: University of Chicago Press, 1995.

Derrida, Jacques. "Economimesis." *Diacritics* 11 (1981): 3–25.

——. *The Ear of the Other: Otobiography, Transference, Translation*. Trans. Peggy Kamuf and Avitall Ronell. Ed. Christie MacDonald. Lincoln: University of Nebraska Press, 1988.

D'Israeli, Isaac. *A Dissertation on Anecdotes*. New York: Garland Publishing, 1972.

Dryden, John. *Sylvae: or the Second Part of Poetical Miscellanies*. London: Jacob Tonson, 1685.

——. *John Dryden: Selected Criticism*. Eds. James Kinsley and George Parfitt. Oxford: Clarendon Press, 1970.

Durling, Dwight Leonard. *The Georgic Tradition in English Poetry*. New York: Columbia University Press, 1935.

Dyer, John. *The Fleece. A Poem. In Four Books*. London: R. and J. Dodsley, 1757.

Eagleton, Terry. *The Function of Criticism: From "The Spectator" to Post-Structuralism*. London: Verso, 1984.

Eilenberg, Susan. *Strange Power of Speech: Wordsworth, Coleridge, and Literary Possession*. New York: Oxford University Press, 1992.

Elfenbein, Andrew. *Romantic Genius: the Prehistory of a Homosexual Role*. New York: Columbia University Press, 1999.

Eliot, George. *Middlemarch: a Study of Provincial Life*. New York: New American Library, 1981.

Ellison, Julie. *Cato's Tears and the Making of Anglo-American Emotion*. Chicago: University of Chicago Press, 1999.

——. "News, Blues, and Cowper's Busy World." *Modern Language Quarterly* 62 (2001): 219–37.

Empson, William. *Seven Types of Ambiguity*. New York: New Directions, 1966.

——. *Some Versions of Pastoral*. New York: New Directions, 1974.

Engell, James. *The Creative Imagination: Enlightenment to Romanticism*. Cambridge, MA: Harvard University Press, 1981.

Farley-Hills, David, ed. *Rochester: the Critical Heritage*. New York: Barnes and Noble, 1972.

Farrell, Joseph P. *Vergil's* Georgics *and the Traditions of Ancient Epic: the Art of Allusion in Literary History*. New York: Oxford University Press, 1991.

Feingold, Richard. *Nature and Society: Later Eighteenth-Century Uses of the Pastoral and Georgic*. New Brunswick, NH: Rutgers University Press, 1978.

Ferguson, Frances. *Wordsworth: Language as Counter-Spirit*. New Haven: Yale University Press, 1977.

Fielding, Henry. *Miscellanies*. Ed. Henry Knight Miller. 3 vols. Oxford: Clarendon Press, 1972–97.

Fineman, Joel. "The History of the Anecdote." In *The New Historicism*, ed. H. Aram Veeser. New York: Routledge, 1989.

Fletcher, Angus. *Allegory: the Theory of a Symbolic Mode*. Ithaca: Cornell University Press, 1964.

Foucault, Michel. *The Order of Things: an Archaeology of the Human Sciences*. Trans. Alan Sheridan Smith. London: Tavistock Publications, 1970.

——. *The Birth of the Clinic: an archaeology of Medical Perception*. Trans. A. M. Sheridan. New York: Pantheon, 1973.

——. *Michel Foucault: Power, Truth, Strategy*. Trans. Meaghan Morris and Paul Foss. Eds. Meaghan Morris and Paul Patton. Sidney: Feral Publications, 1979.

Fowler, Alastair. "The Beginnings of English Georgic." In *Renaissance Genres: Essays on Theory, History, and Interpretation*, ed. Barbara Kiefer Lewalski. Cambridge, MA: Harvard University Press, 1986.

——. "Georgic and Pastoral: Laws of Genre in the Seventeenth Century." In *Culture and Cultivation in Early Modern England*, eds. Leslie and Raylor, 1992.

Fox, Christopher. *Locke and the Scriblerians: Identity and Consciousness in Early Eighteenth-Century Britain*. Berkeley and Los Angeles: University of California Press, 1988.

Freud, Sigmund. *The Standard Edition of the Complete Psychological Works of Sigmund Freud*. Trans. and ed. James Strachey. 24 vols. London: Hogarth Press, 1953–74.

Friedlander, Saul. "Trauma, Transference, and Working Through in Writing the History of the *Shoah*." *History and Memory: Studies in the Representation of the Past* 4: 1 (1992): 39–59.

Friedman, Donald. "Sight and Insight in Marvell's Poetry." In *Approaches to Marvell: the York Tercentenary Lectures*, ed. C. A. Patrides. Boston, MA: Routledge and Kegan Paul, 1978.

Fry, Paul H. "Georgic Comedy: the Fictive Territory of Jane Austen's *Emma*." *Studies in the Novel* 11 (1979): 129–46.

——. *A Defense of Poetry: Reflections on the Occasion of Writing*. Stanford: Stanford University Press, 1995.

Fulford, Tim. *Landscape, Liberty, and Authority: Poetry, Criticism, and Politics from Thomson to Wordsworth*. Cambridge: Cambridge University Press, 1996.

Gallagher, Catherine and Stephen Greenblatt. *Practicing New Historicism*. Chicago: University of Chicago Press, 2000.

Gay, John. *Rural Sports. A Poem*. London: J. Tonson, 1713.

Godwin, William. *Things as They Are or The Adventures of Caleb Williams*. Ed. Maurice Hindle. New York: Penguin Books, 1988.

———. *The Political and Philosophical Writings of William Godwin*. Ed. Mark Philp. 7 vols. London: William Pickering, 1993.

Godzich, Wlad and Jeffrey Kittay. *The Emergence of Prose: an Essay in Prosaics*. Minneapolis: University of Minnesota Press, 1987.

Goldsmith, Steven. "Blake's Agitation." *The South Atlantic Quarterly* 95 (1996): 753–96.

Goodman, Kevis. "Making Time for History: Wordsworth, the New Historicism, and the Apocalyptic Fallacy." *Studies in Romanticism* 35 (1996): 563–77.

———. "'Wasted Labor'? Milton's Eve, the Poet's Work, and the Challenge of Sympathy." *ELH* 64 (1997): 415–67.

Goodridge, John. *Rural Life in Eighteenth-Century English Poetry*. Cambridge: Cambridge University Press, 1995.

Goody, Jack. *The Culture of Flowers*. Cambridge: Cambridge University Press, 1993.

Grainger, James. *The Sugar-Cane*. In *The Poetics of Empire: a Study of James Grainger's The Sugar-Cane*, ed. John Gilmore. New Brunswick: Athlone Press, 2000.

Graver, Bruce. "Wordsworth's Georgic Beginnings." *Texas Studies in Language and Literature* 33 (1991): 137–59.

———. "'Honorable Toil': the Georgic Ethic of *Prelude* I." *Studies in Philology* 92 (1993): 346–60.

Greenblatt, Stephen. *Shakespearean Negotiations: the Circulation of Social Energy in Renaissance England*. Berkeley and Los Angeles: University of California Press, 1988.

Griffin, Dustin. "The Bard of Cyder-Land: John Philips and Miltonic Imitation." *Studies in English Literature 1500–1900* 24 (1984): 441–60.

———. "Redefining Georgic: Cowper's *Task*." *ELH* 57 (1990): 865–79.

Guillory, John. *Cultural Capital: the Problem of Literary Canon Formation*. Chicago: University of Chicago Press, 1993.

Habermas, Jürgen. *The Structural Transformation of the Public Sphere*. Trans. Thomas Burger. Cambridge, MA: The MIT Press, 1994.

Hacking, Ian. *The Emergence of Probability: a Philosophical Study of Early Ideas about Probability, Induction and Statistical Inference*. Cambridge: Cambridge University Press, 1975.

Hagstrum, Jean. "Toward a Profile of the word *Conscious* in Eighteenth-Century Literature." In *Psychology and Literature in the Eighteenth Century*, ed. Christopher Fox. New York: AMS Press, 1987.

Hansen, Miriam "Benjamin, Cinema, Experience: the Blue Flower in the Land of Technology." *New German Critique* 40 (1987): 179–224.

Harlow, V. T., ed. *Colonizing Expeditions to the West Indies and Guiana, 1621–1667*. London: Hakluyt Society, 1925.

Harris, James. *The Works of James Harris, Esq. with an Account of His Life and Character By His Son The Earl of Malmesbury*. Oxford: Printed by J. Vincent, 1841.

Hartman, Geoffrey H. *Wordsworth's Poetry, 1787–1814*. New Haven: Yale University Press, 1964.

——. *Criticism in the Wilderness: the Study of Literature Today*. New Haven: Yale University Press, 1980.

——. *Saving the Text: Literature/Philosophy/Derrida*. Baltimore, MD: Johns Hopkins University Press, 1981.

——. " 'Was it for this . . . ?' Wordsworth and the Birth of the Gods." In *Romantic Revolutions: Criticism and Theory*, eds. Kenneth R. Johnston, Gilbert Chaitin, Karen Hanson, and Herbert Marks. Bloomington: Indiana University Press, 1990.

——. *Minor Prophecies: the Literary Essay in the Culture Wars*. Cambridge, MA: Harvard University Press, 1991.

Hazlitt, William. *The Complete Works of William Hazlitt*. Ed. P. P. Howe. 21 vols. New York: AMS Press, 1967.

Healy, Sean Desmond. *Boredom, Self, and Culture*. Rutherford, NJ: Fairleigh Dickinson University Press, 1984.

Heidegger, Martin. *The Question Concerning Technology and Other Papers*. Trans. William Lovitt. New York: Harper and Row, 1977.

Heinzelman, Kurt. "The Cult of Domesticity: Dorothy and William Wordsworth at Grasmere." In *Romanticism and Feminism*, ed. Anne K. Mellor. Bloomington: Indiana University Press, 1988.

——. "Economics, Rhetoric, and the Scene of Instruction." *Stanford French Review: International Journal of Interdisciplinary Research* 15 (1991): 349–71.

——. "Roman Georgic in a Georgian Age: a Theory of Romantic Genre." *Texas Studies in Literature and Language* 33 (1991): 182–214.

——. "Poetry and Real Estate: Wordsworth as Developer." *Southwest Review* 84 (1994): 573–88.

——. "The Uneducated Imagination: Romantic Representations of Labor." In *At the Limits of Romanticism: Essays in Cultural, Feminist, and Materialist Criticism*, eds. Mary Favret and Nicola Watson. Bloomington: Indiana University Press, 1994.

——. "The Last Georgic: *Wealth of Nations* and the Scene of Writing." In *Adam Smith's* Wealth of Nations*: New Interdisciplinary Essays*, eds. Stephen Copley and Kathryn Sutherland. Manchester: Manchester University Press, 1995.

——. "Millenarial Poetics: Wordsworth's 'Nutting.' " *Raritan* 19 (2000): 148–58.

Herbert, Christopher. *Culture and Anomie: Ethnographic Imagination in the Nineteenth Century*. Chicago: University of Chicago Press, 1991.

Hickey, Alison. *Impure Conceits: Rhetoric and Ideology in Wordsworth's 'Excursion.'* Stanford: Stanford University Press, 1997.

Hollander, John. *Vision and Resonance: Two Senses of Poetic Form*. New York: Oxford University Press, 1975.

Hooke, Robert. *Micrographia: or some Physiological Descriptions of Minute Bodies Made by Magnifying Glasses with Observations and Inquiries thereupon*. London: Printed by Jo. Martyn and Ja. Allestry, 1665.

——. *Philosophical Experiments and Observations*. Ed. William Derham. 1726. Reprint, London: Cass, 1967.

Hume, David. *Essays, Moral, Political, and Literary.* Ed. Eugene F. Miller. Indianapolis: Liberty Fund, 1985.

Hunter, J. Paul. *Before Novels: the Cultural Contexts of Eighteenth-Century English Fiction.* New York: W. W. Norton and Co., 1990.

Hurley, Alison. "The Culture of Conversation: a Social and Literary History of the Eighteenth-Century Watering Place." Ph.D. diss., University of California, Berkeley, 2002.

Irlam, Shaun. *Elations: the Poetics of Enthusiasm in Eighteenth-Century Britain.* Stanford: Stanford University Press, 1999.

Jago, Richard. *Edge Hill, or the rural prospect delineated and moralized. A poem. In Four Books.* London: J. Dodsley, 1767.

Jameson, Fredric. *Marxism and Form.* Princeton: Princeton University Press, 1971.

———. *The Political Unconscious: Narrative as a Socially Symbolic Act.* Ithaca: Cornell University Press, 1981.

———. "Cognitive Mapping." In *Marxism and the Interpretation of Culture*, eds. Cary Nelson and Lawrence Grossberg. Urbana: University of Illinois Press, 1988.

———. *Postmodernism, or, the Cultural Logic of Late Capitalism.* Durham: Duke University Press, 1991.

Jay Martin. *Downcast Eyes: the Denigration of Vision in Twentieth-Century French Thought.* Berkeley and Los Angeles: University of California Press, 1993.

———. *Cultural Semantics: Keywords of Our Time.* Amherst: University of Massachusetts Press, 1998.

———. "Diving into the Wreck." Lecture delivered at the University of California, Berkeley, October 1999.

Johnson, Samuel. *Lives of the English Poets.* Ed. George Birkbeck Hill. 3 vols. Oxford: Clarendon Press, 1905.

———. *The Yale Edition of the Works of Samuel Johnson.* Ed. Allen T. Hazen. 16 vols. New Haven: Yale University Press, 1958–1990.

Johnston, Kenneth R. *Wordsworth and The Recluse.* New Haven: Yale University Press, 1984.

Jones, R. F. *Ancients and Moderns: a Study in the Rise of the Scientific Movement in Seventeenth-Century England.* Saint Louis: Washington University Studies, 1961.

Kames, Henry Home, Lord. *Elements of Criticism.* Edinburgh: Printed for A. Miller, London, and for A. Kincaid and J. Bell, Edinburgh, 1762.

Kant, Immanuel. *Critique of Judgment.* Trans. J. H. Bernard. New York: Hafner Press, 1951.

Kaufman, Robert. "Aura Still." *October* 99 (2002): 45–80.

Kaul, Suvir. *Poems of Nation, Anthems of Empire: English Verse in the Long Eighteenth Century.* Charlottesville: University Press of Virginia, 2000.

Keats, John. *The Selected Letters of John Keats.* Ed. Lionel Trilling. New York: Farrar, Straus, and Young, 1951.

———. *Complete Poems.* Ed. Jack Stillinger. Cambridge, MA: Harvard University Press, Belknap Press, 1982.

Kittler, Friedrich A. *Discourse Networks 1800/1900.* Trans. Michael Metteer and Chris Cullens. Stanford: Stanford University Press, 1990.

——. *Gramophone, Film, Typewriter.* Trans. Geoffrey Winthropp-Young and Michael Wutz. Stanford: Stanford University Press, 1999.

Klancher, Jon. *The Making of English Reading Audiences, 1790–1832.* Madison: University of Wisconsin Press, 1987.

Klapp, Orrin E. *Overload and Boredom: Essays on the Quality of Life in the Information Society.* Westport, CT: Greenwood Press, 1986.

Klein, Kerwin Lee. "On the Emergence of *Memory* in Historical Discourse." *Representations* 69 (2000): 127–50.

Klein, Lawrence E. "Berkeley, Shaftesbury, and the Meaning of Politeness." *Studies in Eighteenth-Century Culture* 16 (1986): 57–68.

——. "Courtly Politesse and Civic Politeness in France and England." *Halcyon* 14 (1992): 171–81.

——. "Gender, Conversation and the Public Sphere in Early Eighteenth-Century England." In *Textuality and Sexuality: Reading Theories and Practices*, eds. Judith Still and Michael Worton. Manchester: Manchester University Press, 1993.

——. *Shaftesbury and the Culture of Politeness: Moral Discourse and Cultural Politics in Early Eighteenth-Century England.* Cambridge: Cambridge University Press, 1994.

——. "Politeness for Plebes: Consumption and Social Identity in Early Eighteenth-Century England." In *The Consumption of Culture 1600–1800: Image, Object, Text*, ed. J. A. Brewer. New York: Routledge, 1995.

Kofman, Sarah. *Camera Obscura: of Ideology.* Trans. Will Straw. Ithaca: Cornell University Press, 1999.

Kristol, Susan Scheinberg. Labor *and* Fortuna *in* Virgil's Aeneid. New York: Garland Publishing, 1990.

Kroll, Richard W. F. *The Material Word: Literate Culture in the Restoration and Early Eighteenth Century.* Baltimore, MD: Johns Hopkins University Press, 1991.

Kuhn, Reinhard. *The Demon of Noontide: Ennui in Western Literature.* Princeton: Princeton University Press, 1976.

Lacoue-Labarthe, Philippe. *Poetry as Experience.* Trans. Andrea Tarnowski. Stanford: Stanford University Press, 1999.

Lamb, Jonathan, Robert P. Maccubbin, and David F. Morrill, eds. "The South Pacific in the Eighteenth Century: Narratives and Myths." Papers from the Ninth Annual David Nichol Smith Memorial Seminar. *Eighteenth-Century Life* 18 (1994): 1–242.

Lamb, Jonathan, Vanessa Smith, and Nicholas Thomas, eds. *Exploration and Exchange: a South Seas Anthology, 1680–1900.* Chicago: University of Chicago Press, 2000.

Landry, Donna. "The Resignation of Mary Collier: some Problems in Feminist Literary History." In *The New Eighteenth Century: Theory, Politics, English Literature*, eds. Felicity Nussbaum and Laura Brown. New York: Methuen, 1987.

Langan, Celeste. *Romantic Vagrancy: Wordsworth and the Simulation of Freedom.* Cambridge: Cambridge University Press, 1995.

——. "Understanding Media in 1805: Audiovisual Hallucination in *The Lay of the Last Minstrel.*" *Studies in Romanticism* 40 (2001): 49–70.

Langford, Paul. *A Polite and Commercial People: England 1727–1783*. Oxford: Clarendon Press, 1989.

Leibniz, Gottfried Willhelm. *The Monadology*. Trans. Robert Latta. New York: Oxford University Press, 1965.

Leslie, Michael and Timothy Raylor, eds. *Culture and Cultivation in Early Modern England: Writing and the Land*. Leicester: Leicester University Press, 1992.

Letsome, Sampson and John Nicoll, eds. *A Defence of Natural and Revealed Religion: Being a Collection of the Sermons Preached at the Lecture founded by the Honorable Robert Boyle, Esq. (From the Year 1691 to the Year 1732)*. London: D. Midwinter et al., 1739.

Levinson, Marjorie. *Wordsworth's Great Period Poems: Four Essays*. Cambridge: Cambridge University Press, 1986.

Levi-Strauss, Claude. *Introduction to the Work of Marcel Mauss*. Trans. Felicity Baker. London: Routledge, 1987.

Lilley, Kate. "Homosocial Women, Martha Sansom, Constantia Grierson, Mary Leapor, and the Georgic Verse Epistle." In *Women's Poetry in the Enlightenment: the Making of a Canon, 1730–1820*, eds. Isobel Armstrong and Virginia Blain. New York: Macmillan, 1999.

Liu, Alan. *Wordsworth: the Sense of History*. Stanford: Stanford University Press, 1989.

——. "Local Transcendence: Cultural Criticism, Postmodernism, and the Romanticism of Detail." *Representations* 32 (1990): 75–113.

——. "The New Historicism and the Work of Mourning." *Studies in Romanticism* 35 (1996): 553–62.

Locke, John. *An Essay Concerning Human Understanding*. Ed. Peter H. Nidditch. Oxford: Clarendon Press, 1975.

Lovejoy, Arthur O. *The Great Chain of Being: a Study of the History of an Idea*. Cambridge, MA: Harvard University Press, 1957.

Low, Anthony. *The Georgic Revolution*. Princeton: Princeton University Press, 1985.

Lowe, Donald M. *History of Bourgeois Perception*. Chicago: University of Chicago Press, 1982.

Luhmann, Niklas. *Art as a Social System*. Trans. Eva M. Knodt. Stanford: Stanford University Press, 2000.

Lukács, Georg. *History and Class Consciousness: Studies in Marxist Dialectics*. Trans. Rodney Livingstone. Cambridge, MA: The MIT Press, 1972.

Lutz, Alfred. "'The Deserted Village' and the Politics of Genre." *Modern Language Quarterly* 55 (1994): 149–68.

Lynch, Deidre S. *The Economy of Character: Novels, Market Culture, and the Business of Inner Meaning*. Chicago: University of Chicago Press, 1998.

Lyotard, Jean-François. *The Differend: Phrases in Dispute*. Trans. Georges Van Den Abbeele. Minneapolis: University of Minnesota Press, 1988.

MacLean, Gerald, Donna Landry and Joseph P. Ward, eds. *The Country and the City Revisited: England and the Politics of Culture, 1550–1850*. Cambridge: Cambridge University Press, 1999.

MacLean, Kenneth. "William Cowper." In *The Age of Johnson: Essays Presented to Chauncey Brewster Tinker*, ed. Frederick W. Hilles. New Haven: Yale University Press, 1949.

Makdisi, Saree. *Romantic Imperialism: Universal Empire and the Culture of Modernity*. Cambridge: Cambridge University Press, 1998.

Manning, Peter J. "'The Birthday of Typography': a Response to Celeste Langan." *Studies in Romanticism* 40 (2001): 71–83.

Markley, Robert. *Fallen Languages: Crises in Representation in Newtonian England, 1660–1740*. Ithaca: Cornell University Press, 1993.

Marshall, David. *The Figure of the Theater: Shaftesbury, Defoe, Adam Smith, and George Eliot*. New York: Columbia University Press, 1986.

——. *The Surprising Effects of Sympathy*. Chicago: University of Chicago Press, 1988.

Marshall, Madeleine Forell and Janet Todd. *English Congregational Hymns in the Eighteenth Century*. Lexington: University Press of Kentucky, 1982.

Marx, Karl. *The Marx–Engels Reader*. Ed. Robert C. Tucker. New York: W. W. Norton and Co., 1978.

Mayr, Otto. *Authority, Liberty, and Automatic Machinery in Early Modern Europe*. Baltimore, MD: Johns Hopkins University Press, 1986.

McCormick, E. H. *Omai, Pacific Envoy*. Auckland, New Zealand: Auckland University Press, 1977.

McGann, Jerome. *The Poetics of Sensibility: a Revolution in Literary Style*. Oxford: Clarendon Press, 1996.

McIntosh, Carey. *The Evolution of English Prose, 1700–1800: Style, Politeness, and Print Culture*. Cambridge: Cambridge University Press, 1998.

McKillop, Alan Dugald, ed. *James Thomson (1700–1748): Letters and Documents*. Lawrence: University of Kansas Press, 1958.

McLane, Maureen. *Romanticism and the Human Sciences: Poetry, Population, and the Discourse of the Species*. Cambridge: Cambridge University Press, 2000.

McLuhan, Marshall. *Understanding Media: the Extensions of Man*. Intro. Lewis H. Lapham. Cambridge, MA: The MIT Press, 1998.

Miles, Gary. *Virgil's Georgics*. Berkeley and Los Angeles: University of California Press, 1980.

Milic, Louis T. "Observations on Conversational Style." In *English Writers of the Eighteenth Century*, ed. John H. Mittendorf. New York: Columbia University Press, 1971.

Milton, John. *John Milton: Complete Poems and Major Prose*. Ed. Merritt Y. Hughes. Indianapolis: Bobbs-Merrill, 1957.

Mitchell, W. J. T., ed. *Landscape and Power*. Chicago: University of Chicago Press, 1994.

Morgan, Michael J. *Molyneux's Question: Vision, Touch, and the Philosophy of Perception*. Cambridge: Cambridge University Press, 1977.

Murdoch, John. "The Landscape of Labor: Transformations of the Georgic." In *Romantic Revolutions: Criticism and Theory*, eds. Kenneth R. Johnston, Gilbert

Chaitin, Karen Hanson, and Herbert Marks. Bloomington: Indiana University Press, 1990.

Nancy, Jean-Luc. *The Birth to Presence.* Trans. Brian Holmes and others. Stanford: Stanford University Press, 1993.

——. *The Muses.* Trans. Peggy Kamuf. Stanford: Stanford University Press, 1996.

Nichols, John. *Anecdotes, Biographical and Literary; Comprizing Biographical Memoirs of William Bowyer, Printer . . .* 9 vols. London: Nichols, Son, and Bentley, 1815.

Nicolson, Marjorie Hope. *The Microscope and English Imagination.* Northampton, MA: Smith College, 1935.

——. *Newton Demands the Muse: Newton's Opticks and the Eighteenth-Century Poets.* Princeton: Princeton University Press, 1946.

O'Brien, Karen. "Imperial Georgic, 1660–1789." In *The Country and the City Revisited,* eds. MacLean, Landry, and Ward.

Ong, Walter J. *Orality and Literacy: the Technologizing of the Word.* New York: Methuen, 1982.

Orwell, George. *A Collection of Essays.* New York: Harcourt, Brace, Jovanovich, 1946.

Pagden, Anthony. *Lords of All the World: Ideologies of Empire in Spain, Britain, and France, c.1500–c.1800.* New Haven: Yale University Press, 1995.

Patey, Douglas Lane. "Anne Finch, John Dyer, and the Georgic Syntax of Nature." In *Augustan Subjects: Essays in Honor of Martin C. Battestin,* ed. Albert J. Rivero. Newark: University of Delaware Press, 1997.

Patterson, Annabel. "Wordsworth's Georgic: Genre and Structure in *The Excursion.*" *The Wordsworth Circle* 9 (1978): 145–54.

——. *Pastoral and Ideology: Virgil to Valéry.* Berkeley and Los Angeles: University of California Press, 1987.

——. "Foul, his Wife, the Mayor and Foul's Mare: the Power of Anecdote in Tudor Historiography." In *The Historical Imagination in Early Modern Britain: History, Rhetoric, and Fiction, 1500–1800,* eds. Donald R. Kelley and David Harris Sacks. Cambridge: Cambridge University Press, 1997.

Paulson, Ronald. *Breaking and Remaking: Aesthetic Practice in England, 1700–1820.* New Brunswick: Rutgers University Press, 1989.

Paulson, William R. *Enlightenment, Romanticism, and the Blind in France.* Princeton: Princeton University Press, 1987.

Perkell, Christine. *The Poet's Truth: a Study of the Poet in Virgil's Georgics.* Berkeley and Los Angeles: University of California Press, 1989.

Peters, John Durham. *Speaking into the Air: a History of the Idea of Communication.* Chicago: University of Chicago Press, 1999.

Pfau, Thomas. *Wordsworth's Profession: Form, Class, and the Logic of Early Romantic Cultural Production.* Stanford: Stanford University Press, 1997.

Philips, John. *The Poems of John Philips.* Ed. M. G. Lloyd-Thomas. Oxford: Basil Blackwell, 1927.

Phillips, Adam. *On Kissing, Tickling, and Being Bored: Psychoanalytic Essays on the Unexamined Life.* Cambridge, MA: Harvard University Press, 1993.

Phillips, Mark Salber. *Society and Sentiment: Genres of Historical Writing in Britain, 1740–1820*. Princeton: Princeton University Press, 2000.

Picciotto, Joanna. "Optical Instruments and the Eighteenth-Century Observer." *Studies in Eighteenth-Century Culture* 29 (2000): 123–53.

——. "Literary and Scientific Experimentalism in Seventeenth- and Eighteenth-Century England." Ph.D. diss., University of California, Berkeley, 2000.

Pigman, G. W. III. *Grief and English Renaissance Elegy*. Cambridge: Cambridge University Press, 1985.

Pinch, Adela. *Strange Fits of Passion: Epistemologies of Emotion, Hume to Austen*. Stanford: Stanford University Press, 1996.

Poovey, Mary. *The History of the Modern Fact: Problems of Knowledge in the Sciences of Wealth and Society*. Chicago: University of Chicago Press, 1998.

Pope, Alexander. *The Poems of Alexander Pope*. Ed. John Butt. New Haven: Yale University Press, 1963.

Potkay, Adam. *The Fate of Eloquence in the Age of Hume*. Ithaca: Cornell University Press, 1994.

Power, Henry. *Experimental Philosophy, in Three Books, Containing New Experiments Microscopical, Mercurial, Magnetical*. London: T. Roycroft, for John Martin and James Allestry, 1664.

Priestman, Martin. *Cowper's Task: Structure and Influence*. Cambridge: Cambridge University Press, 1983.

Prior, Matthew. *The Literary Works of Matthew Prior*. Eds. H. Bunker Wright and Monroe K. Spears. 2 vols. Oxford: Clarendon Press, 1959.

Putnam, Michael C. J. *Virgil's Poem of the Earth: Studies in* The Georgics. Princeton: Princeton University Press, 1979.

Puttenham, George. *The Arte of English Poesy*. London, 1589. Reprint, Kent, OH: Kent State University Press, 1970.

Quinney, Laura. *The Poetics of Disappointment: Wordsworth to Ashbery*. Charlottesville: University Press of Virginia, 1999.

Ramazani, Jahan. *Poetry of Mourning: the Modern Elegy from Hardy to Heaney*. Chicago: University of Chicago Press, 1994.

Redford, Bruce. *The Converse of the Pen: Acts of Intimacy in the Eighteenth-Century Familiar Letter*. Chicago: University of Chicago Press, 1986.

Reiss, Timothy J. *The Discourse of Modernism*. Ithaca, NY: Cornell University Press, 1982.

Roach, Joseph. *Cities of the Dead: Circum-Atlantic Performance*. New York: Columbia University Press, 1996.

Robbins, Bruce. "The Sweatshop Sublime." *PMLA* 117 (2002): 84–97.

Rogers, John. *The Matter of Revolution: Science, Poetry, and Politics in the Age of Milton*. Ithaca, NY: Cornell University Press, 1996.

Ross, David O., Jr. *Virgil's Elements: Physics and Poetry in the* Georgics. Princeton: Princeton University Press, 1987.

Røstvig, Maren-Sophie. *The Happy Man: Studies in the Metamorphosis of a Classical Ideal*. 2 vols. Oslo: Akademisk Forlag, 1954.

Saccamano, Neil. "The Sublime Force of Words in Addison's 'Pleasures.'" *ELH* 58 (1991): 83–106.

Santner, Eric. "History Beyond the Pleasure Principle." In *Probing the Limits of Representation: Nazism and the "Final Solution,"* ed. Saul Friedlander. Cambridge, MA: Harvard University Press, 1992.

Schoenfield, Mark. *The Professional Wordsworth: Law, Labor, and the Poet's Contract.* Athens: University of Georgia Press, 1996.

Schor, Esther H. *Bearing the Dead: the British Culture of Mourning from the Enlightenment to Victoria.* Princeton: Princeton University Press, 1994.

Schor, Naomi. "Blindness as Metaphor." *differences: A Journal of Feminist Cultural Studies* 11 (1999): 76–105.

Scodel, Joshua. *The English Epitaph: Commemoration and Conflict from Jonson to Wordsworth.* Ithaca: Cornell University Press, 1991.

Scott, Joan W. "The Evidence of Experience." *Critical Inquiry* 17 (1991): 773–97.

Scoular, Kitty. *Natural Magic: Studies in the Presentation of Nature in English Poetry from Spenser to Marvell.* Oxford: Clarendon Press, 1965.

Serres, Michel. *Hermes: Literature, Science, Philosophy.* Trans. Lawrence R. Schehr. Eds. Josué V. Harari and David F. Bell. Baltimore, MD: Johns Hopkins University Press, 1982.

———. *The Parasite.* Trans. Lawrence R. Schehr. Baltimore, MD: Johns Hopkins University Press, 1982.

Sessions, William. "Spenser's Georgics." *English Literary Renaissance* 10 (1980): 202–38.

Setzer, Sharon. "Wordsworth's Wanderer, the Epitaph, and the Uncanny." *Genre* 24 (1991): 361–79.

Shakespeare, William. *The Riverside Shakespeare.* Ed. G. Blakemore Evans. Boston: Houghton Mifflin, 1974.

Sharp, Michelle Turner. "The Churchyard among the Wordsworthian Mountains: Mapping the Common Ground of Death and the Reconfiguration of Romantic Community." *ELH* 62 (1995): 387–407.

Shaw, Samuel. *Words Made Visible, or Grammar and Rhetorick Accommodated to the Lives and Manners of Men.* London: B. G. for Daniel Major, 1679.

Shteir, Ann B. *Cultivating Women, Cultivating Science.* Baltimore, MD: Johns Hopkins University Press, 1996.

Sidney, Sir Philip. *An Apology for Poetry.* Ed. Geoffrey Shepherd. London: Thomas Nelson and Sons, 1967.

Simpson, David. *Wordsworth's Historical Imagination: the Poetry of Displacement.* New York: Methuen, 1987.

———. "Public Virtues, Private Vices: Reading Between the Lines of Wordsworth's 'Anecdote for Fathers.'" In *Subject to History: Ideology, Class, Gender,* ed. David Simpson. Ithaca: Cornell University Press, 1991.

———. "Raymond Williams: Feeling for Structures, Voicing 'History.'" *Social Text* 10 (1992): 9–26.

———. *The Academic Postmodern and the Rule of Literature: a Report on Half-Knowledge.* Chicago: University of Chicago Press, 1995.

——. "The Cult of 'Conversation.'" *Raritan* 16 (1997): 75–85.

Siskin, Clifford. *The Historicity of Romantic Discourse*. New York: Oxford University Press, 1988.

——. *The Work of Writing: Literature and Social Change in Britain, 1700–1830*. Baltimore, MD: Johns Hopkins University Press, 1998.

Sitter, John. *Literary Loneliness in Mid-Eighteenth-Century England*. Ithaca: Cornell University Press, 1982.

Smith, Adam. *Lectures on Rhetoric and Belles-Lettres*. Ed. John. M. Lothian. London: Thomas Nelson and Sons, Ltd., 1963.

——. *An Inquiry into the Nature and Causes of the Wealth of Nations*. Eds. R. H. Campbell and A. S. Skinner. 2 vols. Oxford: Clarendon Press, 1976.

——. *The Theory of Moral Sentiments*. Eds. D. D. Raphael and A. L. Macfie. Oxford: Clarendon Press, 1976.

——. *Essays on Philosophical Subjects*. Eds. W. P. D. Wightman and J. C. Bryce. Oxford: Clarendon Press, 1980.

Smith, Bernard. *European Vision and the South Pacific*. New Haven: Yale University Press, 1985.

Smith, Charlotte. *The Poems of Charlotte Smith*. Ed. Stuart Curran. New York: Oxford University Press, 1993.

Smyser, Jane Worthington. *Wordsworth's Reading of Roman Prose*. New Haven: Yale University Press, 1946.

Snel[l], George. *The Right Teaching of Useful Knowledge, to fit Scholars for some honest Profession; Shewing so much skil as anie man needeth (that is not a Teacher) in all knowledges, in one schole, in a shorter time in a more plain waie, and for much less expense than ever hath been used, since of old the Arts were so taught in the Greek and Roman Empire*. London: Printed for W. Dugard, 1649.

Somervile, William. *The Chace. A Poem*. London: G. Hawkins, 1735.

Spacks, Patricia Meyer. *The Poetry of Vision: Five Eighteenth-Century Poets*. Cambridge, MA: Harvard University Press, 1967.

——. *Boredom: the Literary History of a State of Mind*. Chicago: University of Chicago Press, 1995.

Spargo, R. Clifton. *The Ethics of Mourning*. Baltimore, MD: Johns Hopkins University Press, 2004.

Spiegelman, Willard. *Majestic Indolence: English Romantic Poetry and the Work of Art*. New York: Oxford University Press, 1995.

Spitzer, Leo. *Essays in Historical Semantics*. New York: S. F. Vanni, 1948.

Sprat, Sir Thomas. *History of the Royal Society*. Eds. Jackson I. Cope and Harold Whitmore Jones. Saint Louis, MO: Washington University Studies, 1958.

Stafford, Barbara M. *Artful Science: Enlightenment, Entertainment and the Eclipse of Visual Education*. Cambridge, MA: The MIT Press, 1994.

Starr, G. A. "Defoe's Prose Style: 1. The Language of Interpretation." *Modern Philology* 71 (1974): 277–94.

Steinman, Lisa. *Masters of Repetition: Poetry, Culture, and Work in Thomson, Wordsworth, Shelley, and Emerson*. New York: St. Martin's Press, 1998.

Stewart, Susan. *Crimes of Writing: Problems in the Containment of Representation.* Durham: Duke University Press, 1994.

——. *Poetry and the Fate of the Senses.* Chicago: University of Chicago Press, 2002.

Streuver, Nancy S. "The Conversable World: Eighteenth-Century Transformations of the Relation of Rhetoric and Truth." In *Rhetorical Traditions and British Romantic Literature*, eds. Don H. Bialostosky and Lawrence D. Needham. Bloomington: Indiana University Press, 1995.

Summers, David. *The Judgment of Sense: Renaissance Naturalism and the Rise of Aesthetics.* Cambridge: Cambridge University Press, 1987.

Sussman, Charlotte. *Consuming Anxieties: Consumer Protest, Gender, and British Slavery, 1713–1833.* Stanford: Stanford University Press, 2000.

Terada, Rei. *Feeling in Theory: Emotion after the "Death of the Subject."* Cambridge, MA: Harvard University Press, 2001.

Terdiman, Richard. *Discourse/Counter-Discourse: the Theory and Practice of Symbolic Resistance in Nineteenth-Century France.* Ithaca: Cornell University Press, 1985.

Thomas, Richard F. *Reading Virgil and his Texts: Studies in Intertextuality.* Ann Arbor: University of Michigan Press, 1999.

Thomson, James. *The Seasons.* Ed. James Sambrook. Oxford: Clarendon Press, 1981.

——. *Liberty, The Castle of Indolence, and other Poems.* Ed. James Sambrook. Oxford: Clarendon Press, 1986.

Tickell, Richard E. *Thomas Tickell and the Eighteenth-Century Poets.* London: Constable and Co., 1931.

Tillotson, Geoffrey. *Augustan Poetic Diction.* London: Athlone Press, 1964.

Trapp, Joseph. *Lectures on Poetry.* Hildesheim: Georg Olms Verlag, 1969.

Trilling, Lionel. *The Opposing Self: Nine Essays in Criticism.* New York: Viking Press, 1955.

Turner, James. *The Politics of Landscape: Rural Scenery and Society in English Poetry 1630–1660.* Cambridge, MA: Harvard University Press, 1979.

Tylus, Jane. "Spenser, Virgil, and the Politics of Poetic Labor." *ELH* 55 (1988): 53–77.

Vickers, Brian. *Francis Bacon and Renaissance Prose.* Cambridge: Cambridge University Press, 1968.

Vinge, Louise. *The Five Senses: Studies in a Literary Tradition.* Lund, Sweden: LiberLäromedel/CWK Gleerup, 1975.

Virgil. *The Georgicks of Publius Virgilius Maro, Otherwise called his Italian Husbandrie . . . Grammaticallie translated into English meter in so plaine and familiar sort, as a learner may be taught thereby to his profit and contentment.* Trans. A. F[leming?]. London, 1589.

——. *Virgil's Georgicks, Englished by Tho: May, Esqr.* Trans. Thomas May. London: Printed for Thomas Walkley, 1628.

——. *The Works of Publius Vergilius Maro, translated and adorn'd with sculpture, and illus. with annotations by John Ogilby.* Trans. John Ogilby. London: Warren, 1654.

——. *Eclogues, Georgics, Aeneid 1–6.* Trans. H. Rushton Fairclough. Rev. edn. Cambridge, MA: Harvard University Press, Loeb Classical Library, 1986.

——. *Georgics.* Ed. Richard F. Thomas. 2 vols. Cambridge: Cambridge University Press, 1988.

Viswanathan, Gauri. "Raymond Williams and British Colonialism." *Yale Journal of Criticism* 4 (1991): 47–66.

Warner, Michael. *Letters of the Republic: Publication and the Public Sphere in Eighteenth-Century America.* Cambridge, MA: Harvard University Press, 1990.

Warton, Joseph. *An Essay on the Genius and Writings of Pope.* 2nd edn. 2 vols. London: R. and J. Dodsley, 1762.

Weber, Samuel. *Mass Mediauras: Form, Technics, Media.* Ed. Alan Cholodenko. Stanford: Stanford University Press, 1996.

Webster, John. *Academiarum Examen, Or the Examination of Academies, Wherein is Discussed and Examined the Matter, Method and Customs of Academick and Scholastick Learning, and the insufficiency thereof discovered and laid open.* London: printed for Giles Calvert, 1654.

Weiskel, Thomas. *The Romantic Sublime: Studies in the Structure and Psychology of Transcendence.* Baltimore, MD: Johns Hopkins University Press, 1976. Reprint, 1986.

Werkmeister, Lucyle. *The London Daily Press, 1772–1792.* Lincoln: University of Nebraska Press, 1963.

Wilkins, John. *Mercury, or the Secret and Swift Messenger.* London: Printed by J. Norton, for John Maynard and Timothy Wilkins, 1641.

——. *An Essay Towards a Real Character and Philosophical Language.* London: Sa. Gellibrand and Jo. Martyn, 1668.

Wilkinson, L. P. *The Georgics of Virgil: a Critical Survey.* Cambridge: Cambridge University Press, 1969.

Williams, Raymond. *The Long Revolution.* New York: Columbia University Press, 1961.

——. *The Country and the City.* New York: Oxford University Press, 1973.

——. *Marxism and Literature.* New York: Oxford University Press, 1977.

——. *Problems in Materialism and Culture: Selected Essays.* London: New Left Books, 1980.

——. *Politics and Letters: Interviews with the New Left Review.* London: Verso, 1981.

——. *Keywords: a Vocabulary of Culture and Society.* Rev. edn. New York: Oxford University Press, 1983.

Williamson, George. *The Senecan Amble: a Study in Prose Form from Bacon to Collier.* Chicago: University of Chicago Press, 1951.

Wilson, Catherine. *The Invisible World: Early Modern Philosophy and the Invention of the Microscope.* Princeton: Princeton University Press, 1995.

Wood, Gillen D'Arcy. *The Shock of the Real: Romanticism and Visual Culture, 1760–1860.* New York: Palgrave, 2001.

Wordsworth, William. *The Poetical Works of William Wordsworth.* Eds. Ernest de Selincourt and Helen Darbishire. 5 vols. Oxford: Clarendon Press, 1940–49. Reprint, 1966.

———. *The Prose Works of William Wordsworth.* Eds. W. J. B. Owen and Jane Worthington Smyser. 3 vols. Oxford: Clarendon Press, 1974.

———. *The Prelude, 1799, 1805, 1850.* Eds. Jonathan Wordsworth, M. H. Abrams, and Stephen Gill. New York: W. W. Norton and Co., 1979.

———. *Translations of Chaucer and Virgil.* Ed. Bruce E. Graver. Ithaca: Cornell University Press, 1998.

Yolton, John W. *Thinking Matter: Materialism in Eighteenth-Century Britain.* Minneapolis: University of Minnesota Press, 1983.

Youngren, William H. "Conceptualism and Neo-Classic Generality." *ELH* 47 (1980): 705–74.

———. "Addison and the Birth of Eighteenth-Century Aesthetics." *Modern Philology* 79 (1982): 267–83.

Zimmerman, Sarah M. *Romanticism, Lyricism, and History.* Albany: SUNY Press, 1999.

Zippel, Otto. *Thomson's Seasons: Critical Edition.* Berlin: Mayer and Muller, 1908.

Žižek, Slavoj. "I Hear You with My Eyes." In *Gaze and Voice as Love Objects.* eds. Renata Salecl and Slavoj Žižek. Durham: Duke University Press, 1996.

Zupančič, Alenka. "Philosophers' Blind Man's Buff." In *Gaze and Voice as Love Objects,* eds. Renata Salecl and Slavoj Žižek. Durham: Duke University Press, 1996.

NEWSPAPERS

The General Evening Post. July 14–16, 1774, July 19–21, 1774, July 21–23, 1774, July 26–28, 1774, August 6–9, 1774, August 9–11, 1774, September 23–25, 1784, September 25–28, 1784.

The Gentleman's Magazine. 5 (March 1735), 32 (1782).

The London Magazine. 26 (April 1757), 35 (December 1766), 44 (20–22 April, 1775), 49 (August 1780).

The Morning Chronicle and Daily Advertiser. July 16, 1774, July 26, 1774, July 29, 1774, August 5, 1774, August 8, 1774, November 9, 1774, September 30, 1783.

Index

CAMBRIDGE STUDIES IN ROMANTICISM

GENERAL EDITORS
MARILYN BUTLER, *University of Oxford*
JAMES CHANDLER, *University of Chicago*